Frank Forndron, Thilo Liebermann,
Marcus Thurner, Peter Widmayer

mySAP® ERP Roadmap

Business Processes, Capabilities, and
Complete Upgrade Strategy

© 2006 by Galileo Press
SAP PRESS is an imprint of Galileo Press,
Fort Lee (NJ), USA
Bonn, Germany

Copy Editor Nancy Etscovitz, UCG, Inc.,
Boston, MA
Cover Design Silke Braun
Printed in Germany

ISBN 1-59229-071-X
1st edition 2006

Contents

3 mySAP ERP for Midsize Businesses and Industry-Specific Needs

4 SAP NetWeaver and ESA—Architecture Facilitating the Change

5 Transition and Upgrade to mySAP ERP   205

6 Next Generation–Proof Points   237

7 Outlook   271

Appendix

Foreword

By Thomas Baur, Vice President, Head of the Global ERP Initiative at SAP AG

The focus of the past few years, to reduce process and product lifecycle time, is now shifting to the "Next Big Thing," the enablement of flexible and adaptable business process change.

I invite you to read this book to explore the new capabilities that IT makes available to you, and to prepare a roadmap based on these new capabilities so as to ensure the upcoming successful execution of the crossroads of the future—where IT and business interact—enabled by the next generation of Enterprise Resource Planning (ERP) solutions!

In recent years, Business and IT have been moving through "Times of Battle," made even more visible in the latest economic slowdown in which IT has been viewed as a cost-cutting instrument, which is sometimes considered by senior management to be its sole objective. While this is neither the fault of Business or IT, it may potentially lead to a less healthy trend of "outsourcing the CIO and IT" if the changes and opportunities in technology—now represented through solutions based on an enterprise services architecture (e.g., mySAP ERP powered by SAP NetWeaver and the Business Process Platform)—are not considered and adopted.

Senior Management has a clear view regarding its demand toward IT, indicated in recent surveys (e.g., *CIO Magazine*, *The Economist*). CEOs expect that their Chief Information Officer and the IT department provide ideas proactively and support the innovation of the business. Today's existing and upcoming technologies will demand a change in both the role and the responsibility of IT to enable key differentiators supporting senior management's strategies at an accelerated speed. This is only possible if the following disciplines are in place:

▶ These technologies (e.g., SAP NetWeaver, Business Process Platform, concept of the enterprise services architecture) are embedded into the corporate strategy and are fully understood by both Business and IT with their respective impacts.

▶ These two bodies are capable of building a comprehensive and collaborative bridge of joint execution to drive these ideas, as only then can the adaptability and flexibility come to life.

The disciplines are expanding from a heavy-loaded maintenance character of IT to include the competencies of managing the new art of the business process lifecycle, particularly with regard to the following two aspects:

"Commodities" (context processes)—business processes that are necessary to run the business, but are peripheral to the direct value generation of an enterprise and its customers. These processes must be simplified and standardized to provide the basis and flexible option to outsource entirely or partly and within or beyond the enterprise, for example, in shared service centers (typical candidates to such processes are payroll, accounts payable/receivable, inter-company settlements, etc.).

Sustainable differentiation (core processes)—innovative ideas that are, right from the start, embedded and defined on one platform as part of the overall IT strategy, thus enabling scalability, fast project pass through times, and—once they move to "commodities," when being copied by the competition—execution continued at low cost. It may be easier said than done, because this new direction requires a new skill set for both Business and IT, while removing walls, combine silos, and the ability to orchestrate business with much more speed, foresight, agility and adaptability, thereby driving change in all domains: cultural, organizational, collaboration, business process, and technology.

In a nutshell, the paradigm of viewing IT as a strategic cost-cutting element is shifting to seeing IT as an equally important support within the enterprise as are other key business areas. Simply put, IT will return to "being sexy again," thereby serving the key principles of enterprises better.

Paradigms are evolving quickly. Countries that have been viewed as emerging become domain and it is more a question of: "Does a country reflect a strong economic buying power and, thus, could it promote and sustain growth opportunity?" "Does it appear to be a natural place for investing?" Therefore, the key principles that successful companies need to support are:

▶ Consolidation

▶ Globalization

▶ Adaptability and Innovation

So, the reasoning for the change is there, and now, so is the technology. While before such principles have been hard to achieve—most of the time hindered by either a best-of-breed approach with little integration, or via a tight and monolithical integration (hard-wiring of processes) — we are now at the forefront of the next generation of solutions.

Such next generation solutions like mySAP ERP, leading to an enterprise services architecture by the provision of SAP NetWeaver as the basis emerging to the Business Process Platform, will help to ensure that IT will be a valuable asset to the enterprise and a competent partner of the CEO. It will ensure to the CEO that all relevant business information is at hand, plus it will afford him the chance to sense and respond to marketplace parameter changes to drive strategies at an accelerated speed, and ensure that IT will be able to support these strategies at a faster pace and at a much lower cost.

It is the end of huge and long lasting IT projects, and the beginning of a new discipline — the competence to create and enable new processes on the basis of an existing service repository — which will require the start to an up-skill process, ensuring to match the demand of tomorrow, thus, enabling the start of projects with measurable business results at any time in the future. Companies that take this step now will benefit early and more easily due to an evolutionary process; they will move along, while other companies will have to catch up.

This book is intended to shed light on the new perception of ERP — in the way it extends its business processes beyond the border of the enterprise. By providing an evolutionary way in which to see the key benefits of the next generation of ERP solutions, this book will help you to customize the steps of your current deployment of solutions to meet the requirements of the new way forward. More importantly, it will enable you to drive change in the organization more easily, thereby reducing the costs of running operations, and helping you to grow the current solutions significantly.

In order to leverage these opportunities, this book will provide you with a good insight into our upcoming prerequisites, the starting point of the next generation ERP solution, and the roadmap for the evolution of this solution:

▶ Differentiating between context ("commodities") and core (sustainable differentiation) in an initial analysis, thereby enabling a clear planning of your respective roadmap to leverage the next generation ERP solution, SAP NetWeaver, and the enterprise services architecture

- ▶ Understanding the need to build up the architectural skills integral for ensuring a sound basis for this evolution to start at any time
- ▶ Awareness of the requirements for business process composition skills in the new domain of IT, transforming to business analysts or "Hybrid" (resources being business knowledged and IT savvy)

While this book will not have all the answers to your questions, and we do not purport such a claim, it is written by pragmatic people well versed in helping businesses find solutions. It is based on the lifecycle experience—from the start of the development of this next generation solution, its ramp–up period, the general availability, and the first live sites. I am sure that you will be able to take what you need from this book and put it to good use in your daily business.

Enjoy the book!

Thomas Baur
Walldorf, February 2006

Introduction

A new Enterprise Resource Planning (ERP) solution? Which actual benefits can be derived from next generation ERP solutions? What are the differences to traditional ERP solutions? These are only some of the questions that will be addressed and answered in the following chapters.

Thirty years ago, SAP introduced a new era of integrated real-time software for business processing. The products SAP R/2 and, later on, SAP R/3 represented the departure into new dimensions of information technology. Now, the next software generation is ready to continue this success story.

With mySAP ERP, SAP proactively accommodates the challenges that organizations are facing in today's dynamic and volatile business environment. Investments in extending or modernizing IT structures are measured against generating a rapid return on investment and lowering total cost of ownership (TCO). At the same time, the demands on IT are constantly rising. Flexible support of new business models, extension of existing business processes, and maximizing IT capabilities are only a few examples.

mySAP ERP as the next generation solution

Consequently, we must deal with a new quality of demands on next generation ERP systems. These systems are not simply expected to continue increasing organizational efficiency—like traditional ERP systems—but are also expected to serve as an agile platform to flexibly integrate existing and new business models, and act as a seamless unit between ERP and other relevant applications in the organization. This requires an extension of the traditional ERP scope to include all people involved, both internally and externally, comprising customers, vendors, and partners. Meeting these requirements efficiently—and without confining future flexibility—determines the basic expectations toward next generation ERP systems. Along with that is the continued need for the functional depth and breadth of the solution. By offering unparalleled integration capabilities and flexibility for requirements to come, mySAP ERP lives up to these demands. In addition to its industry-specific capabilities and comprehensive process scope, its position as the leading ERP solution on the market is reinforced by the fact that the underlying integration and application platform on which it is built is SAP NetWeaver.

With mySAP ERP, SAP has launched a solution that not only combines more than 30 years of experience in real-time ERP applications, it also ensures continuity and secures previous investments for existing customers by offering comprehensive transition paths that allow for gradual enhancements of existing IT landscapes. Through enabling step-by-step extensions along growing requirements, the often large and costly implementation projects of the past can be cut into concrete implementation steps with clearly defined quick wins and lower costs. Furthermore, new customers can profit from these advantages, whether it be because they're on the lookout for a company-wide next generation ERP solution, or for standardizing existing heterogeneous IT environments.

Target groups
These starting points lead to consecutive questions that are addressed in the chapters to follow. By discussing ERP in a holistic manner, this book is directed at decision-makers and users in IT and business, as well as those users who are interested in the operational and strategic aspects of ERP.

Structure of the book
▶ **Chapter 1**: What are the major challenges resulting from the volatility of our markets and what role does IT play in this dynamic? How can IT live up to the demands resulting from this relationship?

▶ **Chapter 2**: In general, what is the path like to mySAP ERP? What are the major scenarios, business processes, and functional capabilities of mySAP ERP?

▶ **Chapter 3**: To what extent does mySAP ERP cover industry-specific requirements and the specific needs of mid-sized companies toward ERP solutions?

▶ **Chapter 4**: How is a next generation ERP solution defined from a technological perspective, including concepts such as the Enterprise Services Architecture (ESA)?

▶ **Chapter 5**: What are the basic aspects to consider for the transition to mySAP ERP and how are typical transition paths characterized?

▶ **Chapter 6**: How have other leading organizations across the globe conducted the step to mySAP ERP and what are the major benefits they have obtained?

▶ An outlook into future versions of mySAP ERP will conclude this book in **Chapter 7**.

**Frank Forndron, Thilo Liebermann,
Marcus Thurner, Peter Widmayer**
Walldorf, February 2006

1 ERP—at the Heart of the Organization

In today's competitive business environment, just focusing on achieving bottom line efficiency is insufficient. Next generation ERP systems enable organizations to drive both innovation and growth, while concurrently managing efficiency and productivity.

This chapter will provide you with an insight into the history and strategic foundation of Enterprise Resource Planning (ERP) software. You'll learn how next generation IT solutions can be integral to keeping up with or even surpassing the competition, based on the challenges that organizations face in today's business world.

1.1 The ERP Comeback—Here to Stay

For quite a while, we've been hearing that ERP is back, just as if it's having a kind of resurgence. Actually, ERP was never gone!

Although ERP's importance was reduced, and even deemed obsolete during the dot.com revolution and the concurrent flood of new opportunities that resulted, once the dust settled, it became clear that, while e-business did and still does offer many opportunities, it does not cause miracles to happen. The initial prediction of small independent software units, marketplaces and service providers all connected by the Internet, in which organizations no longer needed a solid ERP foundation, did not stand the test of time. Without a doubt, several important lessons, business models, and technologies from that period had a positive impact on business. A major one being that profit, sound cash flows, and a strong administrative backbone are indispensable and will be critical to saving a company that is in dire straits from economic failure.

The Internet boom

And while the demands on IT environments continue to expand, organizations today face tighter controls on their IT budget. "Do more with less" has become a necessary guideline for many organizations. Given this dilemma, topics such as reducing process and IT complexity, increasing transparency, lowering total cost of ownership (TCO), and enabling operations in heterogeneous environments have become fundamental. Having realized this, the organizations have begun (or are already in the midst of) taking full advantage of their next generation ERP solution, reducing the costs of their overall IT infrastructures, and using their e-business applications in a controlled way—focusing on creation of added value.

Best-of-breed decline Along with this came the decline of best-of-breed systems—a phase in which users often unsuccessfully tried to put together and connect various components, which resulted in increasing implementation and system integration costs exponentially. Even today, organizations must deal with the remnants of such activities, by struggling to retrospectively bring their IT structure in line. As predicted, this has led to an increased need for Enterprise Application Integration (EAI) tools, however, while integration tended to be manageable initially, it became increasingly more troublesome with each version upgrade of the individual components. Consequently, more organizations are opting for standardized platforms, giving them enhancement possibilities that reflect their individual requirements. Today's ERP solutions include integrated industry standards such as XML or Java ensuring compatibility—quite a difference from ERP's early years when openness was often subject to technical limitations.

Continued ERP growth The belief that organizations have bought all of the software they need for the foreseeable future is still a rather popular perception, however, it's wrong. The last time that the following laments were popular was in the early 1990s: "There's nothing new left to buy," or "Companies have everything they need." Since then, market growth has been exponential, especially with new applications hitting the market, some of which weren't even conceived back then. Recent market analyses from leading analysts confirm this trend (see also Figure 1.1). The worldwide ERP applications market has reached 26.5 billion USD in 2004 and is forecasted to reach a compound annual growth rate of 8.2% resulting in more than 39 billion USD in 2009. While North America and Europe are expected to grow at rates of 6.4% and 4.3%, Asia Pacific with 15.0% and the rest of the world (ROW) at 19.6% are well above the compound annual rate.[1] To a large extent, this continued growth can be attributed to ongoing strengthened efforts in product innovation by the major vendors attracting customers to further invest in their ERP applications, continued focus on fixed-price implementations, as well as expected exponential growth from small to midsize businesses, many of them making up for previous years in which their IT spending lagged behind usual scales.

---

1 Source: IDC—Market Analysis Worldwide ERP Applications, August 2005

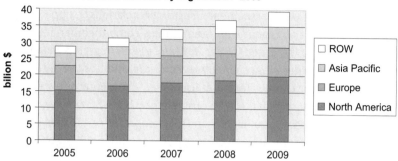

Figure 1.1 Worldwide ERP Applications Revenue Forecast (Source: IDC)

Ten years ago, the concept of enterprise resource planning was just emerging. At that time, the primary application expenditures were for material requirements planning, financial software, basic human resource management, and some limited supply chain planning. With progressively more organizations having acknowledged that they had not fully leveraged ERP, they also become more receptive to the idea of standardizing integrated applications. This, in turn, became a key reason for the rising demand for ERP solutions, and more specifically, for next generation ERP solutions. Accordingly, business processes will be streamlined, simple as well as complex tasks will be automated, and access to relevant information will be made available to the right people at the right time. Organizations that rely on the speed of the information that they receive and distribute will have more obvious benefits of a next generation ERP system than ever before. Those that fail to realize the benefits of an ERP system will continue to struggle with yesterday's applications, which are destined to become obsolete in a dynamic marketplace.

Companies are asking themselves how they can prepare for constant change. The ability to act rather than react will be essential in such an environment. If we look at the past decade's major swings on the economic scale as an indication of future volatility, we can see that companies will have to adopt methods of running their businesses successfully through economic growth periods, as well as through major declines. IT is also susceptible to these changes. Frequently, IT is in the midst of these discussions as organizations recognize that only through leveraging and commanding their IT will they be in a position to achieve or even perfect their strategies, or, at least survive within this new reality. In no other place are these changes within IT more apparent than they are in the area of ERP—the heart and nerve center of the IT ecosystem in every organization. ERP remains the place where areas such as collaborative planning and engineering, e-procurement, customer relations, supply chain, human capital management and Internet sales come together and either a profit or a loss is recorded for the enterprise. An integrated, sound ERP system that provides a transparent view and can monitor the entire ecosystem is the key enabler for an efficient, real-time enterprise. Alternatively, a weak ERP system is like an unstable backbone that causes the rest of the body to become vulnerable and even collapse. As the backbone of an efficient application infrastructure, a next generation ERP solution supports streamlined business processes that lay the foundation for a continued improvement in productivity and profitability, enabling top line growth in addition to being instrumental to containing and reducing IT operating costs.

The evolution of ERP As a result, the significance and importance of ERP in an organization has evolved in the last few years from being a discrete back-end system to being a major vehicle for ensuring efficiency and performance, especially given today's focus on integration within the IT ecosystem and achieving desired business results. Companies that want to effectively manage their key assets will only succeed with a next generation ERP system providing a clear view of their operations.

Of lesser importance during the new economy wave, the relevance of people, finance, operational excellence, and relationships emerged as key priorities across all organizations. Today, all successful companies recognize the value of their intangible assets and the need for efficiency and speed in operations. IT is expected to enable the development and growth of these assets and therefore must live up to this expectation. The demands regularly expressed include compatibility with the existing landscape, a comprehensive target ERP landscape, evolution allowing incremental growth, and the ability to swiftly adjust to a changing ecosystem resulting in a reduced time for business process changes.

The past has also shown that it takes more than a simple collaborative process to manage a company. Firm processes must be in place in the background, which is why ERP is the heart of every company. A company in command of its ERP system is prepared to take on new opportunities. Sustained efficiency gains are particularly important, especially during economically difficult times, when consumers, the public sector, and companies are spending conservatively. Sustainable differentiation enabled through reduced process adaptation is the next step. This, too, explains why ERP has been getting much more awareness recently.

1.2   A Brief History of ERP Applications

Without disregarding any of the remaining market players, the history, as well as the triumph of real-time ERP applications, is intrinsically tied to the success of SAP.

In 1972, the year SAP was founded as a startup in Mannheim, Germany; it was exposed to superior competition in the IT business. Today, SAP is the recognized global market leader in providing collaborative business solutions for all types of industries, for companies of all sizes, and for every major market. With more than 35,000 employees in over 50 countries, 100,000 installations, 12 million users, and thousands of partners, SAP has become the world's largest inter-enterprise software company and the world's third largest independent software supplier.

From startup to global industry leader

With their vision to develop standard application software for real-time business processing, the five founders—Dietmar Hopp, Hans-Werner Hector, Hasso Plattner, Klaus Tschira, and Claus Wellenreuther—embarked on one of the most impressive success stories in the history of the IT industry.

Only one year after SAP's inception, the first financial accounting software was completed. It formed the basis for the continuous development of other software components (in what was later known as the "R/1 system" where "R" stands for real-time data processing). By the end of the 1970s, the development of the SAP R/2 system was in full swing. It saw its market introduction in 1981 and attained the high level of stability of the previous generation of programs. Keeping in mind its multinational customers, SAP designed SAP R/2 to handle different languages and currencies. With this and other innovations in SAP R/2, SAP saw rapid growth materializing with more than 250 customers and over 100 employees at the time the company celebrated its tenth year in business. From the mid '80s onward, the international expansion started to gain momentum with a growing number of subsidiaries outside of Germany.

With development starting in the second half of the '80s, the third generation of SAP's ERP software, SAP R/3, marked the path from mainframe to client/server architecture and was introduced in 1992. While SAP R/2 was well established in the upper and high-end market segment at that time, SAP R/3 was initially targeted at small and mid-size businesses. Along with its introduction, however, came the rapid decline of the mainframe, coinciding with the trend toward downsizing and reengineering. This timely convergence made SAP R/3 the right product at the right

From SAP R/2 to SAP R/3

time, for companies of all sizes—the three-tier client/server concept, uniform appearance of graphical interfaces, consistent use of relational databases, and the ability to run on computers from different vendors made it an overwhelming success throughout the globe and boosted the expansion of SAP. With SAP R/3, SAP spearheaded a new generation of enterprise software—from mainframe computing to the three-tier architecture of database, application, and user interface. Thanks to localized user menus, companies throughout the world could use SAP software. SAP became the first packaged software producer to offer a graphical user interface, replacing mainframe-based systems that still had to be operated using text-based screen templates.

Increasing competition PeopleSoft, a company based in California, started developing applications for human resources, financials, and payroll management in 1987. Competition between SAP and PeopleSoft was particularly intense in the human resources area. Additional competition was presented by the U.S. company JD Edwards, which brought its WorldSoftware ERP suite to market in 1988; from Dun&Bradstreet software, the U.S. market's leading provider of ready-made financial software at the time; and from the Dutch software company Baan, which had originally focused on programs tailored to the manufacturing sector.

By the time SAP celebrated its 25th anniversary in 1997, more than 13,000 people were employed and SAP R/3 had been installed in more than 10,000 systems worldwide. With SAP R/3, SAP released a software suite based on client-server data processing long before the competition. Nevertheless, other companies eventually caught up; at the end of the 1990s, SAP was forced to compete with a number of rivals supplying to the same market segment. The largest of these rivals were the established ERP providers Oracle and Baan. The latter was seeking to expand its product line by acquiring other companies. This strategy proved difficult, however, since Baan had to integrate applications with different architectures into its existing product portfolio. JD Edwards, with its OneWorld ERP software, and PeopleSoft also continued to compete with SAP throughout this period.

The Internet age With the dawning of the Internet age, the user became the focus of software applications, and companies gained the ability to network different computer systems and collaborate across company lines, marking a departure from client/server data processing. In 1999, SAP introduced an all-new product strategy, mySAP.com, an Internet-based platform that companies from any industry and of any size could use to process business transactions. SAP developed mySAP Workplace and paved the way for the idea of an enterprise portal and role-specific access to information. Despite these efforts, SAP's extensive service offerings were unable to cover all of the industry's functional bases. Best-of-breed providers saw the potential for their products, especially in the market for customer relationship management (CRM) and supply chain management (SCM) software. SAP, however, responded swiftly in bringing the solutions mySAP CRM and mySAP SCM to market. SAP locked horns with competitors' i2 and Manugistics on the SCM market, and with Siebel Systems in the CRM market. With respect to portals, SAP competed with specialist software providers like Plumtree, Vignette, and Hummingbird.

In the interim, the Internet hype died down. SAP changed the name of its platform from mySAP.com to mySAP Business Suite. This solution portfolio comprised a broad range of products, including mySAP SCM, mySAP CRM, and mySAP ERP, for example—the next generation ERP solution. To make integration of the suite's various business applications even more flexible, SAP began offering SAP NetWeaver as a central platform in 2003. Initially, only existing SAP applications were integrated on this platform; in an additional step, software from third-party providers could also be integrated. This strategy enabled companies that needed to implement software from different providers, or develop their own solutions, to integrate all of these solutions on a single platform. By releasing mySAP ERP to the market, SAP launched the next generation ERP solution for end-to-end business processes based on Enterprise Services Architecture (ESA) and the underlying integration and application platform, SAP NetWeaver, thereby enabling organizations to integrate people, information, and processes within and beyond the companies' boundaries. A comprehensive integration and application platform, SAP NetWeaver works with existing IT infrastructures to enable and manage change, and drive innovation throughout the organization via a combination of existing systems, all the while maintaining sustainable cost structures.

The mySAP portfolio

mySAP ERP combines the world's most complete, scalable, and effective software for enterprise resource planning with its flexible, open application platform. It is enhanced by industry-specific business processes and best practices based on three decades of SAP's experience. It enables organizations to reduce total cost of ownership (TCO), achieve a faster return on investment (ROI), and benefit from a more flexible IT infrastructure that helps drive productivity and innovation. mySAP ERP offers a complete solution designed to support international operations so that businesses can efficiently and successfully operate and compete on a global scale (see also Figure 1.2). In contrast to the move from SAP R/2 to SAP R/3 in the 1990s, which is best described as a revolutionary step requiring a rip-and-replace of the IT landscape, the move from SAP R/3 to mySAP ERP is an evolutionary step, a transition, which can easily build on existing assets and infrastructures — we'll return to this subject later.

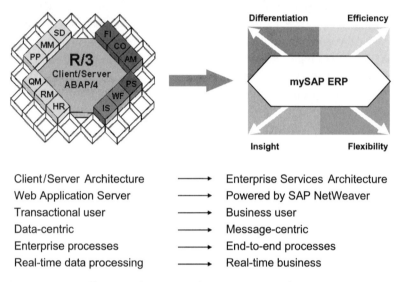

Client/Server Architecture	⟶	Enterprise Services Architecture
Web Application Server	⟶	Powered by SAP NetWeaver
Transactional user	⟶	Business user
Data-centric	⟶	Message-centric
Enterprise processes	⟶	End-to-end processes
Real-time data processing	⟶	Real-time business

Figure 1.2 Key Differences of SAP R/3 and mySAP ERP at a Glance

Today, SAP is the world's leading provider of ERP software, with subsidiaries in over 50 countries. The company faces competition from software industry players like IBM, Microsoft, and Oracle. SAP has multidimensional relationships with IBM and Microsoft, with each party simultaneously assuming the role of customer, partner, and competitor. Microsoft and SAP have worked together since 1993 and are set to underscore their collaboration by the end of 2005 with the release of the joint product Mendocino. While IBM partners with SAP in the database industry, it competes with SAP on the platform market.

1.3 Enabling Business Change

The value that IT creates for organizations has changed. More than a decade ago, SAP and its partner ecosystem delivered efficiency to their customers through best-practice processes. Today, the focal point is definitely shifting to realizing business ideas by finding the right combination of proven best practices and innovative practices.

Completely new demands are being placed on IT. Software must be designed to allow and support the swift adaptation of sophisticated processes spanning within and beyond the organization. It must be capable of mapping entire networks of value generation in order to keep pace with changing conditions. That is the content of Service-Oriented Architectures (SOA), as offered by SAP with its Enterprise Services Architecture (ESA), a main benefit of which is that business-oriented services are supplied, thus leveraging an organization's existing applications and IT infrastructure. ESA is SAP's blueprint for service-based, enterprise-scale business solutions that offer the increased levels of adaptability, flexibility, and openness required to reduce TCO. It combines SAP's experience in enterprise applications with the flexibility of Web services and other open standards. The SAP NetWeaver platform is the technical foundation for ESA. Enterprise Services Architecture elevates the design, composition, and deployment of Web services to an enterprise level to address business requirements. An enterprise service is typically a series of Web services combined with simple business logic that can be accessed and used repeatedly to support a particular business process. Aggregating Web services into business-level enterprise services provides more meaningful building blocks for the task of automating enterprise-scale business scenarios. Enterprise services allow you to efficiently develop composite applications, which are applications that compose functionality and information from existing systems to support new business processes or scenarios. All enterprise services communicate using Web services standards; they can be described in a central repository; and, they're created and managed by tools provided by SAP NetWeaver.

ESA enables companies to have a cost-effective blueprint for composing innovative new applications. It does this by extending existing systems, while maintaining a level of flexibility that makes future process changes cost-effective. ESA moves IT architectures step-by-step to dramatically higher levels of adaptability, and it helps companies move closer to the vision of the real-time enterprise. The promise of ESA is twofold: facilitating business innovation while leveraging existing resources.

After all, it's pointless if organizations have to keep switching to successive generations of software to finally realize the need for flexibility—software that can take years to implement with high migration costs is hardly worth the investment in time and money. A large number of organizations agree that business process management is a permanent process, knowing that their capability to survive in our global competitive markets depends on the prudent management of adjustments and changes. Service Oriented Architectures are the next evolutionary step in business computing and lead to a more flexible configuration and adaptation of business processes.

Furthermore, with the increased need for innovation and differentiation in today's challenging business conditions, executives are under strong pressure. Among the key challenges to accomplish, many competing objectives entail such matters as understanding and anticipating customer requirements and the moves of the competition, encouraging innovation, defining strategic goals, and executing operational plans to improve bottom-line profitability, while simultaneously balancing profitable growth and maintaining operational control. Executives also have to create and sustain an innovation-oriented company culture that nurtures competitive advantage in this increasingly global and ever-changing environment.

Consequently, it is essential that organizations take full advantage of their entire network to fine-tune responsiveness to customer demands and work more efficiently with suppliers and partners, thereby enabling a faster go-to-market of value-added products and services. Sensing market changes and customer requirements in real time and obtaining the ability to adapt and react faster than the competition, while closely managing costs, is key to remaining competitive and enabling sustainable growth.

Now let's be clear on the expectations. Even a next generation ERP solution cannot do the job of teasing out which products and services will differentiate an organization successfully from the competition. Ultimately, the knowledge of the respective markets, industry, and its customers lies within an organization.

So, while making IT more adaptable is essential, ensuring that IT delivers business solutions rather than technology solutions requires that IT must comprehend the business strategy and the challenges ahead. Only then will IT be in the position to take action rapidly and that necessitates a common language between business and IT. This is one of the key objectives that ESA is to deliver: to provide a common language and ensure that the integration of technology is understood by business people as well. By defining the services in a way that they correspond to the individual steps of the business processes, as understood by the business people, they will serve as a common denominator for the road ahead. Having said this, the need to up-skill resources with business process composition skills in this new domain of IT soon becomes apparent, making employees both business and IT savvy.

Thus, once the corresponding strategy and its major steps are defined, a next generation ERP solution like mySAP ERP will greatly facilitate reaching the set goals at distinctly reduced costs when compared with the early days.

1.3.1 The Evolution of Business Requirements

The forces reshaping business are mostly less obvious than one would imagine and tend to take place in the background. Many of the changes introduced during the dot.com revolution had a more substantial impact on our traditional information technology than first envisioned. In "Living on the Fault Line," Geoffrey Moore describes these forces as a series of transitions, shifting power away from things that had long been drivers of value creation to items that were once viewed as secondary or peripheral.

For example, one of the major shifts—the one from assets to information—implies that information about an asset has often turned out to be more valuable than the asset itself. Under such new and extended opportunities, holding information about an asset, for example, in the form of options to buy or sell a certain good, can be much more profitable than holding the asset itself. The leverage that can be obtained from such transactions is distinctly higher than it is from traditional transactions involving the actual ownership of the good. Profiting from these opportunities, however, requires superior information systems that provide decision-critical information at the right time—an issue with which many organizations still struggle.

From assets to information

A recent survey conducted by the CIO Magazine of more than 500 CEOs and CIOs further confirms the trend toward productivity and innovation. The top ranked items of the survey deal with efficiency, productivity, and enabling innovation as the key impacts predicted to be enabled by IT (see Figure 1.3). In other words, IT must proactively envision business opportunities and apply technology to achieve them, in addition to supporting predefined business initiatives—all to enable a company to stay competitive and innovative.

Demands towards IT

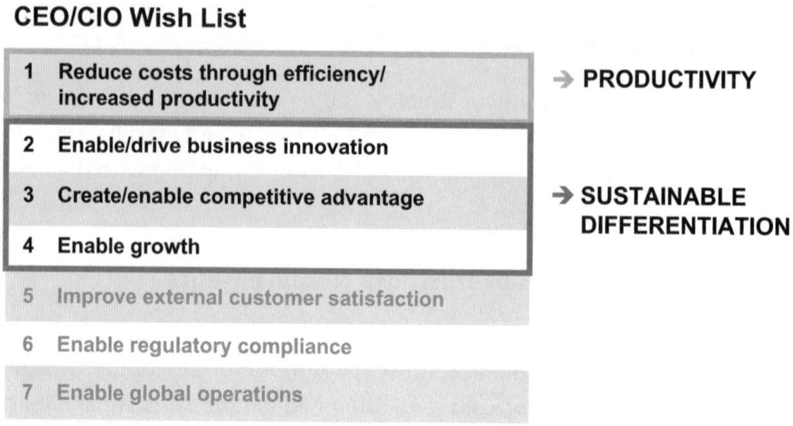

CEO/CIO Wish List

1	**Reduce costs through efficiency/ increased productivity**
2	**Enable/drive business innovation**
3	**Create/enable competitive advantage**
4	**Enable growth**
5	Improve external customer satisfaction
6	Enable regulatory compliance
7	Enable global operations

→ **PRODUCTIVITY**

→ **SUSTAINABLE DIFFERENTIATION**

Figure 1.3 Growth Through Innovation — CEO/CIO Wish List

Reduced time-to-adapt

A key item that is required to live up to this demand is enabling a company's ability to adapt business processes much faster than it had done so in the past. If we look back over several decades, this is analogous to process execution time, which had to be reduced in order to stay competitive back then.

Along with others, technological advancements and real-time business applications have made this a non-issue today where operational processes can be executed within minutes, or even or parts of a second, depending on the process. Consequently, to further reduce process execution time now wouldn't create a considerable advantage for most companies and would therefore not be integral to reaching the set goals. Today, however, many organizations struggle with the time and effort required to adapt business processes to the evolving market and customer demands, often due to heterogeneous IT landscapes in which adapting business processes is a lengthy and costly effort. If we can significantly cut the time and effort required to meet these demands, companies will be freed up to become more competitive by being able to change existing business processes faster or execute new processes when necessary, giving them an advantage over the competition.

Core and context

But why is the ability to quickly adapt existing business processes, or execute new business processes, so essential for innovation and staying competitive? The core and context model introduced by Geoffrey Moore in "Living on the Fault Line" is an excellent way in which to illustrate this point:

The typical issue companies, as well as IT organizations, face is spending too much time on activities that are context-related and too little time on activities that are core. An activity is regarded as core when its outcome directly affects the competitive advantage of an organization and enables the creation of sustainable differentiation, and with this, generates value that customers are willing to pay for. On the contrary, all other activities that do not directly affect these aspects are regarded to be context and need to be performed in a standardized manner that focuses on efficiency. Because these context activities don't create a competitive advantage, there is no sound business rationale to differentiate them further— a company won't get any credit from the market for executing them exceptionally well. Context tasks, in simple terms, do create some value, but they don't add competitive advantage, and therefore, they are typical candidates for outsourcing so as to avoid or remedy a situation whereby most of the scarce resources work on context activities.

Nevertheless, the type of activities that are regarded as core for one company may well be considered to be context for another company, and vice versa, depending on a company's key differentiating products or services.

Both core and context tasks are critical for an organization's productivity and require careful supervision to ensure that the focus lies on activities generating sustainable differentiation and customer value. For this reason, the question arises, "Where do most of the context-related activities come from?"

Actually, in today's markets, technology itself is often the basis for differentiation and this makes imitation a lot easier now than it was in the past. Furthermore, core turns into context over time, simply by the fact that the competition will eventually imitate, or even by copying a product or service that will no longer be a key differentiator from then on, since the other competitors now offer it. Therefore, the effort invested in core activities for differentiation will one day result in context activities. Moreover, the core processes, typically custom processes, are far too intricate to sustain, given the decreased value they now add when turned into a context process over time. A logical consequence to decrease the context activities is to give them to someone for whom this is a core activity, that is, outsourcing the context activities to a service provider that has specialized in doing this type of activity, and thereby freeing up funds and resources for activities that directly impact innovation or support existing key differentiators. A typical example of this would be companies out-

Lifecycle of core and context

sourcing parts, or even the entirety of their production, to a service provider (as regularly observed in technology and design-savvy markets such as mobile phones, laptops, and television sets, or in the automotive industry) so the company could focus instead on activities such as research, design, and marketing.

Outsourcing of context activities Still, as recent surveys show, recombining existing items in a new way, rather than building them entirely from scratch, creates a considerable number of innovations. In this case, activities that have already moved over to the context side can shift back to being core again. This cycle is illustrated in Figure 1.4.

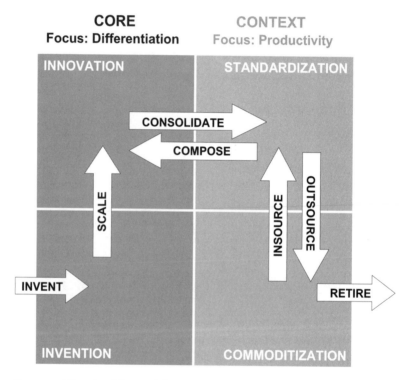

Figure 1.4 Lifecycle of Core and Context Activities

On the basis of the described lifecycle, it is readily apparent that the ability to adapt business processes to changed market conditions quickly is a competitive advantage that is integral for today's companies. If we combine the core and context lifecycle and the most significant contributions expected by IT, we can see that managing both aspects of the lifecycle is a key challenge to be mastered (see Figure 1.5).

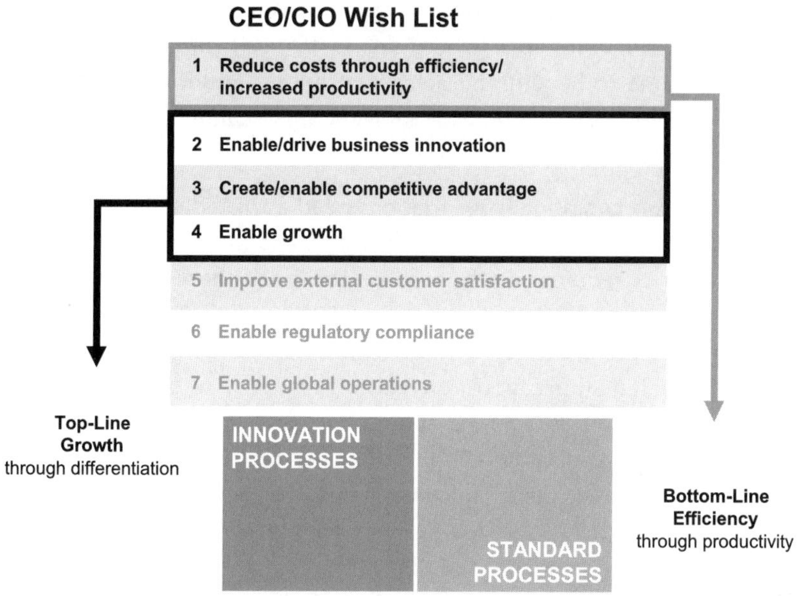

CEO/CIO Wish List

1	Reduce costs through efficiency/increased productivity
2	Enable/drive business innovation
3	Create/enable competitive advantage
4	Enable growth
5	Improve external customer satisfaction
6	Enable regulatory compliance
7	Enable global operations

Top-Line Growth
through differentiation

INNOVATION PROCESSES

STANDARD PROCESSES

Bottom-Line Efficiency
through productivity

Figure 1.5 The Need to Manage Efficiency and Growth Simultaneously

In this context, business application software, through the business processes it enables and the information it provides, is an essential building block helping organizations to achieve their current goals and to prepare for the future. Although not always viewed as a means to differentiation, day-to-day operational efficiency is mission-critical, because it is a key enabler for innovation by freeing up funds and resources for activities focused on exploring and adding new value. Processes supporting new initiatives that deliver innovation, untapped markets, or new products require increasing levels of investment. Organizations have invested billions in legacy and best-of-breed solutions to support day-to-day operations. Many of these organizations are still working hard to successfully implement, deploy, and integrate these solutions to end users in order to achieve a decent return on their investment, while hoping to invest spending in areas where innovative processes can be fostered and improved. Continuous development of both home grown and commercial off-the-shelf software has resulted in a heterogeneous IT landscape for many organizations. Owing to the cost and effort of integration among these disparate systems, the reality for many organizations is that they have a "silo-like" incomplete view of their business. The consequent lack of business insight exposes organizations to numerous problems—spanning from everyday inefficiency and ineffectiveness to regulatory non-compliance and neglected growth opportunities. Increasingly more

Operational efficiency and innovation

organizations these days tend to be cautious and more analytical when making new IT investments, toward clearer defined tactical initiatives that accelerate time to benefit and achieve a quicker return on investment, rather than intricate multimillion dollar implementation projects over several years.

Requirements for ERP To remedy this condition, organizations need a trusted software partner and a flexible technology platform that provides the agility to compose applications as required, with the business insight necessary to quickly adapt to changes without limiting flexibility as organizational requirements evolve in the future. With such an architecture, organizations can build integrated applications on existing services to address market opportunities without worrying about how these services will be implemented. Existing applications and components can be reused, resulting in shorter development and deployment time and reduced costs. mySAP ERP, powered by SAP NetWeaver, with its Enterprise Services Architecture is such a next generation solution.

This leads to several questions:

▶ How is a next generation ERP system differentiating itself from traditional ERP systems in general and with concepts such as ESA?

▶ How can a next generation ERP system such as mySAP ERP serve as a main pillar in supporting organizations to master the challenges ahead?

▶ Which are the key business scenarios and processes that make daily operations efficient and enable innovation?

▶ What are the typical roadmaps to mySAP ERP?

▶ How have other companies conducted the step to mySAP ERP and what are the key benefits they gained from this transition?

We will address these and other questions in the chapters that follow.

1.3.2 Next Generation ERP

For both new customers and existing SAP customers, mySAP ERP offers many benefits. Although the needs of new and existing customers are comparable, some aspects of next generation ERP solutions tend to differ in importance, while other aspects are identically important.

Meeting customer demands New customers typically strive for a quick return on investment (ROI), in months rather than years, and for implementation strategies that cause as little disruption to the operations as possible as they move from legacy applications to a next generation solution. This is a fundamental reason why currently many implementations are broken up into smaller subsequent phases, whereby a smaller scope of the project is realized upfront and then later enhanced with additional scenarios in a second step—both phases are designed to achieve quick wins and reap benefits as early as possible. ERP packaged solutions, predominantly geared at mid-market customers, focus on this need by offering a combination of ERP software, best-practice templates and implementation services at a fixed price, fixed scope, and fixed implementation time (there are more details on packaged solutions in Chapter 3).

The additional focus points for existing SAP customers extend to their existing SAP R/3 landscape and the corresponding previous investments. Because the move from SAP R/3 to mySAP ERP is an evolutionary step, best described as a transition and not a disruptive, revolutionary step like the move from mainframe to client/server architecture, existing customers want to understand how their existing assets can best be leveraged when making the transition to mySAP ERP, along with discovering the key benefits that are achievable when evolving to next generation ERP.

Although the importance of these aspects varies between new and existing customers, the general benefits that can be realized with a next generation ERP solution are appropriate to both.

Among the primary benefits of the next generation ERP solutions is the opportunity (and typically the need) to consolidate, integrate, and standardize the IT landscape with its many technologies and providers built up over the years, be it best-of-breed, home-grown, or any other remnants from the past, where traditionally multiple systems and platforms were used to drive innovation and efficiency. While innovation and growth-related processes were regularly driven by isolated, often custom-built applications, standard processes were run on integrated, however, rather static systems (see also Figure 1.6). With the use of these multiple, disparate platforms, integration between the two types of processes remained a major challenge, characteristically only realized via inflexible or even hard-coded routines that lacked the flexibility and scalability necessary to adapt swiftly to new market requirements.

IT landscape consolidation and integration

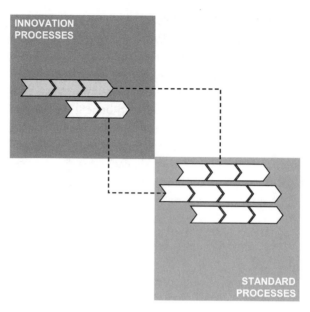

Figure 1.6 Disparate Platforms for Innovative and Standard Processes

Consequently, what is necessary to evolve to the next level is the move from the disparate platforms to one single platform that can support both innovative and standard processes, and can manage efficiency and innovation on a Service-Oriented Architecture (see Figure 1.7).

The superior integration capabilities and scenario coverage of a next generation ERP system—in the form of mySAP ERP and its flexible technology platform—are enabling the required shift. It will allow you to lower corresponding expenditures and free up funds for specific investments in strategic solutions, so you can further enhance operational efficiency and generate more activities with additional value. Therefore, mastering the consolidation is a key step in transitioning to a next generation ERP solution, where technology is intended to result in greater efficiency rather than create another battleground for scarce resources and funds.

Next generation ERP provides both the scenarios and the functionality required and available as services—fundamental building blocks that can be used for modeling company-specific business processes. Furthermore, building new processes, or enhancing existing processes based on these services, is easier than ever before.

Given these objectives, mySAP ERP represents the logical step for organizations to match their future requirements, whether they will implement the full scope at once or, more commonly, use a phased approach. The set of technology options, scenarios, functionality, and incorporation of industry standards such as Java or XML alleviates risks related to system incompatibility or complex integration. This, along with the vendor's continuous research, development, services, and support offerings make it a safe choice for organizations of all sizes and industries. Furthermore, entry barriers have been lowered with more flexible pricing, which also takes into account corresponding previous investments, and focuses on a per-user, per-scenario, or a per-transaction instance, and enhanced packaged solution offerings that are based on best-practice templates, which also decrease implementation time. These packaged solutions, tailored for mid-market customers, have recently been garnering more attention, fuelled by the determination of the major ERP vendors to capture the lion's share of this growing market.

Moving on from the consolidation challenge, it's time to have a first look at the differentiating aspects of next generation ERP solutions, represented by four strategic pillars for the major benefits attainable, while delivering one platform for both innovation-related and efficiency-related processes that connects the entire business ecosystem of customers, suppliers, and partners (see Figure 1.7). **Strategic pillars of mySAP ERP**

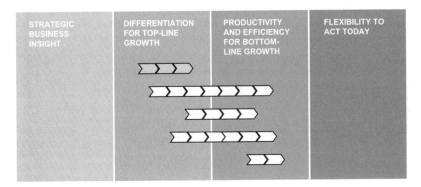

Figure 1.7 The Four Strategic Pillars of mySAP ERP

Embedding analytics in all relevant processes serves the need to obtain relevant information and understand the corresponding activities across the entire value generation network. This allows for once isolated potential areas of concern to engage in business opportunities. Furthermore, the apparent need for compliance with an ever-growing number of regulatory requirements is better served now than ever before. Predefined analytical dashboards provide business guidance, as well as content, which are based on secure, auditable information for authorized roles to **Strategic business insight** support strategic, operational, and compliance activities. mySAP ERP delivers the most comprehensive and efficient corporate governance functionality by enabling organizations to comply with the unique requirements of multiple international standards, including Sarbanes-Oxley, Basel II, and IAS/IFRS, as well as global HR regulations. Because this functionality is tightly integrated, it ensures data integrity and data security, corporate reporting, analysis, and compliance with underlying business process, and transaction systems into a single, complete solution. The result is a sound internal control, and a transparent financial environment that mitigates risk, assures regulatory compliance, and increases corporate trust.

Differentiation for top line growth As we already outlined extensively, focusing on only efficiency is not sufficient in today's competitive markets. Organizations need to keep reinventing and differentiating themselves in order to drive top-line growth. The traditional IT infrastructures have been difficult to manage and lack the flexibility and scalability to adapt quickly to new requirements. mySAP ERP, as the key enabler of business change, provides new scenarios and functionality built on a Service-Oriented Architecture, which provides organizations the flexibility to drive innovation and with it growth, while simultaneously managing operational excellence.

Improved productivity for bottom-line growth Building on top of the improvements in productivity and efficiency already provided by traditional ERP systems, next generation ERP brings operational excellence to the next level by extending the reach of real-time business processes beyond the conventional boundaries of an organization, including employees, customers, supplier, and partners. By offering intuitive web- and role-based portal environments, people are enabled to get their job done faster by providing access to all relevant applications, information, and services. This ensures an easier system-wide access to a single, consolidated, and consistent business process view that offers the information required to react efficiently and respond proactively to market changes.

Flexibility to act today Last but not least, mySAP ERP, powered by SAP NetWeaver technology, offers the flexibility and scalability required to enable, enhance, and deploy real-time business processes that automatically adapt and accelerate business strategies. Furthermore, it allows seamless integration of end-to-end processes into a scalable and adaptable industry solution, with the option to incrementally extend through the right mix of additional customer relationship management (CRM), supply chain management (SCM), or product lifecycle management (PLM) scenarios as the business requires over time. Data from legacy and non-SAP systems can be extended easily to the mySAP ERP environment in order to lower operational costs further, in addition to being well positioned to accelerate business change with new business scenarios and technologies that are emerging from SAP's Enterprise Services Architecture.

All in all, this leads to the conclusion that the footprint of a next generation ERP solution in the form of mySAP ERP has been extended from the traditional footprint of efficiency-related standard processes to innovation-related processes (see Figure 1.8). Therefore, it is providing organizations with all the necessary opportunities to manage sustainable growth while maintaining productivity.

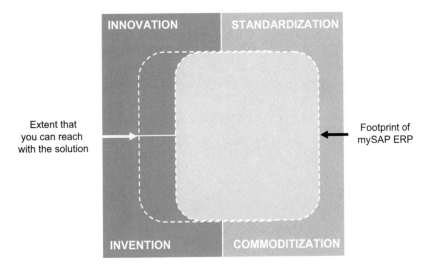

Figure 1.8 Extended Footprint of mySAP ERP

2 The Key Capabilities of mySAP ERP

This chapter looks at the range of processes and functionality offered by mySAP ERP and shows how organizations can gain benefits from deploying these scenarios. But first, we'll explain the path from SAP R/3 to mySAP ERP in more detail.

2.1 From SAP R/3 to mySAP ERP

One way of comparing traditional Enterprise Resource Planning (ERP) and the next generation ERP is to think of an efficiently run office as a traditional ERP and an efficient and agile enterprise as a next generation ERP. SAP and its customers are entering the third generation of ERP—the third time that SAP is leading the way in defining and driving ERP. With the first generation, SAP R/2, SAP brought value to organizations through real-time integration of systems in a central mainframe environment. The second generation, SAP R/3, brought value through standardized business processes in a networked client/server environment. With the third generation, mySAP ERP, SAP brings value to its customers through the integration of heterogeneous environments, with the focus on adaptability and enabling people in an ever-changing environment.

Unlike the move from SAP R/2 to SAP R/3, however, this change is not of a revolutionary nature. It is far more accurate to describe it as an evolutionary step—a step offering a smooth transition, which does not require customers to discard their existing environments (see also Figure 2.1). **An evolutionary step**

In fact, mySAP ERP leverages the second generation by allowing full compatibility with SAP R/3 Enterprise. That means that customers can move into mySAP ERP smoothly, step-by-step, at their own pace, without having to replace systems.

A significant aspect of the new ERP is extendable integration in a heterogeneous environment. For that, SAP NetWeaver, SAP's application and integration platform, offers a state-of-the-art framework to organizations. IT departments can take control of their environments gradually and incrementally by leveraging the power of Enterprise Portals, Exchange Infrastructure, Business Intelligence, and SAP Web Application Server (SAP Web AS) in an Enterprise Services Architecture (ESA). One of the **SAP NetWeaver** chief benefits of this platform is that it allows businesses to respond quickly to new challenges.

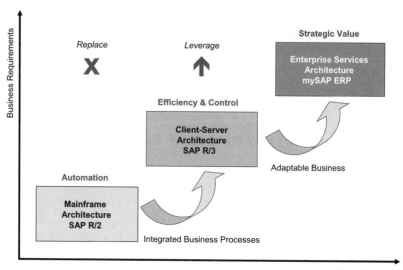

Figure 2.1 Leverage Existing Assets with the Transition to mySAP ERP

With this agility, organizations can gain competitive advantages in the global marketplace and exploit opportunities quickly and effectively. Furthermore, people-centric processing is critical as organizations realize the necessity of leveraging their most important assets. Deploying human capital efficiently is one of the biggest value-creating opportunities and the principal intangible asset that companies have these days. By simply employing the right combination of world-class usability, efficient role definitions, and analytic capabilities, people are enabled to capture the full potential of the ERP environment. Corporate Governance is equally important—a must in a post-WorldCom world in which Sarbanes Oxley, Basel II, IAS/IFRS, and other regulations significantly affect the IT landscape. mySAP ERP focuses on all of these aspects and provides companies with long-term sustainable benefits.

We'll discuss the extended footprint of ERP (see Figure 2.2) further in the coming chapters and give you an overview of how the scenario coverage and functional breadth and depth of mySAP ERP can provide the aforementioned benefits to organizations throughout the world, organizations of all sizes and industries. Moreover, we'll discuss how mySAP ERP and its evolving landscape can enable you to achieve the chosen business strategy and become increasingly successful in an ever-changing world.

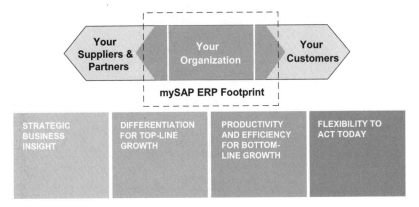

Figure 2.2 Extended Footprint of mySAP ERP

Prior to that, however, it is important that you understand the position of mySAP ERP within the entire SAP solution portfolio.

mySAP ERP is a mySAP solution. In addition to mySAP ERP, SAP offers other mySAP solutions for the areas of Customer Relationship Management (mySAP CRM), Supplier Relationship Management (mySAP SRM), Product Lifecycle Management (mySAP PLM), and Supply Chain Management (mySAP SCM). All these solutions are part of the mySAP Business Suite (formerly known as mySAP.com), as you can see from Figure 2.3.

SAP NetWeaver represents the technology stack provided by SAP to support the mySAP Business Suite and its solutions, as well as other SAP products. Furthermore, SAP NetWeaver and its integration capabilities also allow for the integration of non-SAP products. SAP NetWeaver is delivered with all of the mySAP solutions and consequently, customers can utilize the SAP NetWeaver capabilities for a specific solution.

The principle of the mySAP Business Suite and its solutions is that customers can find the exact solutions they need for their specific requirements. In that context, mySAP ERP can be seen as the first step toward the full suite. A customer that primarily requires best-in-class ERP capabilities will ideally start with mySAP ERP, and by licensing mySAP ERP, the customer will receive the software for state-of-the-art ERP, including SAP NetWeaver.

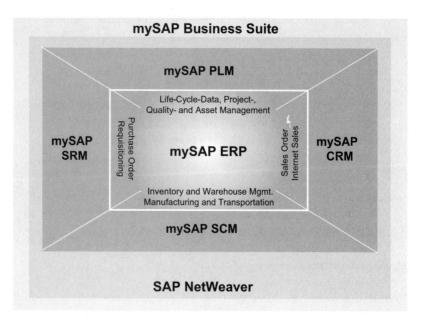

Figure 2.3 mySAP ERP within the mySAP Business Suite

Key capabilities mySAP ERP addresses the core and extended business requirements of midsize and large organizations, whatever their industry or global reach. The solution provides a sophisticated tool that empowers businesses to coordinate, plan, and execute operations activities quickly and effectively in today's challenging business environment. In addition, it gives enterprises better control of their assets and business processes by providing a full suite of software functionality:

▶ Analytics

▶ Financials

▶ Human Capital Management

▶ Operations

▶ Corporate Services

Organizations can extend capabilities to create truly adaptive business systems that support internal business processes, supply chain networks, and collaboration with customers and suppliers, resulting in improved customer relationships and increased revenue, both now and in the future. The mySAP ERP solution map, shown in Figure 2.4, shows the core business processes that the solution supports.

	Self Services			
Analytics	Strategic Enterprise Management	Financial Analytics	Operations Analytics	Workforce Analytics
Financials	Financial Accounting	Management Accounting	Financial Supply Chain Management	Corporate Governance
Human Capital Management	Employee Life-Cycle Management	Employee Transaction Management	HCM Service Delivery	Workforce Deployment
Operations: Value Generation	Procurement / Inventory & Warehouse Management	Manufacturing	Transportation / Sales Order Management	Customer Service
Operations: Support	Life-Cycle Data Management	Program & Project Management	Quality Management	Enterprise Asset Management
Corporate Services	Travel Management	Environment, Health & Safe	Incentive & Commission Management	Real Estate Management

Figure 2.4 mySAP ERP Solution Map Edition 2004

2.2 Analytics

The accelerating pace of business change, increased competition, and growing scrutiny from regulators makes it more important than ever for organizations to have in-depth insight into their business and up-to-date information about their customers, employees, partners, costs, quality, and other aspects of business performance. Organizations are also under pressure to develop innovative products or services, strengthen their market position, and fulfill ever-growing stakeholder and customer demands. To achieve these goals, enterprises need information that is accurate, accessible to the relevant people, and integrated enterprise-wide. The information also needs to consider all business aspects and the impact of change and dependencies.

In short, information must be more than just a collection of enterprise-wide data; it must be "intelligent" information generated by an integrated business intelligence infrastructure. Organizations can then use this information to develop and execute corporate strategies that build value and drive success. The problem is that many organizations have "business intelligence" systems that, over time, have become fragmented, ineffective, complex, and costly to maintain. They cannot be extended to develop new business intelligence applications. And most importantly, the information that these systems provide is unreliable and incomplete at best.

"Intelligent" information

Implementing an integrated business intelligence infrastructure presents a great many challenges, but the benefits are significant. In addition to helping organizations secure a leading competitive edge, the right business intelligence infrastructure can help to reduce costs, ease entry into

Business intelligence infrastructure

new markets, and enable executives to develop more effective competitive strategies and plans for long-term revenue growth.

mySAP ERP offers comprehensive analysis, forecasting, and reporting tools that support human capital management, financial, and operations processes. Key functions include the following:

▶ **Strategic enterprise management**
mySAP ERP enables enterprises to implement strategies quickly and successfully, as well as manage business performance throughout the entire organization. The solution also supports integrated business planning, performance monitoring, business consolidation, and effective stakeholder communication.

▶ **Financial analysis**
The solution also helps organizations define financial targets, develop a commensurate business plan, and monitor costs and revenue on execution.

▶ **Operational analysis**
mySAP ERP facilitates the compilation of detailed operations reports and informed operational decision-making.

▶ **Workforce analysis**
mySAP ERP provides data analysis and reporting tools to analyze and optimize workforce performance, implement and monitor corporate strategy, and evaluate how various scenarios may affect business goals.

2.2.1 Strategic Enterprise Management

Strategic Enterprise Management (SEM) enables companies to implement strategies quickly and successfully, as well as manage business performance throughout the entire organization. SEM also supports integrated business planning, performance monitoring, business consolidation, and effective stakeholder communication.

Holistic performance measurement

mySAP ERP provides comprehensive SEM functionality that offers two primary advantages. First, it delivers a holistic solution that spans the entire performance management cycle—from business planning to performance measurement. Furthermore, by integrating tools for business consolidation, performance measurement, and strategy management with business planning tools, mySAP ERP delivers one of the only closed-loop environments for performance management available today. Secondly, mySAP ERP offers unparalleled SEM functionality in a single solution; few, if any, companies can match this level of functionality without partnering with other providers.

No programming is necessary to utilize SEM via mySAP ERP. The SEM functionality is easy to customize with configuration settings. And with mySAP ERP, employees can make business strategy a part of their daily activities and perform the following functions:

▶ **Business planning and simulation**
mySAP ERP enhances the accuracy and sophistication of a company's financial plans and forecasts while curtailing and simplifying its budgeting and planning processes. This solution allows organizations to update budgets more frequently; meet changing business conditions; and combine traditional, bottom-up budgeting with top-down strategic planning. In addition, the solution encourages a more collaborative budgeting and planning process that involves a greater number of departmental and divisional managers, while at the same time helping companies to integrate strategic, operational, and financial plans to ensure that all business activities are in line with the business strategy.

▶ **Performance measurement**
mySAP ERP provides a management cockpit interface—the ideal framework for reporting performance results. The structure of the interface is predefined yet flexible and enables companies to deliver graphical, numerical, and verbal information to various levels within the organization. Users also benefit from fast access to information in a web-based environment.

▶ **Strategy management**
The solution supports strategy management and provides tools, such as support for a Balanced Scorecard, that help organizations better translate strategy into action by defining and communicating strategies in areas such as product innovation, customer relations, and operational efficiency.

▶ **Accounting consolidation**
mySAP ERP provides comprehensive accounting functions to help companies handle the statutory and management requirements of financial consolidation. This solution offers powerful, ready-to-use tools, preconfigured business content, and sophisticated reporting features that help to streamline the consolidation cycle. The accounting consolidation functions also add significant value to enterprises by providing advanced automation for a fast close, a user-defined data

model, and user-friendly graphical interface, and fully reconciled reporting for both internal and external business groups.

▶ **Risk management**
The solution supports the entire management process—from identifying business risks, administrating risk catalogs, and analyzing and quantifying risks to assigning risks and implementing risk-reducing activities. Furthermore, mySAP ERP supports the setting and monitoring of risk targets, exception reporting, and the development of written assessments.

▶ **Stakeholder relationship management**
mySAP ERP provides functionality for communicating enterprise strategy, current financial results, and strategic initiatives to an organization's stakeholders. It also facilitates the decentralized assimilation of financial figures from subsidiaries in a structured and systematic way.

Increase added value with mySAP ERP

mySAP ERP adds business value in the area of SEM by enabling organizations to control an entire organization using value-based management principles, to set operational objectives, and to convert strategies into actions. The companies have the ability to perform continuous and efficient simulation, planning, and forecasting across an organization, and to accelerate and automate the legal and management aspects of business consolidation. They are also enabled to provide risk forecasts, which are reconciled with business objectives and targets, to collect, structure, and edit relevant external information, and to automatically distribute it to end users on an ongoing basis by using graphical user interfaces that indicate performance measurement and significantly improve communication with stakeholders.

2.2.2   Financial Analytics

mySAP ERP provides financial analytics that help organizations define financial targets, develop a commensurate business plan, and monitor costs and revenue during execution. The comprehensive financial analytics enable businesses to create and simulate value flows in a cross-functional, cross company, or collaborative environment.

mySAP ERP adds business value by supporting comprehensive financial analysis and reporting for a wide range of users—from C-level executives to sales assistants. In addition, the solution helps to improve profitability and increase working capital and cash flow, to ensure more efficient cost controls, and to improve insight via better planning and forecasting.

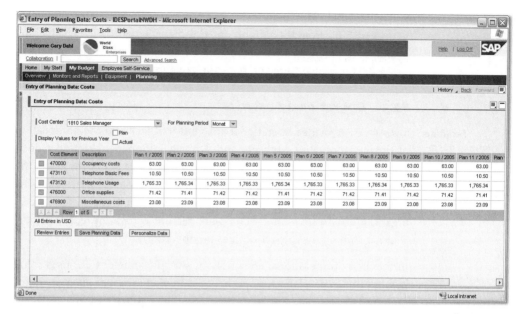

Figure 2.5 Financial Analytics within mySAP ERP

Key functions include the following:

▶ **Financial and management reporting**
mySAP ERP supports a series of standard analyses to meet a wide range of end users' reporting needs, including C-level executives, line-of-business managers, and sales assistants.

▶ **Planning, budgeting, and forecasting**
mySAP ERP also supports traditional budgeting, rolling forecasts, and collaborative planning, such as cost center planning illustrated in Figure 2.5. The analytical planning workbench allows enterprises to model planning scenarios and provides preconfigured planning applications for efficient operational planning.

▶ **Cost and profitability management**
mySAP ERP supports cost and profitability management. It includes functions for the assignment of overhead costs, management of the costs incurred by products and services, and profitability analysis of products and services.

▶ **Working capital and cash flow management**
mySAP ERP supports working capital management via optimized logistics processes and improved liabilities and receivables management. In addition, it supports cash flow management, including cash flow calculations and mid- to long-term planning.

▶ **Payment behavior analysis**
mySAP ERP provides support for the management of receivables by analyzing payment histories and determining the days sales outstanding (DSO), which form the basis for payment optimization.

2.2.3 Operational Analytics

Facilitate informed operational decisions mySAP ERP provides operational analytics that facilitate the compilation of detailed operations reports and support informed operational decision-making. mySAP ERP provides management and employees with the information they need to increase insight into business processes. The mySAP ERP solution also includes sales planning functionality that allows organizations to generate a complete picture across the entire supply chain, including the impact of sales on operations.

In the area of operational analytics, mySAP ERP provides business value by optimizing the entire supply chain; improving revenues via more comprehensive sales planning and monitoring; increasing customer satisfaction through sophisticated quality management and quality monitoring, and providing more detailed, in-depth customer information and more customer-oriented processes. It achieves these benefits by providing operational analytics support in the following areas:

▶ Operations value generation

▶ Operations support

▶ Sales planning and analysis

Added value in "operations" mySAP ERP provides analytics that help organizations generate value in operations. Using this solution, organizations can perform the following functions:

▶ **Procurement monitoring**
mySAP ERP provides various standard analyses and reports to monitor purchasing operations and provide a detailed analysis of purchasing activities and procurement processes.

▶ **Inventory and warehouse management**
The solution supports inventory and warehouse management by assessing an organization's actual stock situation based on quantity- and value-based criteria. In addition, warehouse activities can be analyzed, such as the physical flow of materials and workloads.

▶ **Manufacturing reporting**
mySAP ERP provides various standard reports and analyses detailing production-related information.

► **Order fulfillment analysis**
mySAP ERP supports key performance indicators (KPIs) for transportation and order management, allowing organizations to assess business process performance both internally and externally. The solution provides strategic performance measurements, or distribution statistics needed for supply chain optimization, as well as operative performance measurements that capture day-to-day information necessary for process optimization.

► **Customer service analysis**
The solution facilitates the analysis of *service profitability* by monitoring financial trends, costs, and revenues per customer, as well as service contracts and operations. It also offers *installed-base analysis,* which monitors the volume of orders from one installation and analyzes associated costs, revenues, and profits. In addition, it provides *customer analytics* that help enterprises understand the value of each customer, customer behavior, and levels of customer satisfaction, as well as *warranty analytics*, which provide information about warranty, no-warranty or expired warranty, as well as analyze costs and profits of warranty processes.

To enable operations support, mySAP ERP provides the following analytics functions:

Operations support capabilities

► **Program and project management**
mySAP ERP provides a project information system that helps organizations monitor and control project data. The system provides data with various levels of project details and facilitates the evaluation of multiple, individual, or partial projects. In addition, product design optimization analysis, with its concurrent costing tool, captures and reports on product costs in early product development stages, enabling design-to-cost engineering that can help to optimize costs. Lastly, the mySAP ERP solution supports the calculation of product characteristics and design alternatives.

► **Quality management**
mySAP ERP helps enterprises plan, collect, settle, and evaluate quality-related costs. The solution includes quality management information software that provides data that can be used as a basis for determining standard or user-defined quality scores.

► **Enterprise asset management**
mySAP ERP provides reporting and asset information software as part of its asset lifecycle management capabilities. The software offers a

broad range of reporting features and performs strategic evaluations, including mean time to repair (MTTR) and mean time between repair (MTBR) analyses.

"Sales planning and analysis" functionalities
To support sales planning and analysis, mySAP ERP performs the following:

▶ **Sales planning**
mySAP ERP supports sales target setting by using multiple dimensions and key figures, and making it easy to communicate sales plans across the sales organization. In addition, the solution enables organizations to integrate and consolidate sales planning with marketing or service plans.

▶ **Sales analysis**
The solution also provides sales organizations with an accurate overview of current sales performance and an overview of sales force effectiveness. As a result, management has the information it needs to proactively address trends and measure success or revenue shortfalls.

2.2.4 Workforce Analytics

Workforce analysis and optimization
mySAP ERP provides data analysis and reporting tools, as well as SEM functions, to support HR policy development and decision-making. Companies can analyze workforce data; design, implement, and monitor corporate strategies to optimize the workforce; and continuously evaluate how various courses of action might affect business outcomes. In the area of workforce analytics, mySAP ERP provides a wide range of functionality, including the following:

▶ **Strategic workforce planning and alignment**
mySAP ERP ensures that all business activities are in line with the strategic goals of the enterprise. In the solution's Balanced Scorecard framework, predefined workforce scorecards provide a series of indicators built around general metrics, targets, milestones, and other variables. These workforce scorecards are integrated into department and individual management-by-objective (MBO) documents, helping organizations to align employee goals with business strategies.

▶ **Workforce analysis**
mySAP ERP also provides reporting and analysis tools for operational and analytical reporting. These tools help organizations design and monitor critical success factors by tracking KPIs. Integrated bench-

marking services allow enterprises to analyze cause-and-effect chains and optimize enterprise-wide processes, which helps build customer and shareholder value.

▶ **Workforce cost planning and simulation**
The mySAP ERP solution supports HR professionals in all workforce cost-planning tasks and empowers HR executives to develop effective strategies. Users have access to a broad range of workforce-related data to support accurate planning, and they can continuously monitor actual performance relative to plan. In addition, flexible decision-support resources, such as the ability to simulate multiple planning scenarios or analyze the financial impact of headcount changes, help the HR staff to make more informed business decisions.

▶ **Organizational planning**
mySAP ERP enables companies to simulate, analyze, and experiment with proposed organizational changes. The solution also supports comprehensive succession planning, which is a critical step in safeguarding organizations against future risks.

mySAP ERP provides unparalleled insight into the state of an enterprise's workforce; alerts management regarding overlooked opportunities; helps organizations respond to unforeseen challenges quickly; and enables management to effectively follow through on major initiatives.

2.2.5 New and Enhanced Analytics Functionality

The strategy management process within mySAP ERP supports value-based management, management by objectives, and strategic initiatives. It uses the Balanced Scorecard, shown in Figure 2.6, which provides numerous tools that help organizations to implement strategies efficiently within specific business areas, and communicates strategies and objectives throughout the entire organization.

Briefing Book

The Balanced Scorecard briefing book in mySAP ERP is a new Balanced Scorecard tool that makes it easy to create custom reports that summarize specific Balanced Scorecard data for different audiences. Users simply drag and drop desired data from the Balanced Scorecard into the briefing book, tailoring contents for particular audiences as needed while keeping other Balanced Scorecard data confidential. Briefing book data can be downloaded onto a PC and forwarded to the relevant parties either as a PDF file or as a printout.

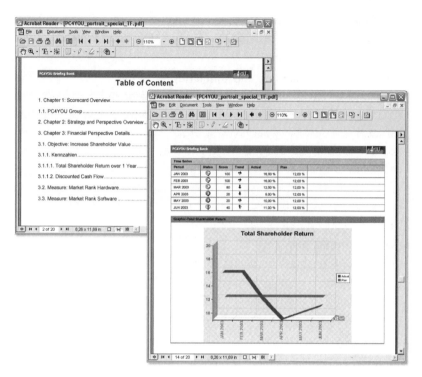

Figure 2.6 SEM Balanced Scorecard—Briefing Book

The Balanced Scorecard briefing book adds value because it:

▶ Enables readers to see only what is of interest to them as knowledge workers or managers, even when they are offline

▶ Combines data from different Balanced Scorecards to meet the individual demands of the recipient

▶ Provides options for formatting the contents professionally using standard data transfer protocol (DTP) software to process the XML data

▶ Provides an easy-to-use, intuitive user environment for creating the briefing book structure

▶ Enables users to structure the contents flexibly to meet unique requirements

▶ Enables users to create different briefing books quickly and easily by copying an existing briefing book and adding the required adjustments

Strategic statutory and management consolidation Consolidation functions in mySAP ERP enable the efficient collection of data from internal and external accounting, and ensure the necessary quality and detail of the data. These functions facilitate an almost fully automatic creation of consolidated financial statements for a broad spectrum of accounting methods, and they do so in compliance with various generally accepted accounting rules (GAAP). External and internal group reporting is based on shared, consolidated data, eliminating time-intensive reconciliation and the synchronization of different sets of data. The result is an efficient, integrated consolidation process for statutory and management reporting that makes a significant contribution to achieving a fast close. mySAP ERP provides the following new functions:

▶ Enhanced integration of statutory and management consolidation

▶ New consolidation of investments

▶ New data collection capabilities

▶ New reporting features, like configurable task logs

The news and enhancements to statutory and management consolidation provide business value in a number of ways. They provide increased support for the full-integration approach to statutory and management consolidation. In addition, new ease-of-use features, such as an ergonomic user interface for manual posting system; the ability to personalize the consolidation workbench; clear definitions of options when customizing; and where-used lists for consolidation units and financial statement items when customizing selections are designed to significantly enhance usability. Total Cost of Ownership (TCO) is also reduced because time-consuming reconciliation processes can be omitted.

In addition, new functions in the consolidation of investments enable a heightened level of automation during the creation of consolidated financial statements on the basis of International Accounting Standards/International Financial Reporting Standards (IAS/IFRS) or US-GAAP (US-Generally Accepted Accounting Principles), resulting in reduced closing times. At the same time, new data collection techniques provide links to SAP and non-SAP systems without the need for custom programming, thus further reducing TCO. And finally, the improved usability and simplified system configuration results in higher user acceptance and faster implementations.

Financial planning, budgeting, and forecasting within mySAP ERP comprises various planning functions, including sales planning, cost center planning, personnel cost planning, investment planning, process and product cost planning, and financial planning. These planning functions are integrated with each other, as well as with balance sheet planning, **Financial analytics** income statement planning, and cash flow planning—the final step in the financial planning and budgeting process.

These enhanced capabilities add business value by:

▶ Replacing Microsoft Excel spreadsheets with direct entries in SAP software

▶ Planning, thereby avoiding consolidation problems

▶ Enabling organizations to define and provide central planning logics (for example, planning functions, layouts, planning processes) and use them decentrally for planning tasks, ensuring uniform editing of planning data

▶ Facilitating the definition of planning and data manipulation functions so that they can be tailored to meet the specific requirements of an organization

▶ Enabling integration with information from transactional systems

▶ Displaying different planning processes and controlling and monitoring them

2.3 Financials

mySAP ERP includes mySAP ERP Financials, which helps organizations achieve these goals by enabling them to process and interpret financial and business data; handle financial transactions; manage business performance, growth, and profit; manage internal controls; and communicate with shareholders. Finance managers have access to all of the tools they need, including support for secure and transparent accounting, streamlined financial supply chain management, and a comprehensive corporate governance solution. Equally important, mySAP ERP enables company-wide control and integration of financial and business information essential to strategic and operational decision-making. By simplifying analyses, improving the management of internal controls, and enabling adaptive changes to business processes, mySAP ERP can help transform financial accounting from a purely administrative function to a globally aligned, value-based management resource.

Success factor mySAP ERP mySAP ERP has contributed to the success of more than 3,200 organizations worldwide. Many of the world's largest construction, service, and R&D projects and programs currently in operation use mySAP ERP to achieve their goals, demonstrating that companies can significantly benefit from an integrated, end-to-end operations support solution. mySAP

ERP offers a unique set of benefits in financial management, including the following:

- Better decision support and business insight via performance measurement and management functions that effectively manage budgets, cash flow, and liquidity. The mySAP ERP solution also helps companies to better understand their business, make more informed business decisions, and manage new business processes that reduce costs and increase the productivity of assets.
- Comprehensive control and improved corporate governance, made possible by functions that manage internal compliance, provide detailed audit support, and ensure faster, more accurate reporting
- Fast closing of accounting books via improved access to all closing activities, automated processes, and intensified collaboration
- Lower operational costs by significantly improving the productivity of accounting, accelerating collection processes, and supporting credit managers with customized user interfaces based on "roles"
- Improved TCO for corporate financial systems by reducing costs of integration and enabling corporate finance departments to react faster to changing business needs

The solution provides capabilities in three key areas that address the complete range of corporate finance needs:

- Financial and management accounting
- Financial supply chain management
- Corporate governance

In addition, mySAP ERP provides financial analytics that are described more fully in Section 2.2.2.

2.3.1 Financial and Management Accounting

Today's finance departments face an increasing challenge to meet reporting requirements, adapt to business change, achieve management objectives, and satisfy shareholder demands. Consequently, pressure has increased on corporate accounting and financial management systems to adapt quickly and remain flexible given changing demands. mySAP ERP addresses these needs by creating a common basis for financial and management reporting.

Financial and management accounting analysis

Specifically, mySAP ERP maintains a set of books that are consistent, reconcilable, and auditable. In addition, the solution creates a common basis for financial and management reporting, thereby reducing data volume and ensuring that internal and external views in accounting can be kept separate, but reconcilable. mySAP ERP also offers customized financial reporting for various user groups, from senior management to administrative staff, as well as the ability to customize the solution using internationally recognized accounting standards. Therefore, the solution can record business transactions while simultaneously simplifying financial reporting for country-specific statutory and company-wide purposes. Through the SAP NetWeaver platform, the accounting function can be integrated with third-party applications or outsourced services; this architecture provides greater flexibility for accounting departments while reducing the cost of maintaining interfaces with external systems or services. Key functions include the following:

▶ **Financial accounting**
mySAP ERP enables the central tracking of financial accounting data within an international framework of multiple companies, languages, currencies, and charts of accounts. The financial accounting capabilities comply with international accounting standards such as GAAP and IAS, fulfill the local legal requirements of many countries, and accurately reflect the legal and accounting changes resulting from European market and currency unification.

▶ **Management accounting**
mySAP ERP enables the valuation and recording of financial data, not only for financial reporting, but also as the basis for all cost- and revenue-related reporting. As a result, analysts and managers can work with the same basic data as the company's financial accountants. Because financial data is tightly integrated with the business processes of ERP's logistics applications, users can also easily obtain detailed information about cost structures and profit margins. Easy access to this data enables management to achieve business goals such as increasing revenue, maximizing customer profitability, and reducing operating costs while increasing efficiency, reducing the cost of goods sold, and improving the visibility of inventory.

▶ **Cost center and internal order accounting**
mySAP ERP records costs incurred during business operations by assigning them to cost centers aligned with managers or organizational units. The solution enables users to plan, record, and analyze actual costs against planned and target costs, and provides sophisticated

functions for detailed analysis of variances. In addition, it uses internal orders to plan, collect, and settle the costs of internal jobs and tasks, and monitors internal orders throughout their entire lifecycle using the SAP system—from initial creation, planning, and posting of all the actual costs to final settlement and archiving.

▶ **Project accounting**
mySAP ERP supports detailed planning of resources and funds, as well as activity monitoring for small-scale projects, such as participation in a trade fair, and large-scale projects, such as building a factory. These capabilities allow project managers to run projects of any size success-fully and efficiently while ensuring that they are executed on time and within budget.

▶ **Investment management**
The solution allows users to manage investments as fixed assets, re-search and development costs, or projects normally run under over-heads. In mySAP ERP, the term "investment" is not limited to only in-vestments that are capitalized for bookkeeping or tax purposes. In this context, "investment" is defined as any measure that initially results in increased costs for the user and can generate revenue or provide other benefits only after a certain time period has elapsed (for example, plant maintenance projects).

▶ **Product cost accounting**
mySAP ERP provides detailed information on the costs of production from the view of the production process itself, allowing organizations to successfully manage their product portfolio. The solution also calcu-lates the cost of goods manufactured (COGM) or cost of goods sold (COGS), and generates this data, which is broken down with each step of the production process. mySAP ERP also automatically gathers and uses product cost information available in other SAP applications and supports the calculation of standard and actual costs.

▶ **Activity-based costing/management**
mySAP ERP supports various methodologies for assigning costs to cost objects (ranging from pro rata allocations of period expenses to causal cost assignments) by using drivers tracked in the mySAP ERP system. Activity-based costing/management (ABC/M) may be embedded within the ERP solution. Alternatively, enterprises can use the solu-tion's Business Information Warehouse (BW) to collect activity drivers in multiple systems and then use flexible formulas to represent the var-ious costing methodologies.

▶ **Profitability accounting and management**
The solution also provides information that organizations can use to evaluate market segments, which can be classified flexibly according to products, customers, or orders (or any combination of them), or according to strategic business units, such as sales organizations or business areas, with respect to the company's profit or contribution margin.

▶ **Profit center accounting**
mySAP ERP can determine profit for internal areas of responsibility using either period accounting or a cost-of-sales approach. Profit center accounting can be enhanced with transfer prices to valuate the exchange of goods between profit centers or legal entities with prices that are different from the legal perspective. This enables mySAP ERP to provide decision support by, for example, representing operational results from different points of view and in different currencies.

2.3.2 New and Enhanced Financial and Management Accounting

Rising demands for stringent corporate governance and accurate financial statements have forced companies to improve the efficiency and effectiveness of their financial and managerial accounting practices. To help customers achieve these goals, mySAP ERP includes the following new capabilities.

New general ledger
Similar to the existing general ledger, the new general ledger in mySAP ERP supports multiple industry and country requirements. With its new technical architecture, the general ledger improves financial reporting transparency, reduces reconciliation and internal communication expenses, and leaves more time for analysis by supporting legal, segment, and management reporting using one consistent, multidimensional database. It also enables finance departments to meet regulatory and compliance rules and to customize accounting practices to meet industry requirements.

▶ **Data structure standardization**
mySAP ERP addresses gaps in previous versions of the general ledger. In particular, the data structure of several ledgers is standardized and provided via the new general ledger in order to reduce redundant data management and streamline analysis.

► **General ledger extensions**

With mySAP ERP, organizations can more easily extend the structure of their general ledger while still leveraging the full support of SAP standard accounting.

► **Online splits**

The new general ledger allows organizations to simplify the generation of financial statements and reports on segments or dimensions that are unique to their industry. Documents are automatically balanced online by any chosen dimension, supporting transparency and fast closes.

► **Real-time integration**

The new general ledger supports real-time integration of financial and management accounting in mySAP ERP. Any postings from management accounting (for example, cost center allocations) are automatically reflected in the general ledger at the appropriate level of detail.

► **Parallel accounting**

mySAP ERP now provides additional functionality for "parallel ledgers" to support parallel accounting and to reduce costs. Organizations can use an identical interface and identical functions to process all ledgers in the general ledger, as well as update ledgers individually or simultaneously.

Enhanced fast close support

Finance departments are under pressure by management and external institutions such as regulators and stock exchanges to reduce the time required to close the books. To address this need, mySAP ERP includes a new closing cockpit for period-end closing of individual financial statements. The closing cockpit assimilates all relevant closing activities, and gives clerks and management a simplified overview of the entire closing process. Financial managers can also schedule and begin the closing process using an intuitive user interface. To enhance the inter-company reconciliation of open items in customer and vendor accounts, mySAP ERP enables users to reconcile open items and intercompany balances in general ledger accounts. Users can also load intercompany data from non-SAP systems via a new interface and then audit, balance, and reconcile this data. Key benefits include the following:

► Reduced costs via automated processes, user collaboration support, and easy access to all closing activities

► Improved employee productivity and reduced costs

► Significantly reduced time to reconcile intercompany activities

► Reduced errors through transparency and support for compliance via a concise overview of the closing status and remaining tasks

2.3.3 Financial Supply Chain Management

mySAP ERP provides comprehensive functions that address the multifac-
eted challenges of credit management, invoicing, collections, cash management, and working capital optimization. mySAP ERP is the first solution of its kind to offer a fully integrated, comprehensive approach to
managing the financial processes for customer, supplier, and intrabusiness
relationships. Designed to work in unison with an enterprise's core financial systems, the mySAP ERP solution delivers immediate value by
extending an enterprise's existing systems infrastructure and supplement-
ing its core financial processes. mySAP ERP provides the following key
functions:

▶ **Electronic bill presentment and payment**
With mySAP ERP, organizations can streamline financial processes with
their customers or suppliers through web-based invoicing, billing, payments, and account inquiry. Web-based financial processes improve
customer access to financial information, extract costs associated with
billing and invoicing, and simplify payments.

▶ **Dispute management**
With mySAP ERP, accounts receivable (AR) departments can leverage
dispute management capabilities to maximize productivity and reduce
settlement time associated with invoice or payment deduction disputes with customers.

▶ **Credit management**
mySAP ERP also enables organizations to gain process efficiency and
effectiveness in their credit department. Credit decisions are automated, and credit ratings are made more visible to those employees
that manage customer relationships.

▶ **Collections management**
mySAP ERP helps organizations prioritize key accounts from a risk perspective and establish customer-centric receivables management.
Automation and prioritization of accounts enable collections departments to remain more productive.

▶ **Cash and liquidity management**
mySAP ERP provides cash managers with more accurate insight into
current liquidity positions. In addition, organizations benefit from
improved forecasting, because they can better understand the status
of important cash inflow and outflow transactions.

- **In-house cash**

  For global organizations that must execute complex sets of international and intercompany payments, an in-house banking capability provided by mySAP ERP simplifies and streamlines multinational cash management.

- **Treasury and risk management**

  mySAP ERP enables finance and treasury departments to work off a common platform, data set, and processes. Treasury accounting is executed in parallel with an enterprise's financial accounting processes, thereby eliminating manual interfaces between these operations.

2.3.4 New and Enhanced Financial Supply Chain Management

Many companies are exploring new business processes to reduce inefficiencies in their finance operations, particularly in the area of financial supply chain management. mySAP ERP supports the following set of new, collaborative financial processes for this area.

With the SAP Credit Management application, enterprises can improve the management of their customers' credit lines, significantly reducing the number of late payments and potential non-payments. The application now meets all of the prerequisites for enterprises deploying a companywide credit management tool, providing features such as automated credit application and approval processes, streamlined credit analysis, and delivery of real-time credit rating information to the credit department (see Figure 2.7). By consolidating customer data from various sources, SAP Credit Management enables centralized customer credit checks and helps organizations minimize customer credit risk. It also performs the following functions:

Credit management

- **Credit limit management and control**

  mySAP ERP manages all business partner master data relating to credit. This data includes the current credit limit, one or more externally calculated values on creditworthiness (for example, credit ratings provided by credit-reporting agencies), the risk class assigned to a business, and order limits.

- **Credit information support**

  The credit information function of mySAP ERP supports credit managers in determining and managing the external and internal credit information on customers. This information primarily serves as input parameters for the credit rules engine in mySAP ERP, which can make credit decisions or automatically calculate credit limits.

► **Credit rules automation**

mySAP ERP offers an option to use rules to automate specific processes in credit management. A credit rules engine helps score the creditworthiness of business partners and determine their credit limit.

► **Credit decision support**

mySAP ERP helps users determine the required data and analyses related to a customer. Data is summarized by customers in a customer credit fact sheet. The mySAP ERP solution also generates reports to analyze the payment behavior or credit history of customers.

Figure 2.7 Credit Manager Portal

Electronic bill presentment and payment — Through the SAP Biller Direct application, mySAP ERP enables companies to deploy web-based billing, invoicing, account management, and payment services via their Internet portals. The application supports authorization of automatic payment debits via the Internet. In addition, this web-based application allows businesses to collaborate with their customers and trading partners and eliminates the need to manage paper-based and EDI-based payment methods. A portal that allows suppliers to view invoices and payments has also been added. SAP Biller Direct supports the complete communication process—from bill presentation to discrepancy handling and final reconciliation. Companies benefit from the following:

- ▶ Reduced billing and settlement transaction costs
- ▶ Improved payment and exception processing
- ▶ Improved cash flow
- ▶ Integrated data in accounts receivable and accounts payable, eliminating the need to reenter information
- ▶ Reduced accounting errors on the customer side
- ▶ Reduced processing time on the supplier side

The SAP Collections Management application enables companies to prioritize customer accounts from a risk perspective and capture promise-to-pay agreements or disputes. This enhancement to mySAP ERP allows a collections department to accelerate the collections process by unifying and simplifying the identification of open customer invoices, account status, and invoice information. Organizations benefit from the following:

Collections management

- ▶ Reduced days sales outstanding (DSO)
- ▶ Improved liquidity and liquidity forecasting
- ▶ Flexibility to collect receivables via different collection methods
- ▶ Increased efficiency in collecting receivables that must be handled in special ways
- ▶ Improved customer relationships resulting from customer-oriented receivables management

The SAP Dispute Management application enables enterprises to process receivables-related disputes. Organizations can structure and streamline the process of dispute resolution and reduce processing time via an entirely electronic communication process. Dispute management capabilities are integrated into accounts receivables, sales and distribution, mySAP CRM and the SAP Business Workflow tool (including email notification). Users can also automatically create dispute cases for underpayments generated by the electronic account statement. The correspon-

Dispute management

dence function enables companies to send standard letters, faxes, and email automatically for improved customer interaction. Finally, customers can create dispute cases directly inside the application and monitor the status of their dispute. These functions offer the following benefits:

▶ Reduced days sales outstanding (DSO)

▶ Reduced days deduction outstanding (DDO)

▶ Improved liquidity and liquidity forecasting

▶ Accelerated processes via automation

▶ Improved customer relationships via targeted inquiries and fast processing of complaints

▶ Reduced costs via early identification and notification about possible problems in the logistics value chain or internal processes

In-house cash The SAP In-House Cash application enables global enterprises to efficiently manage intra-group and external payment transactions by setting up a virtual house bank. International businesses can centrally process payments made by their affiliates by netting and consolidating internal accounts. The application can be used to pay external business partners on behalf of subsidiaries, or to forward incoming payments from external business partners to the appropriate subsidiary. New enhancements include integration with cash management and treasury management components, new in-house cash payment orders, flexible routing, and new currency conversion capabilities. In addition, the application supports international payments with real-time exchange-rate information. Customers realize the following benefits:

▶ Reduced complexity of intercompany netting and payments

▶ Accurate current accounts forecasting for cash managers

▶ Easy integration of intercompany payments with the treasury management platform

▶ Flexible payment-routing capabilities that can be adapted to business needs

Cash and liquidity management The SAP Cash and Liquidity Management application integrates the treasury function with electronic banking, customer relationship management, and financial processes. The application improves liquidity, maximizes yields on financial assets, and simplifies multicurrency management. It also manages liquidity mid- and long-term, streamlining the planning process and comparing planning data with real-time data from the cash management component. The application adds business value because it does the following:

▶ Simplifies reporting and forecasting of cash flow in any currency and in any business unit

▶ Facilitates better decision-making by supplying accurate cash data faster

▶ Supports accurate cash reporting for corporate governance projects

▶ Increases the management of working capital by generating position reports on time

▶ Automates cash flow reporting

The SAP Treasury and Risk Management application offers a comprehensive set of functions for managing financial transactions and risk. The application supports financial deals and position management, from trading and back-office processing to data transfer and financial accounting, minimizing the need for workarounds. Users can leverage flexible reporting and evaluation capabilities for analyzing financial transactions, positions, and portfolios. Automation capabilities help to accelerate and streamline financial processes across the enterprise. The application also improves financial insight by calculating market-to-market values and other key figures such as value-at-risk. Equally important, it helps to control credit and settlement risk, and also measures and manages foreign exchange and interest rate exposures. New functions in SAP Treasury and Risk Management also improve compliance with the International Financial Reporting Standards (IFRS) and Financial Accounting Standards (FAS), including hedge accounting, and support the Sarbanes-Oxley Act and country-specific regulations. New financial products for foreign exchange trading have also been added. Key benefits include the following:

Treasury and risk management

▶ Greater transaction support

▶ Improved corporate controls by integrating treasury with finance and accounting

▶ Improved ability to manage cash flow and liquidity

▶ Significant cost reductions by eliminating the costs of maintaining technical or process interfaces between treasury and finance

▶ Real-time insight into corporate treasury operations

2.3.5 Corporate Governance

Corporate governance is the system by which corporations are directed and controlled. In addition to specifying the distribution of rights and responsibilities among different participants in the corporation, such as the board, managers, and shareholders, it defines the rules and procedures for making corporate decisions and the internal controls and financial reporting standards needed to maintain high-quality standards and monitor performance. mySAP ERP supports organizations that take a rigorous approach to corporate governance by helping them comply with rules and regulations. The solution reduces the overall cost of managing internal controls and enhances adherence to financial reporting standards and laws, such as the United States' legal requirements included in the Sarbanes-Oxley Act (SOA). Key corporate governance capabilities in mySAP ERP 2004 include the following:

▶ **Reporting control**
mySAP ERP provides a comprehensive set of reporting controls that are configurable and secure.

▶ **Audit information support**
mySAP ERP provides a set of functions that support and streamline internal or external audits.

▶ **Data retention**
A data retention tool is included in mySAP ERP to provide tools capable of extracting period-dependent financial data, as well as the information required to support financial transactions.

▶ **International accounting standards support**
mySAP ERP currently offers all necessary functions for performing parallel valuation using International Accounting Standards (IAS) and national reporting regulations.

▶ **Fast close support**
The solution also provides a comprehensive set of functionalities to support fast close initiatives, including financial portals, management cockpits, intercompany reconciliations, accrual engines, business consolidations, and a schedule manager.

With these capabilities, mySAP ERP provides businesses with the foundation necessary for supporting superior corporate governance business practices, as well as reducing the costs of achieving compliance in financial and managerial reporting.

2.3.6 New and Enhanced Corporate Governance

One of the challenges facing finance organizations today is complying with an increasing number of national and international legal requirements for financial reporting and corporate governance. Statutes like the Basel II and the Sarbanes-Oxley Act increase workloads and operational costs in finance organizations. mySAP ERP provides comprehensive functions that reduce the overall cost of managing internal controls and ensure adherence to standards and corporate governance laws. New capabilities that support corporate governance include the following:

mySAP ERP now includes Management of Internal Controls (MIC) capabilities that support the documentation, assessment, and testing of internal controls needed to fulfill the requirements of Sections 302 and 404 of the Sarbanes-Oxley Act, as well as the "Committee of Sponsoring Organizations of the Treadway Commission I (COSO)" framework and other internal control initiatives. These capabilities provide scheduling functionality and workflow-supported issue remediation capabilities to ensure on-time disclosures and reduce internal communication and administration expenses related to compliance.

Management of Internal Controls

Predefined and customizable management reports provide management, as well as internal and external auditors, with a wide variety of reports; from a high-level overview of the status of internal control to detailed analyses (see Figure 2.8). Key benefits include the following:

▶ Reduced internal communication and administration expenses for compliance documentation

▶ Streamlined assessment procedures and tracking of issue remediation, which reduces costs and improves service levels

▶ Improved management reporting that highlights issues prior to legal and regulatory reporting deadlines in order to reduce the risk of non-compliance

mySAP ERP includes the Audit Information System (AIS), an auditing tool kit for external and internal auditors that provides an interface between the auditor and the SAP system landscape. The interface supports auditors who may be less familiar with the SAP system and it delivers several predefined roles. AIS improves the quality of the auditing process, particularly in the areas of internal and external systems and business auditing, tax audits, and data protection. Users can export document data and account balances in flat files for further analysis.

Audit information support

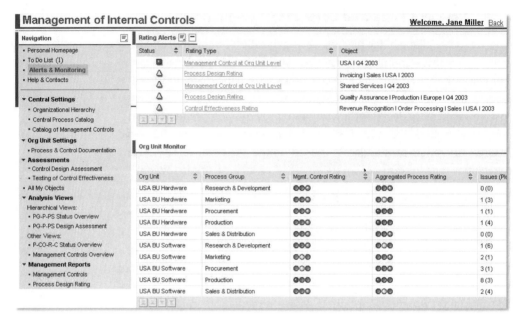

Figure 2.8 MIC Capabilities in mySAP ERP

Enhancements to the AIS include new roles that support two different business audit approaches:

▶ An *account-oriented approach* that provides a balance sheet, an income statement, and segment reporting, as well as internal activity allocation and a consolidated financial statement

▶ A *process-oriented approach* that supports two different processes: from order to cash and from purchase to order

The solution offers a wider range of preconfigured business audit functions and provides the following benefits:

▶ Accelerated auditing by providing functionalities for system and business audits

▶ Reduced risk of noncompliance by including a drill-down audit trail to the document level, which enables the identification of exceptions

▶ Enhanced user productivity by displaying structured reporting controls

▶ Significantly reduced costs associated with auditing an SAP system

Support for whistle blower complaints To help companies comply with Section 301 of the Sarbanes-Oxley Act, SAP has added a new functionality supporting the complete process of "whistle blowing." The whistle blower complaints function, illustrated in

Figure 2.9, provides an exemplary complaints form that customers can configure according to their own specific requirements and internal policies, as well as federal laws. Because this function leverages existing portal technology (if available) and users need no additional training, it provides an affordable way for companies to fully address the legal requirements of the Sarbanes-Oxley Act and thereby reduce the risk of noncompliance.

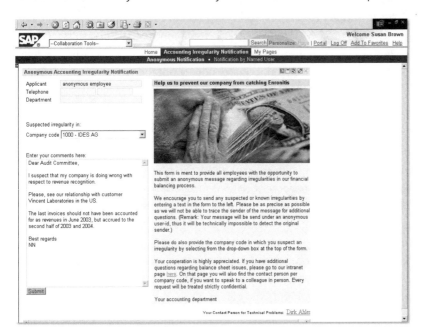

Figure 2.9 mySAP ERP Whistle Blower Portal

2.4 Human Capital Management

mySAP ERP delivers a comprehensive solution for Human Capital Management (HCM) by providing the following functionalities:

▶ **Employee lifecycle management**
mySAP ERP supports employees through every phase of their employment with an organization. The solution helps businesses identify and retain top performers, leverage their talents, align employee goals with corporate goals, and maximize the impact of training.

▶ **Employee transaction management**
mySAP ERP enables enterprises to streamline and integrate essential HCM processes, including administration, payroll, time management, and legal reporting, in order to lower IT costs. The solution supports global requirements and has been customized for over 50 countries.

▶ **HCM service delivery**

mySAP ERP allows workforces to share knowledge quickly and to build collaborative, interactive relationships via mobile, help desk, portal, and voice channels.

▶ **Workforce deployment**

mySAP ERP facilitates workforce deployment. The solution allows organizations to create project teams based on skills and availability, monitor project progress, track time, and analyze results. It also enables organizations to ensure that resources are not wasted on ineffective projects, thereby increasing profitability via more efficient workforce management.

Competitive edge with the shift from HR to HCM

To gain a competitive edge, enterprises must align all corporate resources—including human capital, or employees—with the enterprise's overall business processes, goals, and strategies. This requires transforming traditional human resources (HR) functions into a comprehensive Human Capital Management (HCM) program that integrates employees, business processes, and technologies with business goals and objectives, and that maximizes the value of an organization's human capital by increasing its contribution to the business. HCM views employees as key assets of the corporation, and seeks to ensure their optimal development and deployment with the goal of increasing their active commitment, productivity, engagement, and retention.

A strategic, carefully designed, and properly executed HCM solution offers far more than just cost reductions and productivity enhancements: it can bring about a transformation that dramatically impacts business results. HCM improves employee productivity, job satisfaction, and retention by:

▶ Matching employees to projects and careers that meet their skills and interests

▶ Recognizing and developing the skills of future leaders

▶ Identifying learning needs and delivering appropriate training

In addition, HCM enables employees to maintain their own personal information and control many administrative transactions and other processes, which were previously handled by the HR staff so that HR can focus on value-generating projects instead of administrative activities. Most importantly, HCM improves each employee's contribution to corporate goals by aligning employee skills, activities, and incentives with measurable business objectives and the strategies to reach them. At the same time, it provides employers with the tools to measure, manage, and reward team and individual contributions. When properly designed and executed, effective HCM programs ensure that all employees contribute according to their full potential and further business objectives.

Transforming the traditional HR function into a comprehensive HCM program impacts enterprises at all levels. In addition, it requires integrated, enterprise-wide tools that support the following activities:

mySAP ERP HCM supports all enterprise levels

▶ Aligning corporate strategies with management, team, and individual goals throughout the enterprise

▶ Developing streamlined HR processes that seamlessly integrate across global operations

▶ Accelerating workforce-related decisions with real-time information

▶ Supporting employees and managers throughout the employee lifecycle

▶ Deploying the right people to strategic initiatives quickly and efficiently

▶ Enabling employees to manage collaborative processes

By fully leveraging integrated HCM tools, organizations benefit from improved insight into—and control over—increasingly virtual workforces. In addition, they can adapt their workforce and IT investments faster and more easily in response to changing business conditions. Equally important, organizations can significantly improve productivity as employees focus more time on value-added activities and leverage the personal empowerment enabled by HCM.

mySAP ERP delivers leading-edge HCM capabilities that integrate fully with existing business systems and can be customized to match an enterprise's specific requirements. Designed for a global marketplace, mySAP ERP Human Capital Management (mySAP ERP HCM) includes comprehensive support for local best practices and regulatory requirements, as well as payroll functions, for over 50 countries.

HCM today

"SAP continued to chalk up big wins largely due to the global applicability of its products," said Albert Pang, enterprise applications research lead at IDC. "SAP's strengths are in the global HR automation capabilities for an array of industries, and the ability to support the HR demands of over 50 countries, while at the same time integrating information and processes from diverse global offices in a single system."

(IDC Document # 29803, "Worldwide Human Resources Management and Payroll Processing Applications Forecast and Analysis", 2003–2007)

With 35 plus years of experience in ERP, SAP supports an HCM customer base that exceeds 9,000 customers in over 50 countries, managing more than 54 million employees. Over 11 million employees now actively use the management tools and employee self-service functions in mySAP ERP. Table 2.1 summarizes the comprehensive benefits that mySAP ERP delivers throughout an organization.

Organizational Group	Benefits
C-level executives	▶ Reduced administrative costs and greater efficiency ▶ Improved alignment of human capital with business objectives ▶ Increased productivity throughout the organization
Line-of-business managers	▶ Comprehensive HR management and decision-making ▶ Improved information sharing and visibility ▶ Enhanced collaborative relationships and networking ▶ Support for compliance requirements
IT management	▶ Low cost of ownership ▶ Investment protection through integration with all mySAP™ Business Suite solutions and the SAP NetWeaver™ platform ▶ Simplified IT infrastructure
Employees	▶ User-centric approach for improved usability and increased empowerment ▶ Improved communication, collaboration, and information sharing ▶ Wide range of access options to support multiple work styles

Table 2.1 Key Benefits of HCM Functionality

HCM incorporates processes for recruiting, deploying, developing, motivating, and retaining valuable employees, among others, and seeks to improve all of these processes from end to end. mySAP ERP provides HCM capabilities in the following four areas:

- ▶ Employee lifecycle management
- ▶ Employee transaction management
- ▶ HCM service delivery
- ▶ Workforce deployment

In addition, mySAP ERP also provides workforce analytics capabilities that are described more fully in Section 2.2.4.

2.4.1 Employee Lifecycle Management

mySAP ERP provides functions that automate and optimize all phases of the employee lifecycle. Consequently, companies can find the best people, develop and leverage their talent, align their efforts with corporate objectives, maximize the impact of training efforts, and retain top performers. Key functions include the following:

Functions for all phases of the employee lifecycle

- ▶ **Recruiting and talent management**
  mySAP ERP includes the SAP E-Recruiting application, which combines the latest technology with best-practice know-how in an integrated solution that enables organizations to optimize their recruiting processes and develop a sophisticated talent relationship management system. This solution can handle everything from worldwide recruiting and applicant-tracking processes to local reporting. It helps business find the right people and coordinate team collaboration to identify and evaluate candidates. In addition, SAP E-Recruiting offers a full range of integration options to other enterprise applications, as well as to complementary third-party service providers, such as job boards and resume processors.

- ▶ **Enterprise learning management**
  mySAP ERP includes the SAP Learning Solution, which provides a comprehensive enterprise learning platform capable of managing and integrating business and learning processes and supporting both e-learning and classroom training, as well as synchronous and asynchronous collaboration. It is fully integrated with mySAP ERP and includes content authoring, content management, and learning management capabilities, as well as a learning portal. The SAP Learning Solution offers back-office functionality for competency management and comprehensive assessment for performance management. It also offers strong analytical capabilities, including support for ad-hoc reporting. The application uses a comprehensive learning approach to deliver knowledge to all stakeholders and tailors learning paths to an individual's educational

needs and personal learning styles. Interactive learning units can be created with SAP Tutor, a training simulation tool that is also available.

▶ **Performance management**
With mySAP ERP, organizations can integrate team and individual goals with corporate goals and strategies. In addition, management-by-objective documents can be linked directly to performance reviews, appraisals, and compensation administration. Employee development tools help to identify and implement career and development plans that directly relate to the organization's core business strategy. The solution helps motivate employees to achieve corporate goals, standardizes employee reviews and appraisals, and provides functions to support the performance-oriented compensation process.

▶ **Compensation management**
mySAP ERP makes it easy for companies to implement innovative reward strategies, such as performance- and competency-based pay, variable pay plans, and long-term incentives reward programs. In addition, companies can perform comparative compensation package analysis based on internal and external salary data to ensure competitiveness in the marketplace.

2.4.2 Employee Transaction Management

Employee trans-actions and regulatory requirements

mySAP ERP helps organizations streamline and integrate essential employee transactions and processes, as well as support global compliance with regulatory requirements. In addition, mySAP ERP helps IT organizations deliver better services at a lower cost. Key employee transaction management functions include the following:

▶ **Employee administration**
mySAP ERP supports all basic processes related to personnel and employee information management. Via a centralized database, employees and management always have instant access to current, consistent, and complete information that can support HR- and business-related decisions.

▶ **Organizational management**
mySAP ERP supports key processes for managing and disseminating organizational structure and policy information.

▶ **Expatriate management**
mySAP ERP supports all processes involved in international employee relocation—from the planning and preparation of global assignments to personnel administration and payroll for global employees.

▶ **Benefits management**
  mySAP ERP supports diverse plan definitions and automatically tailors
  benefit offers to individual employees.

▶ **Time and attendance management**
  mySAP ERP facilitates effective time-management strategies and provides convenient tracking, monitoring, record keeping, and evaluation
  of time data.

▶ **Global payroll**
  mySAP ERP handles complex payroll processes and supports current
  legal regulations for over 50 countries worldwide, ensuring compliance with regulatory requirements for reporting purposes. Advanced
  features address considerations such as national currency, multiple languages, collective agreements, and reporting.

2.4.3   HCM Service Delivery

mySAP ERP provides a number of new and enhanced self-service capabil-   **Self-services**
ities and roles that increase employee efficiency and productivity. For   **functions**
more information on HCM-related self-services functions provided by
mySAP ERP, please refer to the "Self Services" section of this document in
Section 2.7.

2.4.4   Workforce Deployment

Effective workforce management requires consistently deploying the   **Optimal**
right people with the right skills to the right positions at the right time.   **workforce**
mySAP ERP improves workforce efficiency and increases profitability by   **deployment**
allowing organizations to create project teams based on skills and availability, as well as monitor and analyze progress and results in order to
ensure that resources are not wasted on ineffective projects. Key workforce deployment functions within mySAP ERP include the following:

▶ **Project resource planning**
  mySAP ERP provides comprehensive support for project resource
  planning, including a workforce-scheduling application designed for
  professional service organizations that ensures employees are assigned
  to appropriate jobs, projects, and teams.

▶ **Resource and program management**
  mySAP ERP unifies project management, time tracking, financial data,
  and employee skills information in a portfolio management paradigm,
  with capabilities that include resource management, project portfolio
  management, project execution, and skills management. mySAP ERP is

an integral contributor to workforce deployment solutions across other SAP solutions, enabling businesses to create project teams based on skills and availability, monitor project progress, track time, analyze results, and much more.

▶ **Call center staffing**
mySAP ERP supports call center scheduling based on forecasted call volume and shift schedules.

2.4.5 New and Enhanced Human Capital Management

Recruiting and talent management

Attracting, recruiting, and retaining the right people are the cornerstone of an organization's success. Successful recruitment relies on strong long-term relationships with both current and potential employees and the ability to locate appropriate positions for talented individuals both inside and outside the organization. New features and enhancements to the SAP E-Recruiting application included with mySAP ERP offer innovative support for talent relationship management, as well as traditional central recruitment functions. These include the following:

▶ **Talent relationship management**
mySAP ERP supports comprehensive talent relationship management with functions that include talent planning, sourcing, evaluation, hiring/reassignment, and retention. Recruiters benefit from enhanced search-and-match functions (see Figure 2.10), clear classifications of candidates by ranking, and communication options such as newsletters and questionnaires. Candidates benefit from an intuitive user interface and new features, including employee referrals.

▶ **Applicant tracking**
The solution offers enhanced requirements management, with support for candidate rankings by recruiters, as well as candidate and application administration. Organizations benefit from extended support for handling unsolicited applications, as well as advanced searches for ideal candidates. The efficiency of hiring managers is improved by comprehensive self-service support, including the ability to create and submit job requirement profiles for approval; use approval workflows for requirements profiles; view candidate short lists and profile and application data; and respond to questionnaires about candidates.

▶ **Analytics**
Up-to-date information is necessary to ensure long-term effectiveness of recruitment processes. mySAP ERP delivers a broad range of reports

and analyses specifically designed to meet recruitment needs, including standard reports, ad-hoc reporting, and evaluations based on key performance indicators (KPIs), as well as important figures such as time to hire and time to offer versus acceptance rate. In addition, comprehensive planning functions enable the analysis of various sourcing strategies and alternative recruitment concepts. Enhancements to the SAP E-Recruiting application included with mySAP ERP enable organizations to create faster and more efficient hiring processes, resulting in a better internal and external corporate image that attracts higher-quality candidates and helps retain talented employees. In addition, as their recruitment processes improve, businesses come to rely less on costly sourcing and are able to reduce administrative and operational costs. The automated, streamlined processes enabled by SAP E-Recruiting also make it easy to outsource specific recruitment tasks or the entire recruitment functions itself.

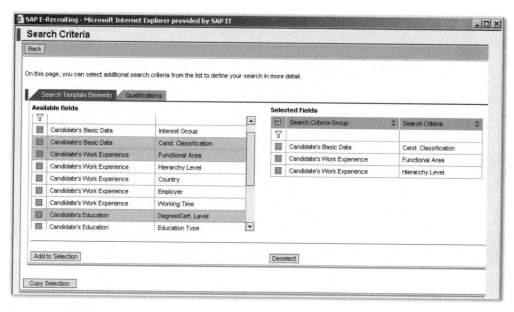

Figure 2.10 SAP E-Recruiting—Search Functionality

Performance management support within mySAP ERP helps to motivate employees to achieve corporate goals; standardize employee reviews and appraisals; and simplify performance-oriented compensation while enabling managers to identify employees whose contributions do not meet the requirements of their position. Enhancements include the following:

Performance management

▶ **Performance appraisal management**

Organizational changes, varying tasks, and changed project assignments often mean that employees are reviewed by new appraisers.
New maintenance features allow appraisal documents to reflect organizational changes, such as new managers or changes to the validity
period of the appraisal document. In addition, mandatory process participants can now be defined.

▶ **Employee development**

mySAP ERP enables organizations to link business objectives and
employee appraisals directly to employee development and training
management applications, enabling organizations to include training
and development plan steps as objectives in the appraisal document.

▶ **Improved attachment processing**

Support for file attachments ensures that documents associated with
employee appraisals, such as documentation of a certain achievement
or notes taken during the performance feedback period, can be added,
displayed, and deleted in a web-based environment.

▶ **Appraisal calibration**

Methodical calibration processes ensure fairness in employee appraisals and compensation packages and provide important decision support for succession management and individual promotions. Comparative overviews of appraisal results are available as reports and graphics.

▶ **Template management**

Appraisal processes vary depending on employee position and responsibilities. By enabling organizations to link different appraisal templates
to different groups of employees, mySAP ERP helps businesses ensure
that employees are fairly and appropriately reviewed.

Learning management

To meet the demands of global business activities, shorter product life-
cycles, and accelerated time to market, employees require immediate
access to the specialized training that they need to effectively perform
their jobs. In addition, increasing worker mobility and decentralization
demand that learning opportunities must be available anytime and anywhere. The SAP Learning Solution in mySAP ERP provides a comprehensive, enterprise-wide learning platform that is capable of integrating business and learning processes to deliver optimal e-learning and classroom
training for internal and external users (see Figure 2.11).

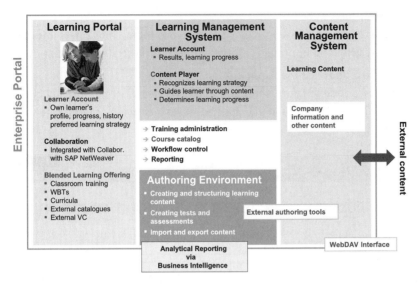

Figure 2.11 Learning Management

Enhancements include the following:

▶ **Collaboration features**
mySAP ERP leverages components of the SAP NetWeaver platform to deliver enhanced collaboration tools for online learning. mySAP ERP supports both synchronous collaboration (for example, instant messaging, chat, shared contact list, and application and desktop sharing) and asynchronous collaboration (team news, team calendar, team tasks, and document sharing), making online learning experiences more effective.

▶ **Content integration**
Training administrators can coordinate, integrate, and communicate with external and internal content providers through a web-based interface. In addition, they can customize teaching and learning scenarios by using Web services to integrate external functions and services into the learning platform.

▶ **Content authoring**
Simplified authoring processes, including separate views for subject matter experts and instructional designers, ensure that course developers can focus their efforts on developing content rather than on learning complicated tools. A learning strategy preview and wizards, including a configuration wizard and an import wizard, accelerate the development of new course material.

▶ **Portal-based access**

A new Section 508-compliant portal layout for learners offers intuitive navigation and improved response speed, as illustrated in Figure 2.12.

▶ **Correspondence management**

Correspondence functions and multiple delivery methods, such as sending notifications in PDF format, make it easy to communicate with learners.

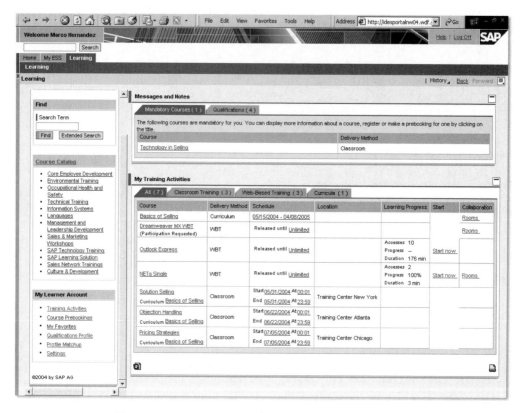

Figure 2.12 Section 508—Compliant Portal Layout

These enhancements result in an even more comprehensive platform that increases employee motivation and value to the business. Enterprises that focus on the education of their employees strongly benefit from the seamless, comprehensive integration of the SAP Learning Solution into mySAP ERP. In addition, because mySAP ERP offers a complete, comprehensive solution for blended learning with all components integrated into a single product, companies realize lower TCO.

2.5　Operations

mySAP ERP includes mySAP ERP Operations, which offers comprehensive support for managing and enhancing both internal and external operations. Operations functions and benefits are organized into two categories:

▶ **Operations value generation**
mySAP ERP provides end-to-end logistics for complete business process cycles, such as "purchase-to-pay" cycles and "make-to-order" cycles. By supporting a variety of core business processes in this way, mySAP ERP helps organizations improve their entire logistics operation and add value to the business.

▶ **Operations support**
To streamline complete business process cycles, mySAP ERP also provides logistics operations management functions that ensure operations run smoothly, fulfill all quality demands, and comply with all relevant regulations and standards. These functions help to reduce downtime, enable better decision-making, and increase customer loyalty while improving product quality, cost, and time to market.

Figure 2.13 shows the key operations capabilities provided by mySAP ERP.

Figure 2.13　Operations Capabilities within mySAP ERP

2.5.1　Operations Value Generation

Seamless integration of all enterprise processes

mySAP ERP seamlessly integrates enterprise operations functions—including purchasing, warehouse management, manufacturing, sales, service, and fulfillment—to provide businesses with comprehensive, current information about internal and external processes. A wide range of flexible management and analytical tools offers better insight, improved planning, and more accurate control of enterprise-wide processes to help organizations adapt to changing market and business requirements rapidly and more easily. Role-based interfaces and flexible portal environments make it easy for employees at all levels to access the information and applications they need; and support for collaborative communities enables the coordination of activities of business partners and customers within the organization.

More than 21,600 businesses worldwide rely on the integrated, end-to-end operations capabilities of mySAP ERP to plan, manufacture, distribute, and support products and services in all major industries. Businesses that utilize mySAP ERP can realize the following benefits:

▶ Reduced costs

mySAP ERP helps businesses decrease operating costs by converting time-consuming, manual processes into streamlined, online functions. Sophisticated analytical and management tools help businesses to match supply with demand, in addition to improving overall enterprise planning.

▶ Better asset utilization

mySAP ERP supports planning and strategic asset deployment that frees resources and reduces order cycle times. Therefore, businesses can improve manufacturing resource utilization, reduce excess inventories, and better meet shifts in customer demand.

▶ Increased revenue

With support for customer-focused initiatives (such as online availability checks, individual pricing information, and earliest delivery date), rapid response to customer demand, and improved customer service, mySAP ERP helps businesses realize greater revenue opportunities and improve customer satisfaction.

▶ Improved adaptability

mySAP ERP offers enterprise-wide visibility, performance management, and accurate forecasting to help businesses reduce planning cycles and lead times, enabling faster response to opportunities and continuous process improvements.

▶ **Enhanced employee productivity**
Customizable interfaces, portals, and self-services' capabilities within mySAP ERP ensure that employees have easy access to information and tools so they can perform their jobs more efficiently and effectively.

To help businesses fully realize these benefits, mySAP ERP provides capabilities in the following key areas:

▶ Procurement

▶ Inventory and warehouse management

▶ Manufacturing

▶ Transportation

▶ Sales order management

▶ Customer service

mySAP ERP improves procurement processes by facilitating plan-driven and ad-hoc purchasing, complete inventory management, and intelligent reporting on all procurement activities. In addition to providing supplier relationship management tools, mySAP ERP enables supplier selection and qualification, contract negotiations, bid invitations, and vendor evaluation. mySAP ERP supports not only traditional processes such as requisitioning, purchase order management, and invoice verification, but also innovative features such as self-service requisitions for maintenance, repair, and operations (MRO) material and services. Support for process variant optimization allows individual categories of material or services to be procured in the most appropriate way; for example, the subcontracting process supports the delivery of components required by outsourced manufacturing steps, and procurement through invoicing plans helps to improve rental and leasing processes. **Procurement**

mySAP ERP offers the following benefits for procurement:

▶ **Reduced raw material and procurement expenses**
mySAP ERP helps businesses better monitor material availability status, resulting in minimized procurement costs.

▶ **Optimized inventory turns**
By providing accurate reporting of real-time inventory availability, mySAP ERP helps organizations improve inventory utilization.

▶ **Increased productivity**
By automating routine tasks and by automatically determining sources or converting requisitions into purchase orders, mySAP ERP enables ongoing evaluation and optimization of procurement processes.

mySAP ERP supports and improves processes at warehouses and distribution facilities, and it can be used locally to improve the functions of an individual warehouse, or as part of an integrated, decentralized, enterprise-wide management system. As illustrated in Figure 2.14, all major areas of inventory and warehouse management are supported, including the following:

▶ Workload planning

▶ Wave picking and order consolidation

▶ Direct radio frequency and bar code scanning

▶ Handling unit management (compliant with EAN/UCC 128)

▶ Enhanced task management

▶ Resource optimization and control

▶ Monitoring and alert generation

▶ Cross docking

Figure 2.14 Warehouse Management within mySAP ERP

Combining delivery and warehouse information with data from customers, suppliers, and logistic service providers delivers accurate, up-to-date information to all partners, thereby improving visibility and reducing errors. Internet-enabled collaborative features support the following: online shipment tracking; web-based execution of packing functions on the warehouse floor; online delivery confirmation and automated discrepancy handling throughout the invoicing process; and Advance Shipping Notifications (ASNs) so that suppliers can provide delivery and packing information to the receiver prior to an order's arrival.

mySAP ERP offers the following benefits for inventory and warehouse management:

▶ **Improved facility management**
Real-time stock keeping and stock evaluation help businesses to better track, manage, and plan inventory and warehouse status.

▶ **Accelerated collaboration**
By supporting Internet-based collaboration, mySAP ERP enables rapid transactions, cost reductions, and increased transparency among trading partners.

▶ **Improved decision-making**
By providing rapid, accurate data access and real-time reports, mySAP ERP provides managers with the data they need to make informed decisions.

With support for all manufacturing strategies for businesses in the discrete, process, and consumer products industry, mySAP ERP helps enterprises manage the full range of manufacturing activities—from planning to execution and analysis—in a single, end-to-end system. mySAP ERP delivers all elements of a customer-oriented manufacturing management system and is fully compatible with Just-in-time (JIT) and Kanban[1] methodologies.

Manufacturing

By combining information from a variety of business processes (including planning, cost accounting, human resources, materials management, warehouse management, plant maintenance, and quality management), mySAP ERP supports the development and execution of efficient production plans and ensures that accurate, comprehensive information is available at any time to those who need it. Businesses can share manufacturing information across the enterprise and supply networks to coordinate production processes and promote cooperation. In addition, data from plant process-control and data-collection systems can be incorporated as well, enhancing decision-making by including accurate production data.

---

1 Kanban is a Japanese term. The actual term means "signal." It is one of the primary tools of Just-In-Time systems. It signals a cycle of replenishment for production and materials, and maintains an orderly and efficient flow of materials throughout the entire manufacturing process. It is usually a printed card that contains specific information such as part name, description, quantity, etc.

Benefits of mySAP ERP for manufacturing include the following:

▶ **Decreased costs**
mySAP ERP can help reduce manufacturing costs in a number of ways. Accurate manufacturing information results in increased productivity and reduced errors, while role-based user interfaces reduce supervision costs and improve the efficiency of shop floor task distribution. A single, master data model throughout the enterprise results in a lower rate of obsolescence and faster time to market.

▶ **Increased flexibility**
By supporting different production strategies, such as engineer-to-order, configure-to-order, make-to-order, and make-to-stock models, mySAP ERP helps businesses rapidly respond to customer demands.

▶ **Improved visibility and insight**
mySAP ERP establishes a continuous flow of information across engineering, planning, and execution, and it documents each step in the production process. Order change management capabilities track customer order revisions and new versions of Bills of Material (BOM) to ensure that up-to-date information is available throughout manufacturing. Moreover, the combination of easy-to-use analysis tools with comprehensive, real-time data enables managers to make informed decisions.

Transportation mySAP ERP helps businesses to meet shipping requirements and manage the multiple processes and reports required by foreign trade effectively. Flexible options for consolidating deliveries into shipments include rule-based automation, manual consolidation, and collaborative order combination through the Internet; in addition, the optimization logic from mySAP SCM can be used to further improve shipping choices. Support for collaborative tendering lets businesses tender directly into the transportation service provider's system. Consequently, organizations can integrate information from partners into their business processes and better control transportation plans.

Benefits of using mySAP ERP for transportation management include the following:

▶ **Increased invoice accuracy**
mySAP ERP helps businesses develop accurate, detailed freight cost calculations, which are essential for verifying invoices to and from transportation service providers.

▶ **Reduced transportation costs**
mySAP ERP enables accurate management of transportation costs, with support for settling costs for multiple transportation providers, posting both costs and accruals, and billing specific shipment costs directly to the customer.

▶ **Enhanced management of foreign trade**
Foreign trade management capabilities handle declarations for several authorities in the European Union, North American Free Trade Agreement (NAFTA) organizations, the European Free Trade Association (EFTA), and Japan, and make it easy to identify savings that can be gained by trading with countries that are preferred partners. In addition, business transaction simulation helps businesses analyze the effects of potential exports and problems, such as embargoes or boycotts.

mySAP ERP provides superior insight into sales back-office processes, including handling inquiries, quotations, order generation, and processing, as well as contract and billing cycle management. Businesses benefit from a complete overview of the customer lifecycle, including order status, billing, payment, and credit management. In addition to the back-office features, mySAP ERP also supports Internet sales, sales entered through mobile devices such as handhelds, and basic call center functionality.

Sales order management

mySAP ERP includes the following sales order management functions:

▶ **Quotation and order management**
mySAP ERP supports inquiry, quotation, and order management, including product configuration; flexible pricing and automated price calculation; product determination; online product availability checks; substitution for obsolete products and proposals; free goods and selling bundles; and fulfillment process tracking.

▶ **Contract management**
The solution also provides contract management capabilities and provides support for generating and managing long-term agreements; compiling follow-up sales documents based on contract agreements; and automatically locating related contracts during order entry, with data replication into follow-up orders.

▶ **Billing management**
mySAP ERP supports billing management, including support for compiling billing documents, flexible rebate calculation, and integration with mySAP ERP Financials.

Benefits of mySAP ERP for sales order management include the following:

► **Enhanced customer relationships**
Sales order management with mySAP ERP improves customer relationships by streamlining the sales process; employees have immediate access to all relevant information and can easily answer customer questions and provide up-to-date information about orders and quotations. Support for several types of sales processes helps meet customers' unique requirements; and integration with mySAP ERP supply chain functionality helps ensure that customer demands such as delivery data or requested batches and quality are addressed. Furthermore, online available-to-promise (ATP) checks provide reliable delivery due dates for customer orders.

► **Reduced financial risks**
mySAP ERP offers several ways to reduce financial risks with effective sales order and financial management, including support for customer credit checks and credit card handling. Integration with mySAP ERP Financials offers benefits that include identifying and addressing sales orders that are blocked by exceeded credit limits.

► **Improved billing efficiency**
mySAP ERP offers a billing portal to provide a single point of entry for all customer information and provides tools to process invoices and create credit and debit memos.

► **Improved agility and responsiveness**
mySAP ERP offers analytics that enable businesses to quickly recognize trends. This information can then be used to rapidly adjust and improve processes, take action to strengthen customer relations, and assess future opportunities.

Customer service mySAP ERP supports the complete customer service cycle, from post-sales support through initial product installation, ongoing support services, billing, and revenue recognition. mySAP ERP performs the following:

► **Installation and configuration management**
mySAP ERP supports installation and configuration management, including definition of product hierarchy, customer installed base, service location sites, serial number management, measurements and counter readings, document management, and engineering change management of the installed base at the customer site.

► **Service contract and entitlement management**
Support for service contract and entitlement management within mySAP ERP includes configurable service products and pricing, which

are also linked to installed-base products. Plan costs can be compared to the actual costs incurred for the life of a service contract.

▶ **Service planning**

mySAP ERP helps to improve resource and workload planning with support for planned services, which maintain and manage all data pertaining to ongoing, scheduled, and anticipated service requirements. As a result, enterprises benefit from greater visibility into resource demand, which enables more accurate forecasting and planning.

▶ **Service request and order management**

mySAP ERP records and monitors quotations, service requests, validates service entitlement, and tracks costs for in-house and field repairs. The solution supports processes such as escalation management, and provides tools for recording known issues, creating audit trails of what activities have been performed, and identifying the location of customer products that have been returned for repair. mySAP ERP also enables the capture of diagnostic information from various products for analysis, and provides organizations with performance reports about products and service levels.

▶ **Mobile service**

With support for mobile asset management, mySAP ERP enables the maintenance of field service information offline by using a mobile device such as a laptop or a personal digital assistant (PDA). Consequently, field engineers can access the tools and data they need to perform their jobs effectively.

▶ **Warranty management**

mySAP ERP includes warranty management functions that allow employees to process warranty, goodwill, service, recall, and parts claims from service providers. In addition, mySAP ERP enables automatic processing for most claims and can be used to support overall business analysis functions. Support for warranty claims processing enables the recovery of costs associated with warranty work from original equipment manufacturers (OEMs) and component suppliers.

The benefits of customer service management with mySAP ERP include the following:

▶ **Enhanced customer relationships**

By providing personnel with access to comprehensive customer and product information in a single, easy-to-use interface, mySAP ERP improves customer service by ensuring that representatives have access to the information and tools they need to provide services at the customer site.

▶ **Improved service processes**
mySAP ERP increases the visibility of customer service processes. In addition, it helps businesses manage and track all product manufacturing, sales, and service information to support improvements in maintenance, product recalls, and new product design. Companies can deliver fast and efficient superior service to achieve a competitive advantage. With the availability of mobile technology, technicians in the field can report their activities faster, resulting in quicker and more accurate billing and reporting.

▶ **Reduced costs**
By supporting data entry from field employees and streamlining service personnel planning, mySAP ERP reduces administrative efforts and improves employee efficiency.

2.5.2 New and Enhanced Operations Value Generation Functionality

Creating corporate value requires more than simply generating more revenue; true value generation is based on improving all aspects of a company's operations (including manufacturing processes and employee productivity), as well as a commitment to inspiring customer loyalty. mySAP ERP helps businesses meet these challenges by simplifying and accelerating business processes to reduce costs and enhance productivity, improving collaboration with partners, and providing innovative support for customers in all their communications with the organization.

Self-service "requisitioning"
Support for self-service *requisitioning* within mySAP ERP empowers employees throughout the enterprise to create and manage routine requisitions by themselves, including self-service requisitions for maintenance, repair, and operations material and services. Catalog content management in mySAP ERP helps to accelerate the ordering for frequently requested services, projects, and materials, and improves compliance with company purchasing rules. Self-service *requisitioning* improves procurement speed and responsiveness, while freeing up the purchasing department to focus on strategic tasks by reducing administrative burden.

Order processing using RFID
Radio frequency identification (RFID) supplements or replaces bar codes with electronic tags that store and transmit unique identifying information for individual items, cases, or pallets to readers deployed at warehouses and distribution facilities. RFID tagging is now required by some

of the world's largest retailers, including Tesco, METRO, Wal-Mart, and others. By eliminating line-of-sight requirements for scanning and allowing multiple tags to be scanned at once, RFID speeds up product and order handling, reduces hands-on processing, and minimizes errors. Together, with the SAP Event Management application, RFID support within mySAP ERP improves the visibility of stock levels and the execution status throughout the supply chain, enabling the identification of quality and process improvements.

RFID support within mySAP ERP contributes to the following benefits:

▶ **Minimized hands-on processing**
mySAP ERP decreases the need for human intervention in outbound order processing, resulting in improved accuracy, shorter fulfillment cycles, and reduced employee workload.

▶ **Instant stock verification**
Support for RFID within mySAP ERP can help businesses verify that product stock is available to meet fulfillment requirements by ensuring that accurate, up-to-date stock information is available throughout the enterprise.

▶ **Improved stock and order accuracy**
mySAP ERP makes it easy to use RFID information to verify the contents of an order before it leaves the warehouse, improving order accuracy and significantly reducing losses.

Manufacturers often face legal requirements to document where a product was produced, what components were used, and whether quality standards were met. mySAP ERP supports batch tracking, eliminating the need to manage batch inventory. Manufacturers of consumer products or cars and their suppliers frequently encounter legal and customer requirements for store data that pertains to materials procured from vendors, and is used in production and delivered to customers. Enabling recall actions is a mandatory and critical issue for these industries. mySAP ERP can manage all required data such as material tracking numbers thereby supporting legal regulations.

Documentary batch

mySAP ERP provides business value by:

▶ **Addressing the most important legal requirements**
mySAP ERP offers comprehensive search features that facilitate the traceability of products.

▶ **Reducing costs**

mySAP ERP supports the traceability of material flow, which significantly reduces total cost of ownership (TCO).

▶ **Simplifying internal logistic processes**

mySAP ERP fulfills the tracking requirements of many industries without the need to manage inventory in batches.

Internet sales mySAP ERP provides powerful e-commerce capabilities that can be expanded in an easy, cost-effective manner in line with business growth. Organizations can run a complete sales process on the Internet, and provide business-to-business (B2B) and business-to-consumer (B2C) customers with personalized and interactive online self-services (see Figure 2.15).

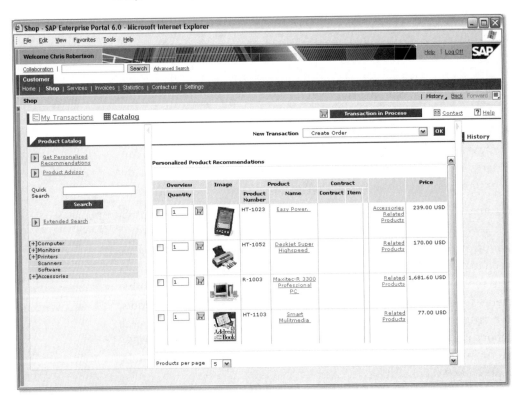

Figure 2.15 Internet Sales

Benefits include the following:

▶ **Increased revenues**

mySAP ERP enables businesses to use the Internet as a profitable channel for sales and interaction. Web shops can be easily integrated.

► **Improved customer service**

mySAP ERP provides a convenient, easy-to-use experience, supporting customers with online product configuration, shopping basket features, product availability checks, and secures transactions as well as order status and tracking.

► **Simplified sales processes**

mySAP ERP supports a variety of end-to-end sales processes with easy-to-use interactive self-services for customers.

► **Reduced total cost of ownership**

E-commerce in mySAP ERP is fully integrated with existing mySAP ERP processes and systems, enabling the leveraging of existing investments to support e-commerce activities.

mySAP ERP enables sales professionals to access front- and back-office business processes and to manage critical sales activities in the field using standard PDAs or other handheld devices (including those with bar code scanners). In this area, mySAP ERP provides the following functions:

Mobile sales for handhelds

► **Customer management**

With mySAP ERP, sales professionals can enter, view, and modify detailed customer information, and view sales order history for each customer.

► **Sales order management**

mySAP ERP enables sales staff to take sales orders via bar code scanners; search, create, and modify sales orders; and list or sort sales order partners.

► **Material management**

Support for material management for mobile sales enables staff to view material lists or details for a specific material, search material, and display customer-specific prices.

Benefits of support for mobile sales include the following:

► **Increased data entry accuracy**

Using bar code and RFID technologies instead of keystrokes ensures that data is entered rapidly and without errors.

► **Simplified and accelerated processes**

By enabling sales professionals to create orders in the field, mySAP ERP accelerates order entry and fulfillment.

► **Reduced data maintenance and administrative burden**
Because data from the field is entered directly in mySAP ERP, the reentering of field information in back-office or other systems is no longer
necessary.

2.5.3 Operations Support

mySAP ERP Operations is a key solution of mySAP ERP that delivers an
enterprise-wide solution for operations management, with field-proven
methods for improving product quality, cost, and time to market. mySAP
ERP helps organizations align all operations activities with business objectives and provides a solid, scalable foundation for future enterprise
growth. In addition to driving innovation across organizations, mySAP
ERP provides the following benefits:

► **Improved decision-making throughout the organization**
By combining powerful, flexible analytical tools with comprehensive,
enterprise-wide operations data, managers can make solid, fact-based
decisions for areas such as portfolio management, occupational health
and safety, product safety, product quality, and enterprise asset management.

► **Maximized plant and equipment performance**
mySAP ERP supports comprehensive asset management for optimally
maintaining plants and equipment, deploying them to support appropriate projects, and complying with safety and regulatory standards.

► **Enhanced customer satisfaction**
By improving all business processes—including product design and
development, manufacturing, and customer service—mySAP ERP
ensures that products and services meet or exceed customer demands.

► **Rapid, cost-effective time to market**
Efficient, enterprise-wide operations support accelerates the product
development cycle, enabling businesses to develop and maintain a
competitive edge when responding to changing marketplace
demands.

► **Improved internal and external collaboration**
mySAP ERP ensures that all internal and external team members and
partners have immediate access to relevant data, enabling rapid
response to changes or issues that arise.

► **Reduced risk exposure**
Comprehensive quality management capabilities ensure that all
aspects of product development meet stringent quality requirements.

▶ **Lower total cost of ownership for technology infrastructure**
mySAP ERP is easily integrated with other mySAP Business Suite solutions, including mySAP Customer Relationship Management (CRM), mySAP Supplier Relationship Management (SRM), and mySAP Supply Chain Management (SCM), ensuring the free flow of accurate information throughout the enterprise. In addition, mySAP ERP can be integrated with product development tools, including various CAD products, and can provide visibility and management capabilities for all aspects of the product development process.

To help enterprises fully realize these benefits, mySAP ERP provides operations with support capabilities in the following key areas:

▶ Lifecycle data management

▶ Program and project management

▶ Quality management

▶ Enterprise asset management

With mySAP ERP, organizations can manage all product-related data, including product structures, documents, recipes, and associated configuration and change management processes. mySAP ERP can be integrated with product development technologies, including CAD, and comes pre-integrated with office applications and analytical tools to ensure that product development staff can change product information when necessary with the most appropriate tools for the task. mySAP ERP helps businesses manage the full range of product lifecycle data, including the following:

Lifecycle data management

▶ Early development materials, including documents and specification data

▶ Design, planning, and production materials, including engineering documents, materials, Bills of Material (BOM), recipes, and routings

▶ Service and maintenance materials, including installed-base information, asset, and equipment data

By providing transparent, enterprise-wide access to product lifecycle data, mySAP ERP offers the following benefits:

▶ **Reduced costs and error rates**
mySAP ERP reduces the number of applications required to support operations, resulting in fewer errors and lowered costs.

▶ **Enhanced decision-making support**
mySAP ERP provides designers, planners, and product managers with immediate access to accurate, up-to-date, relevant product and project data, which helps to ensure that their decisions are based on the best available information.

▶ **Improved NPDI processes**
By integrating people and information into a single, streamlined process, mySAP ERP helps improve new product development and introduction (NPDI) and enables efficient, successful product launches (see Figure 2.16).

▶ **Enhanced collaboration**
Support for a collaborative work environment enables everyone in the enterprise to contribute appropriately at each stage of a product's lifecycle.

NPDI Process

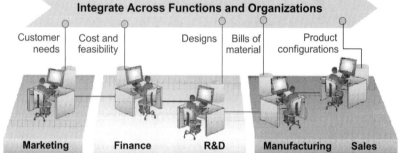

Figure 2.16 NPDI Support within mySAP ERP

Program and project management
Effective program and project management helps to improve collaboration and communication among internal and external participants in the product development process, resulting in efficient processes that expedite time to market and satisfy customer demand. mySAP ERP helps organizations plan, manage, and control all program and project parameters, including project structures, timelines, costs, and resources for projects of any size in any industry. Real-time document exchange and status information ensures that staff and managers have the information necessary to evaluate progress and make informed decisions at every stage, while comprehensive project overviews help organizations manage the enterprise-wide product portfolio. Furthermore, program and project manage-

ment information can be integrated with supply chain management and procurement systems to ensure that necessary materials are available at the right price and at the right time. mySAP ERP offers the following benefits in program and project management:

▶ **Rapid time to market**
Improved project management capabilities and integration with supply chain management systems reduce the time to design, develop, manufacture, and ship new products.

▶ **Reduced product development costs**
Access to consistent, accurate data helps organizations improve project management efficiency and reduce errors, resulting in lower development costs.

▶ **Optimized purchasing**
Integrating project information with supply chain management and procurement systems minimizes material costs and maximizes purchasing efficiency.

▶ **Improved budget management**
Detailed cost overviews help to ensure accurate budgeting; access to real-time project information helps managers identify and address potential budgetary adjustments in advance.

▶ **Better resource allocation**
Accurate profitability analysis helps organizations focus resources on strategically important activities.

▶ **Improved collaboration**
Improved collaboration throughout the organization and supply chain makes it easier to adapt projects to changing markets and customer needs, to drive product innovation, and to explore new market opportunities.

Comprehensive quality management functions within mySAP ERP help businesses meet customer demand for superior products by supporting quality processes related to product development, production, change management, and service and maintenance issues across the organization. By integrating quality information with logistics and manufacturing, mySAP ERP can help extend quality processes beyond the enterprise borders to all elements of the extended supply chain, resulting in higher quality products and faster product releases at reduced costs.

Quality management

As shown in Figure 2.17, mySAP ERP delivers a unified approach to total quality management, with a complete range of features and functions that help businesses control and maintain quality and react quickly when unexpected issues arise throughout the product lifecycle:

▶ **Quality planning**
mySAP ERP supports quality engineering during product evaluation, design and development, validation, and launch.

▶ **Quality assurance and control**
mySAP ERP enables efficient quality assurance and control for procurement, production, final inspection, and storage.

▶ **Continuous improvement**
mySAP ERP supports quality improvement capabilities throughout sales, distribution, service, and disposal.

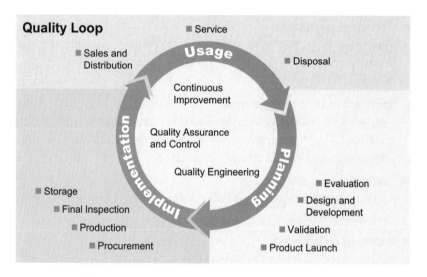

Figure 2.17 Quality Management within mySAP ERP

The benefits of quality management with mySAP ERP include the following:

▶ **Optimized product development**
Incorporating quality engineering practices into all stages of the product lifecycle reduces time to market; improves product analysis, planning, and management; and maximizes the quality of both processes and products.

▶ **Increased customer satisfaction**
Quality assurance, control, and improvement capabilities ensure the overall quality of products, services, and processes, resulting in products that meet or exceed customer expectations.

▶ **Reduced inspection costs**
Quality management features improve the inspection process with support for multiple kinds of inspections—including goods receipt inspections, in-process checks, recurring batch inspections, and others. mySAP ERP offers flexible methods of organizing, recording, and reviewing inspection data, including the use of Internet and mobile devices to enter results of field inspections or inspections of hard-to-access assets.

▶ **Enhanced quality throughout the supply chain**
Incorporating business partners into the quality management process ensures that all elements in the process meet quality requirements and reduces the need for product correction.

▶ **Improved regulatory and standards compliance**
Quality management features provide manufacturers with the comprehensive documentation of quality control processes required by ISO 9000 and other industry standards, such as Good Manufacturing Practice (GMP) guidelines and other regulations governing the food and drug industry.

▶ **Lower total cost of ownership**
By incorporating all quality management functions in a single solution and eliminating the need for multiple, third-party applications, mySAP ERP reduces system complexity.

To maintain a competitive advantage, organizations must maximize the use of every available asset, as well as ensure that every piece of equipment and all facilities operate at the highest level of performance and efficiency. Enterprise Asset Management (EAM) helps ensure that effective decisions are made during the complete asset lifecycle—from specification and design, procurement, and deployment, to maintenance and eventual disposal (see Figure 2.18). mySAP ERP helps minimize downtime, accelerates time to market, and improves revenues by ensuring that assets are deployed, utilized, and serviced in such a way as to maximize their contribution to enterprise goals.

Enterprise asset management

mySAP ERP offers enterprises the following benefits in EAM:

▶ **Reduced operating costs**
By better tracking and managing operations, safety, maintenance, and expenses, businesses can reduce overall operating costs and make informed capital investment decisions.

► **Minimized equipment downtime**

mySAP ERP helps improve plant and equipment performance and reduce equipment downtime with comprehensive support for maintenance planning, preventive maintenance, and rapid identification of items needing repair. As a result, businesses improve asset planning, operation, maintenance, and replacement processes, and reduce the need to maintain large inventories of spare parts.

► **Strategic asset deployment**

mySAP ERP provides organizations with comprehensive, accurate asset information, enabling managers to match appropriate assets with production requirements. Consequently, the most efficient assets are deployed for each project, ensuring optimal performance and reduced production costs.

► **Increased support for fact-based decision-making**

Managers can make fact-based operation and maintenance decisions supported by mobile or portal-based access to accurate information, enabling improved maintenance and upgrade management and rapid equipment repair.

► **Improved environmental, safety, and regulatory compliance**

By enabling organizations to plan and organize equipment maintenance intervals, mySAP ERP helps businesses meet industrial health and safety measures, as well as comply with regulations and industry standards.

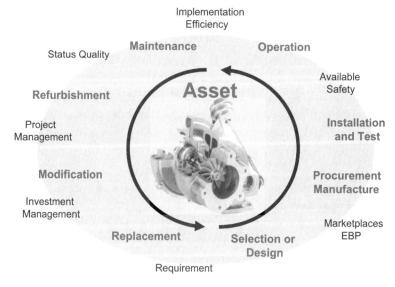

Figure 2.18 Asset Lifecycle Management

2.5.4 New and Enhanced Operations Support Functionality

Lifecycle data management

Successful organizations continually strive to leverage and improve industry best practices for product design and engineering. These enterprises realize that creating value in today's economy requires efficient internal and external collaboration, solid customer and partner relationships, and effective utilization of all available information sources, as well as management tools to increase productivity, profitability, and innovation.

New and enhanced Lifecycle Data Management (LDM) features in mySAP ERP simplify and accelerate development processes and document management, enabling improved collaboration and cost reductions at every step of the product lifecycle. Overall benefits of LDM capabilities include the following:

Better collaboration and cost reduction

▶ Lower TCO resulting from reduced administrative and operational costs

▶ Rapid time to market with faster, more efficient development processes

▶ Improved communication with vendors and customers via secure connectivity and enhanced collaboration tools

▶ Reduced administrative burden and training costs via improved data and document management

New trial capabilities in SAP Recipe Management integrate trial definition, planning, execution, and monitoring during development in laboratories, pilot plants, and handoffs to production. All data related to recipes and formulas, research and development, production, and environmental health and safety can be included in a single environment. Support for pilot plants and production lines have been enhanced to allow fully automated transformation to Production Planning-Process Industry (PP-PI) recipes. In addition, new support for process orders simplifies the use of process management objects.

Trails in recipe management

Together, these enhanced development functions enable faster product development and improved product consistency. The following functions are also supported:

▶ **NPDI process support**
New functions provide NPDI process support with recipes, specifica-

tions, formulas, materials, and production operations generated by the recipe development environment.

▶ **Recipe creation**
The application enables rapid access to objects and functions, as well as support for faster calculations, resulting in more efficient recipe creation.

▶ **Trial development**
Integration with SAP project management and workflow solutions improves control of the trial development process and results in faster time to volume.

▶ **Information access**
mySAP ERP makes it easy for users to access information from previous efforts, including existing recipes and formulas, resulting in a more efficient development process.

Simplified document management The new SAP Easy Document Management application, which is installed on individual users' computers, simplifies and speeds up document management and maintenance time, and makes it easier for users to benefit from the sophisticated document management capabilities that are already available in mySAP ERP. New group structures facilitate team and group work and enhance collaboration. And users benefit from intuitive, simplified, and flexible document management capabilities such as drag and drop and hierarchical folder displays similar to those in Microsoft Windows Explorer. SAP Easy Document Management is so easy to use that even occasional users require only minimal training.

Internal and external document access Enhanced document-sharing features in the Document Management System (DMS) provide internal and external users with transparent, up-to-date documents such as design drawings and contracts, and support efficient document retrieval across multiple repositories. Therefore, decision-makers have secure, immediate access to the information they need. Electronic search techniques reduce labor costs when multiple or diverse storage systems are involved. Equally important, the DMS supports the integration of documents into business processes and enables collaboration through a web-based platform for engineering and logistics. Collectively, these capabilities reduce access times and labor costs for routine tasks, and increase overall efficiency.

CAD integration New features allow users to access and edit CAD document structures directly in a CAD system, or from within mySAP ERP, enabling the inclusion of new product information in business processes at an early stage. CAD integration supports a variety of industry-standard CAD systems, including Pro/Engineer, CATIA, Inventor, and others; and because SAP partners develop each interface, businesses are assured seamless integration. CAD integration supports enterprise-wide collaboration with concurrent engineering and versioning, enabling multiple users to simultaneously process an assembly, and allowing the status of several processes to be saved in the system. In addition, CAD integration provides a single access point to all CAD documents, making it easier for all users to access the resources they need, when they need them. Enhanced viewing options include tabbed pages for different views, and the ability to view two- and three-dimensional files (such as drawings and CAD models) in a single view. The CAD integration also simplifies routine tasks with automatic bills of material; visual version control; mass check-in/check-out; and check-in/check-out assistant capabilities.

A new product-modeling environment in mySAP ERP simplifies the process of defining and maintaining product models that require variant configuration, and addresses the challenge of managing products under continual development. Variant configuration support ensures the efficient management of necessary product data by enabling product-modeling experts to quickly adapt to market demands, and by allowing business users to review and modify the product model as needed. The product modeling software is fully integrated with planning, pricing, order processing, availability checking, production, fulfillment, billing, and financial reporting, and ensures a consistent view of the product in sales orders, production plans, and profitability analyses.

Product modeling for configurable products

The collaboration folders (cFolders) application enables users to work on product design and development data in virtual teams with external partners and suppliers. Because they support vertical integration with knowledge management and collaboration systems, these collaboration capabilities help to generate effective external collaboration for product development and engineering. Additional features of cFolders include the following:

Collaboration with partners and suppliers

▶ Structured collaboration support for sharing a variety of objects and documents, with the ability to view two- and three-dimensional objects

▶ Secure collaboration through encrypted files, assuring data confidentiality and integrity even when shared with external partners

▶ Integration with other systems (such as DMS and BOM processing) and collaboration tools such as WebEx's online meeting system ensures flexible access to related information and meetings for all participants

▶ Integration with Microsoft Windows Explorer to simplify access for occasional users

Guided procedures mySAP ERP makes it easy for organizations to replace inefficient, paper-based processes with automated business workflow solutions. As shown in Figure 2.19, guided procedures within mySAP ERP enable businesses to create customized electronic forms that have the same look and feel as traditional paper forms, but can be completed and submitted online.

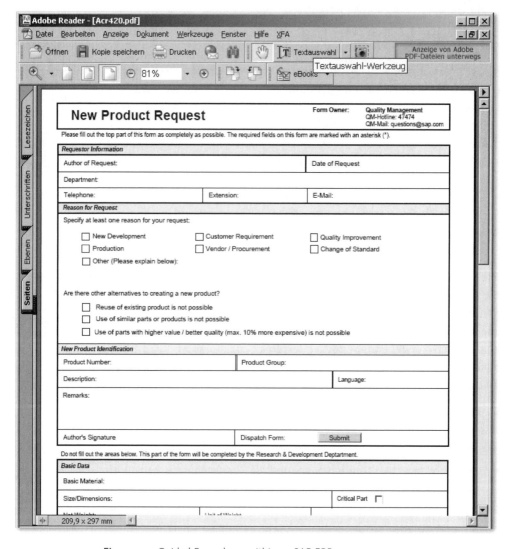

Figure 2.19 Guided Procedures within mySAP ERP

In addition, guided procedures support flexible business processes by allowing employees to change the workflow process (such as where a form is submitted or what other processes are triggered as a result) dynamically, ensuring that the enterprise can respond appropriately to exceptions. Benefits of guided procedures within mySAP ERP include the following:

▶ **Improved business processes**
Replacing paper forms with electronic versions ensures that information is rapidly delivered to all the appropriate personnel and systems, without requiring copying, manual delivery, or data reentry. Therefore, accurate information flows more freely through the enterprise.

▶ **Enhanced responsiveness**
Because workflows can be modified as needed to meet business requirements—without requiring costly or time-consuming programming efforts—business units are better equipped to change their processes to meet changing requirements.

▶ **Reduced administrative burden**
Easy-to-use electronic forms that employ a similar look and feel to paper versions help relieve employees of time-consuming data entry. In addition, because information is automatically delivered to the next step in the workflow, employees are no longer burdened with concerns regarding routing.

Program and Project Management

One of the challenges that businesses face today is launching innovative, high-quality products with a shorter time to market, while at the same time keeping overall product costs down. Today, more complex IT environments, increasing customer demands for "market-to-one," and the need for intensified collaboration with partners require that businesses have better process management and more accurate, transparent financial data for development activities. The enhancements to the program and project management capabilities of mySAP ERP provide the following benefits:

▶ Better collaboration with business partners

▶ Greater financial transparency and cost reductions

▶ Faster product development resulting from improved project modeling

▶ Reduced costs for training and software integration

cProjects Through the collaborative projects (cProjects) suite, mySAP ERP offers support for collaborative product development processes from the planning phase to product (or process) validation based on the Stage-Gate process methodology. Users can now share information with partners through Microsoft Project integration and uploads, create project snapshots and simulation versions, and assign substitutes for their tasks while on vacation. Usability enhancements include a customizable interface and the ability to perform mass maintenance of task lists and checklists. In addition, users can now share information with collaborations used in bidding scenarios and link not only to complete collaborations, but to single folders within a collaboration as well.

The cProjects suite also provides the following:

▶ The ability to split large projects into individual subprojects, which facilitates modeling projects based on responsibilities

▶ Standardized project reporting, which saves time by automatically including all available information in a status report

▶ Support for SAP Easy Document Management, which reduces cost of ownership by leveraging existing investments in document-sharing technologies

▶ Simplified access to project structures and documents through Microsoft Windows Explorer and Microsoft Office, which reduces training costs and improves usability for occasional users

▶ Easy access to collaborative projects from other software packages through Web services, which simplifies implementation and customization

Resource-related down payments and billing In long-term projects, services rendered can often be billed only after they have been approved, or after the customer confirms the progress of the project. In most contracts, the customer and contractor agree on down-payment dates. Often, these payments don't generate revenue. mySAP ERP enables organizations to create down-payment requests analogous to the functions offered by resource-related billing.

In addition, mySAP ERP makes it easy to bill services between different organizational units. In the past, businesses that could not bill services between company codes within a single controlling area were required to use a reconciliation ledger, which often led to delays in invoicing. Now organizations can bill the requesting company code for services provided using a resource-related billing document.

Quality Management

Customer demands for product personalization and product quality are increasing, while businesses are producing new and diversified products and services at a record pace. These trends are forcing organizations to cut time to market and minimize costs. To succeed in this environment, businesses must find ways to meet and even exceed customer expectations—a challenge that requires a relentless focus on product, service, and process quality. mySAP ERP enhancements in quality management are designed to support current best practices and provide the following benefits:

▶ Improved system performance and flexibility

▶ Support of current Good Manufacturing Practice (GMP) and Good Laboratory Practice (GLP) guidelines

▶ Improved data management and data integration

▶ Faster development processes and simplified studies

Support for advanced product quality planning

Advanced Product Quality Planning (APQP) is a Stage-Gate driven approach to structured project management required by various standards, such as ISO TS 16949 in the automotive industry. Enhancements in mySAP ERP that support APQP include the automatic assignment of objects, such as inspection plans or routings, up to the control plan. Additional object links can be used to assign inspection lots and attach or create quality notifications, for example, triggering a failure mode and effect analysis, or Failure Mode and Effects Analysis (FMEA).

Trail-specific stability studies

Planning, executing, and evaluating laboratory trials are critical product development steps in the processes industries, especially food and beverage. Businesses are required to conduct stability studies using samples taken from different trials, as well as perform quality inspections. Recipe management can now handle inspection characteristics, trials, and trial-specific stability studies. These enhancements help to establish the connection between trial management and quality management in mySAP ERP. The solution allows product developers to initiate stability studies more efficiently using building blocks with fixed planning parameters such as time intervals, storage conditions, or testing plans. In addition, the solution:

▶ Integrates quality-relevant information into the product development process

▶ Supports current Good Manufacturing Practice (GMP) guidelines and industry standards such as ISO TS 16949

▶ Simplifies and accelerates the planning of stability studies via reusable building blocks

Quality assurance and control New quality assurance and control enhancements in mySAP ERP provide improved sample management capabilities, including extended selection options for sample work lists, extensions to the master record, and archiving of sample data in alignment with the overall SAP archiving concept. Archival functions are particularly important for service laboratories that provide sample analyses upon customer request, as well as process industries that use the quality management application and Laboratory Information Management Systems (LIMS), and that handle large numbers of samples and drawings each day. In addition, the solution:

▶ Supports current Good Manufacturing Practices and Good Laboratory Practices (GMP/GLP) guidelines for regulated industries, such as the pharmaceuticals industry (which must keep sample records for long periods of time for tracking purposes)

▶ Delivers better system performance by removing mass data from the system, resulting in less real-time data

▶ Improves usability and user acceptance

Quality improvement To help businesses address the ongoing challenge of quality improvement, a number of enhancements are available in mySAP ERP and in other SAP software and third-party offerings. Quality manuals can be maintained with the SAP Easy Document Management application, which simplifies updates and document management. In addition, businesses can now use the SAP Business Intelligence (SAP BI) component of the SAP NetWeaver platform to analyze stability studies.

Enterprise Asset Management

To meet customer demands quickly and cost effectively, organizations must exploit every asset available to them—including those within the extended supply chain. Simultaneously, they must also ensure that their equipment and maintenance procedures comply with safety and work regulations. To meet these challenges, organizations need reliable, current asset information and innovative ways to optimize and maintain those assets throughout their entire lifecycle. mySAP ERP enhancements in enterprise asset management allow businesses to implement automated, standardized processes that reduce administrative and operational costs, and provide more flexible ways to access and edit asset data. Consequently, organizations can ensure that they are using their assets to their full potential.

The SAP Mobile Asset Management solution delivers access to critical, role-based information and services anytime and anywhere. SAP Mobile Asset Management provides a suite of tools tailored to meet the needs of plant maintenance and customer service field engineers—key players in the asset management lifecycle. This complete, offline mobile solution provides ready-made scenarios that help field technicians perform their daily activities at customer sites. SAP Mobile Asset Management can be used with either a laptop or a standard PDA device. The solution offers:

Mobile Asset Management

▶ Fast, easy access to timely information anywhere, anytime

▶ Tools that enable field technicians to resolve problems faster

▶ Reduced costs per work order

▶ Elimination of paper-based orders

▶ Simplified access to usage-related stock information

In addition, technicians can enter data directly on-site, which provides the following benefits:

▶ Increased data-entry accuracy (for example, notification or counter reading data)

▶ Lowered risk of losing data

▶ Reduced administrative time spent reentering field information in the back office

▶ Reduced total cycle times—from job completion to invoice submission—resulting in greater cash flow for the business

In capital-intensive industries such as oil and gas, chemicals, mining, and utilities, maintenance typically accounts for 50% of operating costs. Organizations trying to establish their maintenance cost budget face a number of complex issues. In most cases, interdependent data, such as actual maintenance costs, planned maintenance costs, and maintenance-related budget data are insufficiently integrated, making data analysis difficult. In addition, planning is quite time-consuming, because it is usually performed manually or in nonintegrated environments such as Microsoft Excel. In either case, managers don't have the tools they need to measure continuous improvement.

Maintenance cost budgeting

Maintenance cost budgeting within mySAP ERP allows users to define a maintenance budget based on data residing in a firm's ERP systems. This solution helps businesses reduce maintenance costs and now offers a number of enhancements, including the following:

▶ Automated and standardized budgeting processes

▶ Fast, integrated overviews of all necessary asset lifecycle management functions

▶ A new, intuitive user interface for improved efficiency

2.6 Corporate Services

In the current market situation, organizations are under enormous pressure to cut costs while meeting stakeholder expectations for continued growth, innovation, and financial success. Businesses are challenged to reduce costs wherever possible and to avoid taking risks that might lead to unexpected and unbudgeted expenditures. In addition, organizations are expected to achieve high levels of financial transparency, develop and adhere to strict fiscal policies, and comply with a range of regulatory standards. Businesses will benefit from enterprise-wide tools that aid in the planning and the administration of the critical corporate areas of travel management; environment, health, and safety; variable compensation plan management; and real-estate management.

Travel management

Travel management presents unique challenges for corporations that want to reduce costs and streamline administrative processes. Pressure to reform traditional travel policies is increasing, as changes in compensation and pricing models from suppliers, Global Distribution Systems (GDS), and travel agencies are forcing companies to examine the ways in which they plan and finance corporate travel.

Traditional travel management policies often make it difficult for travel managers to ensure that employees select the most appropriate travel services, or for travel management to monitor policy compliance. Businesses will benefit from travel management tools that enable the following:

▶ Deliver cost transparency and improved strategies for cost control

▶ Ensure that employees choose travel services through preferred airlines, hotel chains, and car rental companies

▶ Simplify travel expenses for employees

▶ Help the organization to monitor policy compliance

▶ Integrate travel costs into corporate financial accounting

Environment, health & safety

As products and processes continuously change, so do the laws and rules that regulate them. Global businesses must contend with frequent changes in the number and complexity of Environment, Health, and

Safety (EH&S) regulations and their consequences. These regulations may impact nearly every area of an enterprise, including purchasing, new product development, manufacturing, sales, distribution, service, and maintenance. Regulatory changes may require alterations to work areas, which can immediately impact industrial hygiene and safety, as well as the occupational safety of employees. Organizations will benefit from technology solutions for EH&S management that enable the following:

▶ Production of safer products

▶ Creation of safer workplaces and reduced risks for employees

▶ Environmental protection

▶ Compliance with all relevant national and international regulations

Incentive and commissions management

Organizations also face challenges in the management and payment of variable compensation plans, which account for some of today's greatest corporate expenditures. The most effective variable compensation plans rely on supporting technologies that can evolve with a business and offer sufficient scalability to accommodate organizational changes, product launches, mergers, or acquisitions.

Businesses will benefit from compensation management solutions that do the following:

▶ Promote collaboration in the achievement of organization-wide goals with support for variable compensation plans that reward efforts appropriately

▶ Improve accuracy and streamline program administration by automating compensation programs

▶ Increase productivity by reducing the time spent on plan management and performing error prone manual calculations

Real-estate management

Real-estate management is another area that presents challenges for businesses interested in controlling costs, particularly large organizations. Businesses for which the management of commercial space is a core competency will benefit from process support and automation that aid in streamlining and improving business functions. Managers of residential real estate will benefit from tools that help avoid vacancies and reduce costs associated with real-estate development, rentals, and property management. Businesses that manage any kind of corporate, commercial, or residential real estate will benefit from solutions that offer the following:

- ▶ Greater flexibility and higher quality through enhanced data transparency

- ▶ Better cost and land-use management

- ▶ Improved investment strategy through accurate cost- and revenue-performance data

- ▶ Enhanced management of integrated property portfolios

- ▶ Better rental property management methods

- ▶ More versatile reporting and analyses

- ▶ Integration of accounting and logistic functions with property management functions

Corporate Services today mySAP ERP offers an ideal solution for companies intent on improving the monitoring and administration of travel management; environment, health and safety; incentive and commissions management; and real-estate management. The mySAP ERP Corporate Services solution delivers leading-edge capabilities to help organizations effectively manage these business-critical functions, and it supports regulatory compliance, particularly in the area of EH&S. The solution is tailored to meet the needs of both global and national organizations.

While many solutions are available to support individual functions such as travel management or incentives and commissions, most lack integration with enterprise-wide business systems and processes. mySAP ERP is powered by the SAP NetWeaver platform, which enables integration of applications, processes, and data throughout the enterprise.

mySAP ERP performs administration and management functions in the following key areas:

- ▶ Travel management

- ▶ Environment, health, and safety

- ▶ Incentive and commissions management

- ▶ Real-estate management

2.6.1 Travel Management

Travel management functions New service fees and security charges may cause the cost of business travel to rise by as much as 20% over the next few years. Businesses that want to prevent travel costs from spiraling out of control must examine their travel-booking processes, analyze and redefine travel policies, and increase employee compliance with these policies.

Travel management functions within mySAP ERP provide an end-to-end solution for managing business travel that can help organizations define and improve their travel procedures and accelerate the adoption of changes throughout the enterprise. There are also travel management features to help travel agencies operate more efficiently and strengthen client relationships.

mySAP ERP offers the following features for travel management:

▶ **Travel planning and online booking**
mySAP ERP enables business travelers to book flights, hotels, cars, and country-specific rail options, as well as look up related information. In addition, the solution fully supports communication with travel agencies, making interactions more efficient.

▶ **Travel expense accounting**
With easy-to-use functions that accelerate the processing of travel expense statements and streamline accounting and settlement processes, mySAP ERP reduces the administrative workload associated with travel expense accounting. The SAP Mobile Time and Travel solution enables offline access to expense reports, allowing travelers to create new reports and enter receipts.

▶ **Travel planning**
Online booking is controlled by corporate travel policy parameters, helping travel managers to bundle travel volumes to preferred providers and negotiated fares. Better compliance with travel policies facilitates a better negotiation position for central travel service procurement and has an immediate effect on direct purchasing costs.

▶ **Travel expense management**
Management can implement effective travel policy strategies and easily control travel budgets for the global enterprise or institution, ensuring internal policy compliance as well as national legal and tax compliance.

▶ **Travel management reporting**
mySAP ERP supports decision-making and facilitates the development and implementation of new strategies for reducing costs and creating a more efficient travel policy. Preconfigured reports help businesses consolidate valuable data for supplier negotiations to cut direct purchasing costs even further.

Organizations benefit from the following:

▶ **Higher adoption rates through end-to-end processes**
The consistent, easy-to-understand user-interface design used across all process steps minimizes employee learning curves, results in higher acceptance rates, and reduces training costs.

▶ **Improved compliance**
mySAP ERP makes it easy for businesses to define and implement travel policies, as well as help to ensure that employees choose policy-compliant travel options. As a result, the solution helps organizations apply expense policies consistently throughout the enterprise and prevent unnecessary expenses via efficient control processes and audits.

▶ **Improved information access and deeper insight**
With mySAP ERP, travel managers, purchasers, and controllers have immediate access to all the information they need to make informed, effective decisions.

▶ **Increased accuracy**
The elimination of most manual data entry significantly reduces the potential for errors in entering and processing travel-related information.

2.6.2 Environment, Health, and Safety

Environment, health, and safety functions

Enterprises in a variety of industries are subject to multiple local, national, and international laws and regulations that stringently control the proper treatment of hazardous substances. These businesses must ensure effective planning and management of operational processes that involve the use and handling of dangerous raw materials and by-products of finished goods. In addition, it is imperative that these organizations provide proper safeguards to protect customers, neighboring communities, and the environment. mySAP ERP supports environment, health, and safety professionals with functions that do the following:

▶ **Identify and minimize employee health risks**
mySAP ERP enhances employee health and safety with complete support for industrial hygiene, safety, and occupational health functions. In addition, it helps to ensure compliance with government safety regulations.

▶ **Support preventive healthcare**
The occupational health function includes a medical service that records all relevant health protocol data, allowing businesses to track

employee health care and monitor the results of medical examinations and diagnoses.

▶ **Ensure product safety and hazardous substance management**
mySAP ERP offers specific product-safety functions, including automatic product composition calculation, rule based Material Safety Data Sheets (MSDS) authoring, automatic MSDS generation, global label management capabilities, and MSDS shipping. In addition, mySAP ERP includes inventory reports for hazardous substances, as well as a substance information search system that can block or approve the purchase of hazardous materials.

▶ **Track dangerous goods**
mySAP ERP helps companies store and manage regulatory data, classify dangerous goods, perform checks during transport, and compile and update dangerous goods documentation. This data can be automatically supplied to other applications for use in delivery notes and packing lists. mySAP ERP can automatically identify appropriate transportation channels (road, rail, sea, or air), and ensure that shipments comply with regulations before leaving the premises.

▶ **Manage waste disposal**
With management features that help ensure the efficient disposal of both hazardous and no hazardous waste, mySAP ERP enables organizations to comply with all relevant waste disposal laws and regulations. The solution provides basic features for managing waste data. Other functions help users create hazardous waste permits, choose suitable disposal firms, allocate disposal costs among internal departments, and ensure that authorized waste quantities are not exceeded.

Organizations benefit from the following:

▶ **Improved safety**
By supporting full compliance with regulations and standards, mySAP ERP helps businesses produce safer products, protect customers and communities, and provide safe workplaces that reduce risks to employees.

▶ **Lower costs**
mySAP ERP helps organizations minimize financial risks associated with noncompliance and avoid costly downtime associated with unexpected events.

▶ **Enhanced corporate image**
Years of costly branding efforts can be tarnished by reports of noncompliance; by helping to ensure that organizations are compliant with

regulations, mySAP ERP helps businesses promote and maintain a positive public image. In addition, meeting or exceeding regulatory compliance requirements can provide a competitive edge by helping businesses differentiate themselves from other players in their industry.

▶ **Optimized business processes**
mySAP ERP can help businesses improve a variety of business processes, such as simplifying the management of dangerous goods, improving administrative processes such as MSDS, and providing access to external content providers.

2.6.3 Incentive and Commissions Management

Incentive and commissions management functions

Successful companies must set clear targets for their internal and external sales forces, offer effective compensation for sales efforts, and provide methods for sales personnel and management to track performance. Incentive and commissions management features within mySAP ERP are designed to help organizations develop effective incentive programs, including sales and brokerage commissions, profit sharing, and bonuses. With mySAP ERP, businesses can determine the appropriate balance between fixed and variable pay, the mix of incentive pay arrangements (such as bonuses versus commissions), and methods for calculating commissions and other incentives based on expectations for individual sales groups.

To help businesses achieve the desired results from variable compensation programs, mySAP ERP offers the following:

▶ **Flexible methods to align pay with performance objectives**
mySAP ERP helps organizations implement variable pay schemes, where appropriate, and align incentives and commissions with business objectives. In addition, the solution also supports tactical, short-term incentive programs and commissions amendments.

▶ **Compensation calculation for various levels**
With mySAP ERP, organizations can calculate compensation for individual business transactions (such as the conclusion of a sales contract), or at an aggregated level (such as quarterly sales volume). Compensation can be scaled (increased for specific volumes of sales), time-bound (increased for sales made within a specified time period), or divided among two or more sales people working as a team. The solution can also automatically identify and calculate the appropriate compensation for indirect participants in commissions, such as sales representatives' managers at various levels of the company's hierarchy.

▶ **Sales tracking and monitoring**
By integrating information from sales-processing and financial systems with Customer Relationship Management (CRM), channel partner, and sales automation systems, mySAP ERP makes it easy to track, monitor, and reward sales efforts throughout the enterprise. The solution also enables organizations to identify and reward sales performance that is strategically important to the business.

Organizations benefit from the following:

▶ **Improved productivity**
Effective tools for plan administration, execution, and reporting help commission administrators perform more effectively.

▶ **Increased sales force motivation**
By providing commission recipients greater insight into the impact of performance on compensation, mySAP ERP helps motivate sales forces to perform their best.

▶ **Deeper management insight**
With improved calculation and forecasting for compensation costs, managers are better able to make informed decisions.

2.6.4 Real Estate Management

While real estate is usually an organization's second largest operating cost (after payroll), it is often not visible to management at the enterprise level, despite the associated expense. In addition, competition and volatility within the real estate marketplace places significant demands on property management, while real estate's inherent inflexibility can make it difficult to effectively manage properties in business environments that rely on speed and adaptability. Businesses will benefit from real-estate management tools that improve management efficiency and make it easy to address changing requirements such as those caused by acquisitions and mergers.

Real estate management functions

With tools to streamline and manage every stage of the real estate portfolio lifecycle, mySAP ERP provides strategic and operational support for corporations to effectively manage property and real estate investments. mySAP ERP offers real-estate management functions, such as simplified service charge settlements and improved correspondence, which provide enterprises with greater management flexibility, visibility, and control of rental space and contracts. Closely integrated with financial accounting and product lifecycle management, mySAP ERP also helps businesses manage properties as efficiently as possible while increasing customer satisfaction.

Key functions include the following:

▶ **Property acquisition and disposal**
mySAP ERP offers tools to support all aspects of real estate management, including buying, building, leasing, and selling properties.

▶ **Property portfolio management**
Support for managing property portfolios helps property managers define the real-estate infrastructure and manage business partner relationships.

▶ **Commercial management**
mySAP ERP supports real-estate contract management, management of sales-based rent, service charge settlements, adjustments of conditions, and giving notice and renewing contracts.

▶ **Technical management**
mySAP ERP provides support for all processes related to building operations, including service management, administration of available spaces, modernization, refurbishment, and building maintenance.

▶ **Controlling and reporting**
By providing powerful tools to define investment strategies through accurate cost and revenue performance data, mySAP ERP improves the way that businesses manage integrated property portfolios and provides complete cost visibility.

The solution offers a variety of features to support different real estate management requirements, including the following:

▶ **Commercial real-estate management**
To help commercial real estate managers achieve greater returns on their investments, mySAP ERP supports key activities such as project development, contract management, leasing support, property management, and management of open- or closed-end real estate funds.

▶ **Facility management**
mySAP ERP offers a range of features to help enterprises that provide facilities management services, including support for building control systems and infrastructure services.

▶ **Residential real estate management**
To aid residential real estate managers, mySAP ERP supports a range of management activities for rental properties (both publicly subsidized

and privately financed), as well as tools for managing property construction and rentals.

2.6.5 New and Enhanced Corporate Services Functionality

Travel Management

New and enhanced features for travel management make it easy for employees to access a range of travel services directly, as well as benefit from better support for travel expense reimbursement.

As illustrated in Figure 2.20, mySAP ERP offers a web-based interface that provides a single access point of entry for all employee self services functions for travel and expenses, including requesting approval for business trips; booking flights, hotels, and rental cars in accordance with corporate guidelines; entering expense claims per corporate policy and assigning them to cost objects, such as a cost centers and project numbers; managing claims for per diems and receipts; handling advances; attaching receipts via credit card clearing; recording itineraries; and more.

Employee self services for travel and expenses

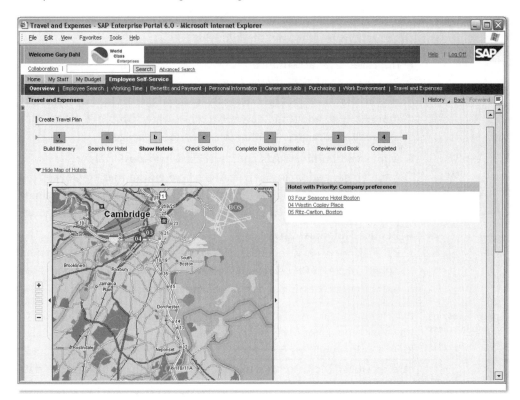

Figure 2.20 Self-Service Travel within mySAP ERP

New self-service travel management functions include the following:

- Integration of maps to support hotel and airport searches, indicating exact distances to destination address
- Integration of airline and car rental logos, hotel images, and amenities information in availability searches
- Integration of external web content regarding current visa, health, security information, and important travel news
- Integration of company-specific texts and links to inform travelers about important policy information
- A new self-service function that maintains personal traveler profiles
- Easy entry of non-travel-related expenses such as monthly cell phone bills or entertainment expenses
- Features that enable users to check imported credit card data for subsequent assignment to expense reports
- Country-specific versions that ensure all employees have access to the most relevant information for their destination

Organizations benefit from the following:

- **Improved user acceptance**
  Because mySAP ERP offers an easy-to-use interface and comprehensive access to employee travel information and tools, employees are more likely to adopt the new services, which will improve compliance and reduce administrative burdens for travel managers.

- **Minimized training costs and decreased help-desk calls**
  Intuitive navigation and new features help ensure that employees can use travel self-services functions without requiring significant training or additional support.

- **Reduced administrative costs**
  By making it easy to enter and process travel-related information online, mySAP ERP decreases the need for manual data entry and the number of processing and reimbursement cycles.

Improved options for mobile access
Enhancements to SAP Mobile Time and Travel provide better support to traveling employees who need to enter expense information through their laptops while working offline. Offline users can also attach credit card receipts directly to expense reports, which reduce the need for data entry and ensures accurate exchange rates when traveling internationally. Employees can also use receipt itemization functions to break down complex receipts, such as hotel bills, into individual components.

Environment, Health, and Safety

New and enhanced environment, health, and safety features make it easier for organizations to provide safe workplaces and products, as well as protect the environment.

The open content connector in mySAP ERP helps organizations—from all types of industries—comply with regulations by providing easy access to relevant scientific and regulatory data from outside content providers. The feature relies on an open, standardized interface that allows customers to choose from a wide range of content providers, and do so while reducing maintenance costs.

Data import from external content providers

Incentive and Commissions Management

New and enhanced functions in incentive and commissions management deliver improved communication with commission recipients, new reporting features, and wider integration with mySAP CRM. This integration facilitates an end-to-end compensation calculation cycle, beginning with the assimilation of data in the CRM system and ending with the final reporting of compensation results. Consequently, commission administrators can improve productivity with more effective compensation planning, executing, and reporting. At the same time, commission recipients are better motivated with detailed information about the impact of performance on compensation.

Support for comprehensive incentive compensation plan management contains four major elements:

Management of incentive compensation plans

▶ A commission recipient database listing all personnel who are eligible for commissions.

▶ Standard commission contracts, which are a series of predefined templates for standard commissions. Changes to a standard commission contract are automatically updated to any individual commission contracts based on the modified contract.

▶ Individual commission contracts for each commission recipient defined in the database. The contracts are based on standard commission contracts; however, they may be modified on a contract-by-contract basis to meet any unique requirements.

▶ An organizational hierarchy that allows employees to automatically derive the recipient of the respective indirect commission (for example, the manager) from the recipient of a direct commission (for example, a sales representative).

By supporting a set of standard contracts that can be used to create individual contracts, and by ensuring that changes to standard contracts are updated throughout the system, mySAP ERP helps to ensure consistency in incentive compensation plans and reduces administrative burdens for commission analysts when implementing new guidelines throughout the enterprise.

Calculation of variable compensation

mySAP ERP now supports the calculation of both direct sales commissions and incentive compensation. Direct sales commission processing enables businesses to calculate commissions based on sales activities or financial bookings, where each sales order or invoice triggers the calculation of a commission. This transactional commission processing is suitable for businesses with large volumes of transactions. For incentive compensation, mySAP ERP supports the calculation of commissions based on aggregated data, such as the overall revenue of a sales team for one or more sales periods.

Both of these features support the following:

▶ Participation determination, which creates incentive calculations for multiple recipients within a single calculation process

▶ Valuation calculation, which supports the alignment of individual compensation with corporate goals by identifying the business value of each commissionable activity, thereby providing a basis for determining appropriate compensation

▶ Remuneration calculation, which determines the amount of individual commissions to be paid

▶ Posting, which defines due dates and commission periods

Compensation results analysis

With a variety of data analysis tools (including drill-down reports) and integration into other SAP software (including SAP Business Intelligence, mySAP CRM, and SAP Enterprise Portal), mySAP ERP enables key groups within an organization to perform comprehensive analysis of compensation programs and their results. Key benefits include the following:

▶ Commission administrators benefit from an immediate overview of changes to incentive compensation plans and their impact on financial calculations.

▶ Management groups gain insight into the financial impact of incentive plans and their effect on the performance of commission recipients. Additionally, managers can judge the success of various incentive compensation plans by a variety of measures, such as the degree to which the plans align individual goals with corporate goals.

► Commission recipients gain online access to their expected payments and can simulate potential payments for specific activities.

Real Estate Management

Enhancements to real estate management in mySAP ERP simplify all aspects of property management, while new reporting functions expand its analytical features and enable organizations to create detailed real estate reports. In addition, the real estate management features are more tightly integrated with accounting features in mySAP ERP.

mySAP ERP provides a link between the architectural view (for example, the overall occupancy capacity) and the real view (for example, the actual use of the property). This link allows organizations to better manage the allocation and utilization of rental and pooled office and factory space.

Owner occupancy management

With mySAP ERP, managers can enter the reasons why a vacancy has occurred (and the date it occurred) into the posting parameters. The solution makes it easy to identify the appropriate account and cost center assignments.

Rental vacancy management

Rent adjustments can be made in accordance with representative lists of rents and comparable objects. This feature can be used to adjust rents for company-owned property and for objects belonging to third parties.

Rent adjustments

If meters are assigned to settlement units (or master settlement units) or pooled spaces, the metered costs can be divided among the rental units and assigned accordingly.

Service charge settlements

The number of the real estate contract also appears on the incoming payment transaction so that tenant accounts are displayed in standard reporting for financial accounting. In addition, organizations can record installment agreements in the system by breaking down open items in financial accounting into smaller amounts at a later time. Additional features include malfunction reports that can be created directly from real estate objects and used by the plant maintenance function in mySAP ERP. The software also allows group real estate master data to be entered into sets to facilitate reporting, cost planning, and revenue on real estate objects. Alternatively, data can be entered and changed manually.

Improved data integration

A number of new standard reports are available with mySAP ERP. For example, analysis with mySAP ERP provides new reports for plant maintenance (costs on maintenance orders), asset accounting (depreciation of real estate objects), and controlling (costs on internal orders for real estate objects). In addition, rent invoices can be printed from the periodic

Improved reports and invoicing

postings function and dispatched to tenants. Line items on the invoice are grouped together, and the invoice number is based on the real estate document.

Customers benefit from the following:

▶ Shorter vacancy durations and reduced frequency of vacancies through more effective property management

▶ Improved and accelerated reporting and accounting due to a clearer framework for diverse service charges and costs

▶ Simplified data management and reduced complexity, which supports better decision-making and business insight

▶ Increased efficiency through automated processes

▶ Flexible space and room management by leveraging integration with Computer-Aided Facilities Management (CAFM) systems

2.7   Self Services

ERP applications have made a significant contribution to organizational efficiency and effectiveness, largely due to the improved integration of processes and information throughout an enterprise. However, organizations must continually modify business processes in order to leverage new opportunities in global markets, and address the requirements of worldwide information access. Two key trends currently drive business change:

▶ **Decentralization**
In many organizations today, standard information and processes are centralized so that employees can easily access information, anytime and anywhere. But, to make the system work, employees across the enterprise must be willing to input locally held, business-critical information. Today, employees are prepared to use ERP systems to access and add relevant information, as long as they can do so quickly and easily.

▶ **Business process automation**
Automating routine tasks is critical for organizations that want to generate additional value from existing resources. Business process automation liberates skilled professionals from routine administrative work so that they can focus on improving value-added business processes and strategies.

Both of these trends require organizations to do more than integrate their back-end technology systems; addressing these kinds of changes requires businesses to modify "people processes," or the activities that employees perform on a daily basis to do their jobs. Enterprises can benefit by incorporating these "people processes" into the underlying technology on which their business relies. Doing so ensures that employees can access the tools they need to perform their jobs effectively, while enabling a free flow of information throughout the organization.

In the past, the use of technology to improve personal interactions with an organization was focused on improving the customer experience with customer self services; these services allowed customers to interact with the business on their own terms and schedule. However, today's forward-thinking enterprises realize that supporting internal "people processes" with appropriate technologies results in higher employee productivity.

Businesses will benefit from transactional systems that not only provide a wide range of features and functions to support professional employees, but also enhance productivity for all employees and improve competitiveness by offering business process automation and enhanced self services.

mySAP ERP provides innovative self-services functionality that can significantly improve organization performance and user productivity. mySAP ERP not only supports professional business processes, but also simplifies tasks for all key functional areas of mySAP ERP. Automated processes and improved workflow help employees to execute their tasks efficiently and accurately—even with applications that they seldom use. Self services are especially well suited for processes that involve the assimilation of specific information from transactional systems (reports, market analyses, sales figures, and so on) or typical, routine activities such as requesting verifications, corrections, and approvals, or recording activities and leave.

Self-services functionality provided by mySAP ERP offers the following benefits:

▶ **Improved productivity and efficiency**
mySAP ERP simplifies tasks and eliminates process steps and paperwork. As a result, error rates are reduced, data consistency is increased, and employees across the enterprise can access vital information and tools anytime, anywhere.

► **Reduced costs**

By increasing productivity and optimizing workflow throughout the organization, transaction and administration costs can be significantly reduced and operational costs lowered.

► **Increased employee motivation**

By automating routine tasks, mySAP ERP enables employees to focus on strategic, high-value efforts where they can make the greatest contribution, thereby improving their motivation and morale. Furthermore, a highly usable interface increases employee acceptance and allows even untrained staff to use self-services functions.

The benefits of self services have been highlighted by an SAP AG/Deloitte Consulting study conducted in 2003. The study examined the use of self-services applications in the areas of leave requests, travel management, seminar administration and booking, and approval for further education. Data was taken from the personnel area, employees, and executives. The potential savings averaged around 60% in terms of time and costs compared to the normal HR processes. An investment calculation yields a dynamic amortization time of less than one year and a Return on Investment (ROI) of 480% in the analysis period of five years. The basis for these calculations is the potential savings realized, due to the optimization of HR processes in a fictitious company with 10,000 employees.

mySAP ERP offers self-services functionality in three key areas:

► Employee Self Services (ESS)

► Manager Self Services (MSS)

► Centralized employee interactions

2.7.1 Employee Self Services

mySAP ERP provides functionality for Employee Self Services (ESS) that enable employees to manage a variety of tasks that would otherwise be handled by others, such as creating, viewing, and modifying various kinds of data related to their job functions. It also empowers employees to update HR information, such as entering information about life and work changes. Altogether, more than 40 international and over 40 country-specific scenarios are available. SAP ESS within mySAP ERP meets the needs of today's global, mobile workforce with the following functions:

▶ **Working time management**
mySAP enables employees to enter their own working time, allocate the time-to-work breakdown structure (WBS) elements such as cost centers, check how much leave they have available, request leave, and more.

▶ **Travel management**
With mySAP ERP, employees can create travel requests and submit them directly to their manager (or the department that coordinates travel). After employees return, travel expenses can be recorded and assigned to cost centers or customer sales orders.

▶ **Life and work event management**
Through mySAP ERP, employees can receive step-by-step guidance for viewing personal, payroll, benefit, and other professional information. The solution also prompts them to enter any necessary personal data.

▶ **Benefits management**
mySAP ERP makes it easy for employees to manage their own benefits information by enabling them to check which benefit plans they are currently enrolled in, view previous benefit plans, and enroll in new ones. Employees can modify details of the benefits plan, including costs, contributions, and investments, and display information regarding dependents and beneficiaries.

▶ **Purchasing**
mySAP ERP enables employees to directly request the purchase of goods and services they require for maintenance, repair, and operations (MRO).

▶ **Job searching**
With mySAP ERP, the HR department can post a list of open positions within the organization, including job descriptions and requirements. Employees can also apply for positions, create attachments that contain their application documents and photographs, and view the status of their applications.

▶ **Payment tracking**
mySAP ERP enables employees to display past and current remuneration statements, provides an overview of the awards they have been granted, and displays and prints complete compensation statements.

▶ **Personal information management**
mySAP ERP enables employees to manage the personal information that their organization requires, such as home address, bank information, marital status, family member names and dependents, and previ-

ous employers. Various country-specific services, which are standard with mySAP ERP, comply with local requirements.

▶ **Training**
Locating appropriate training courses is easy with mySAP ERP, because the solution allows employees to view all available training and business events, as well as register online and submit attendance requests for approval.

▶ **Career management**
mySAP ERP enables employees to keep their list of qualifications current by making it simple to edit and display their skills profile (which details qualifications, talents, and knowledge, including the proficiency level and any dates associated with each skill). Employees can also display and review their performance appraisals.

Benefits of ESS functions within mySAP ERP include the following:

▶ **Improved employee motivation and satisfaction**
Employees who can access and update their own information—including training opportunities, open positions, and skills profiles—are empowered to take more control of their careers. This sense of empowerment can improve participation in the workplace and motivate employees to deliver their best efforts to the organization. Therefore, employees are more satisfied with the organization and eager to improve its bottom-line results.

▶ **Reduced administrative burdens and costs**
Because employees can handle their own routine HR interactions, including data entry, HR data is more accurate and the HR department can now focus on strategic tasks instead of managing basic service requests.

▶ **Improved operational efficiency and lower costs**
The self-services functions provided by mySAP ERP increases employee efficiency, reduces necessary headcount for support staff, and results in lower administrative costs.

2.7.2 Manager Self Services

mySAP ERP provides functionality for Manager Self Services (MSS), which help managers throughout the enterprise to quickly and easily accomplish their goals in areas such as budgeting and personnel responsibility. These manager "tools" can have a profound impact on organizations, because they make managers more efficient, effective, and proactive. SAP MSS also enables managers to run their departments more in line with an organization's core business objectives.

mySAP ERP enables central departments such as human resources to personalize the presentation of information in each manager's portal so that individuals can quickly and easily find their unique information on their own virtual desktop (that is, the portal).

mySAP ERP supports the following self-services management tasks:

▶ **Budgeting**
mySAP ERP helps managers fulfill their cost and budget responsibilities, including annual budget planning, budget monitoring, cost analysis, service requests (for example, for correcting postings), and more. The solution also provides managers with decision support and support for cost management tasks.

▶ **Staffing**
mySAP ERP helps managers handle administrative and planning functions for Human Capital Management (HCM), and provides support for HR processes such as recruitment, annual employee reviews, and compensation planning. Managers can handle a variety of approval processes within mySAP ERP, such as the approval of shopping carts.

Benefits of MSS functions within mySAP ERP include the following:

▶ **Increased user productivity and efficiency**
mySAP ERP offers a new user interface that helps administrators complete routine duties quickly so that they have more time for strategic, high-value tasks. In addition, by helping managers adhere to defined processes and guidelines for HR and other activities, mySAP ERP ensures that standards are consistently applied and goals are reliably communicated throughout the enterprise.

▶ **Informed decision-making**
Key performance indicators (KPIs) and warnings enable managers to take action before a situation becomes critical. In addition, by providing analytical information to managers, mySAP ERP facilitates strategic decision-making and planning.

▶ **Enhanced consistency**
By helping managers adhere to defined processes and guidelines for HR, financial services, and other business areas, mySAP ERP ensures that standards are consistently applied and goals are reliably communicated throughout the enterprise.

2.7.3 Centralized Employee Interactions

mySAP ERP provides functionality that enables an Employee Interaction Center (EIC), which helps employees and HR staff interact more efficiently through a *central point of contact* for HR requests. Employees have access to a single, unified source of information, and EIC agents and HR staff can easily access information and tools to deliver consistent, personalized services across multiple communication channels. To use the EIC on a project base, customers must have either mySAP ERP and mySAP CRM, or mySAP Business Suite in place.

EIC functionality offers significant benefits to HR departments and managers:

▶ Contact management
The solution provides functions that allow HR staff to manage and process all information about employee requests, as well as track contact history.

▶ Activity and case management
mySAP ERP enables HR staff to record and process each procedural step and follow-up activity for individual employee requests. In addition, it helps HR staff to combine related requests into a single follow-up procedure, which improves overall staff efficiency.

▶ Knowledge management
The knowledge management function provides the HR department with enterprise intelligence to improve contact-handling efficiency and expedite resolution of employee requests.

▶ Analytics
mySAP ERP provides analytical functions that help managers identify opportunities to increase efficiency and employee satisfaction, optimize the interaction center's efficiency, evaluate ROI, and ultimately reduce costs.

▶ Workflow management
The solution supports escalation and routing rules to help managers define which supervisors, support staff, and departments should receive various incoming requests. This functionality also ensures that service commitments are fulfilled as quickly and efficiently as possible.

▶ Alerts and scripting
mySAP ERP provides alerting and scripting functions that notify HR staff of open requests and guide them through business processes that comply with corporate standards.

The EIC functionality provided by mySAP ERP delivers the following benefits throughout the enterprise:

► **Increased employee satisfaction**
mySAP ERP makes it easy to ensure that each employee receives prompt, personalized answers to issues or requests, resulting in increased employee satisfaction. It also ensures that HR employees have access to the tools and information needed to deliver high-quality service.

► **Reduced HR costs and increased productivity**
By providing HR generalists with the tools they need to resolve issues quickly on first contact, mySAP ERP allows them to respond to a higher volume of employee requests in a given time period. As a result, HR employees have more time and flexibility to focus on strategic, value-added initiatives with a greater potential impact on the bottom line.

► **Improved service levels**
mySAP ERP provides managers with tools to monitor the contact center environment in real time, allowing them to react immediately to meet business needs and define the way that information requests are routed through the enterprise. This increased insight and responsiveness helps organizations maintain the highest service levels for HR.

2.7.4 New and Enhanced Self-Service Functionality

mySAP ERP offers new, consistent navigation for all self-services functions, making them even more user-friendly and intuitive. It has been designed to improve the usability of the application via simple and intuitive user guidance. All pages have the same "look and feel," and the new self services home page gives users more guidance. Every application is explained, and users can navigate throughout the application from explanatory text. To simplify complex processes, mySAP ERP also now provides roadmaps to direct users through processes in a step-by-step format.

Employee Self Services

The Employee Self Services home page, shown in Figure 2.21, provides employees with an overview of all areas where Employee Self Services are offered (for example, benefits and payment, working time, and so on). Employees can access specific information about important applications or actions in the individual areas. They can also use this page to navigate to the self services.

ESS home page

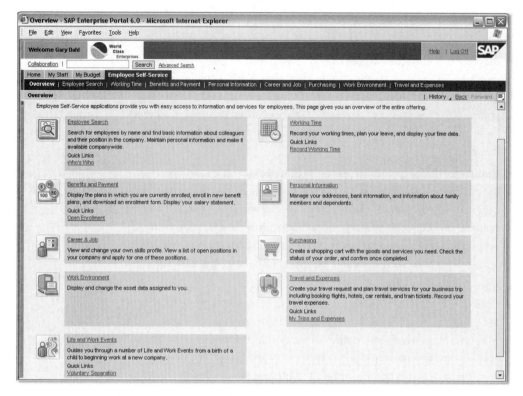

Figure 2.21 Employee Self Service Home Page

ESS area pages   Each area is represented by an area page, such as the "career and job" page, which can be accessed from the ESS home page. An area page contains the applications for the respective area and brief information about the applications. Additional information in the form of text, HTML pages, or links to additional information can also be integrated.

Key areas for Employee Self Services include the following:

▶ Work Environment

▶ Employee Search

▶ Working Time

▶ Travel and Expenses

▶ Life and Work Events

▶ Benefits and Payment

▶ Personal Information

▶ Purchasing

▶ Career and Job

mySAP ERP provides functionality that enables time administrators to reduce the effort involved in processing messages that arise due to incorrect postings at time-recording terminals. In a graphical weekly overview, employees can, for example, correct duplicate postings and add missing postings and account assignments. In addition, optional control functions and an approval procedure enable time administrators to check the postings entered, as well as change and delete them manually.

Time posting corrections

Manager Self Services

mySAP ERP enables managers to control the process of staffing the right people in their area of responsibility and to trigger the administrative steps that are part of this process. This functionality is integrated with SAP E-Recruiting.

Recruitment

mySAP ERP offers new equipment management functions to support a variety of tasks. In addition, it provides support for new internal service requests that make it easy for managers to handle repairs, losses, scrapping, pickups, and equipment theft. Supported equipment management functions include the following:

Equipment management

▶ **Inventory management**
Support for equipment information ensures that managers are well informed about physical inventory in their areas of responsibility.

▶ **Employee transfers**
mySAP ERP ensures that managers are aware of the equipment assigned to employees who are transferred to other departments or leave the organization.

▶ **Equipment lifecycle management**
mySAP ERP provides functionality that enables managers to use internal service requests for managing repairs; changing assignments for employees, cost centers, and organizational units; and tracking information about losses. As a result, managers and other employees can manage the equipment lifecycle process more efficiently (see Figure 2.22).

▶ **Monitoring**
mySAP ERP provides managers with monitors to track cost centers, internal orders, and projects. The monitors generate rule-based alerts to warn managers of critical situations.

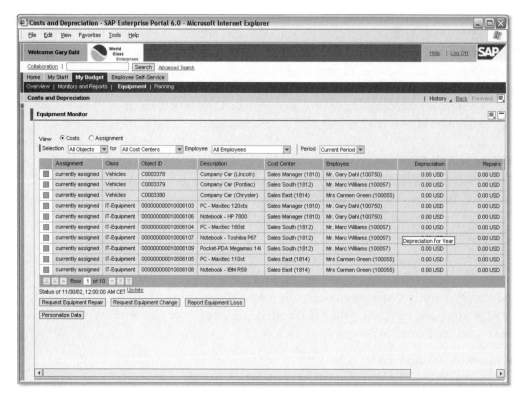

Figure 2.22 Equipment Monitor

Organization planning processes

Collaborative features enable managers to work directly with business unit analysts.

Approval processes

Electronic approval processes for shopping carts, purchase requisitions, purchase orders, and travel requests replace paper forms, thereby helping managers to approve or deny these items and reduce cycle time.

Portal management capabilities for IT staff

Interactive forms powered by Adobe help to lower implementation costs and enable organizations to implement their forms more easily and quickly. Programming skills are no longer required to make these types of changes.

Role-based Capabilities in Human Capital Management

Support for role-based access within mySAP ERP ensures that employees can readily access the crucial data, applications, and analytical tools required to perform their job functions efficiently and effectively. New and enhanced roles include the following:

The HR executive role provides a portal designed specifically to meet the needs of HR executives. This role provides executives with a central point of access to all relevant information that supports strategic HR decision-making processes, including key figures, budgets, and processes. Information is available through a template-based, standardized interface that eases navigation. HR executives can subscribe to key data that meets their interests, as well as navigate to original data sources for further information. In addition, executives can automatically monitor key figures such as budgets and processes, and receive alerts when the data exceeds defined threshold values. The portal can be customized to address special needs of individual HR executives.

HR executive role

The compensation specialist role in mySAP ERP addresses the needs of HR employees who are responsible for evaluating, developing, adapting, and promoting effective compensation policies that are aligned with organizational strategies. These employees act as internal service providers to advise HR and line managers on compensation-related issues. In addition, they are responsible for devising guidelines and local compensation strategies for international companies. The compensation specialist role within mySAP ERP supports the following functions:

Compensation specialist role

▶ **Compensation administration**
mySAP ERP provides comprehensive support for displaying and editing employee compensation-related data, activating planned and approved compensation adjustments, and transmitting the information to payroll.

▶ **Long-term incentive plan administration**
Support for Long-Term Incentive (LTI) plans includes the ability to display and edit employee compensation and LTI-related data, administer all LTI-relevant data for employees, and generate reports about LTI plans and status.

▶ **Budgeting**
Budgeting capabilities enable compensation specialists to manage activities related to budgets for compensation reviews, such as merit increases, bonuses, variable pay, and stock options. Approved budgets can be used as a control instrument during the compensation review and planning process performed by the individual line managers. A budget reassignment tool helps compensation specialists to adjust the budget if organizational changes occur after the budget is released.

▶ **Job pricing**

To ensure that employees receive fair compensation, mySAP ERP supports a variety of job-pricing activities, including performing salary surveys, importing job and salary data from salary survey providers, salary benchmarking, assessing market data, and defining market-based standards. If job pricing indicates that a salary structure should be adjusted, the compensation specialist can adjust the salary structure accordingly and submit it for review.

Role-based Capabilities in Operations

Plant or production manager role

Plant or production managers must be able to view and modify information related to production, exceptions, personnel, revenue, costs, budget planning, and other processes for one or more plants. The new plant manager role within mySAP ERP aggregates plant management information from a variety of sources on a single page, providing a concise overview of the facility's operational status that makes it easy to identify and implement appropriate actions.

Purchasing agent role

Purchasing agents, who are responsible for processing and issuing purchase orders and order acknowledgments, must ensure that the purchase of external goods and services meets delivery, quality, and price requirements. By helping purchasing agents to address routine functions, such as assigning sources to requisitions or converting requisitions to orders, the purchasing agent role within mySAP ERP enables personnel to focus on strategic activities such as improving relationships with suppliers.

The purchasing agent role within mySAP ERP provides status information for procurement processes on a single portal page. The role provides ready access to information and tools so that the purchasing agent can perform the following activities:

▶ Check messages

▶ Determine sources for purchase requisitions

▶ Convert purchase requisitions into purchase orders

▶ Print purchase orders

▶ Create Requests For Quotation (RFQs)

Internal sales representative

Internal sales representatives typically maintain master customer data; compile quotations, contracts, and orders; and perform other administrative tasks to support the sales team. In addition, sales teams may require information pertaining to customer care, sales data, sales support, order fulfillment, and reporting functions.

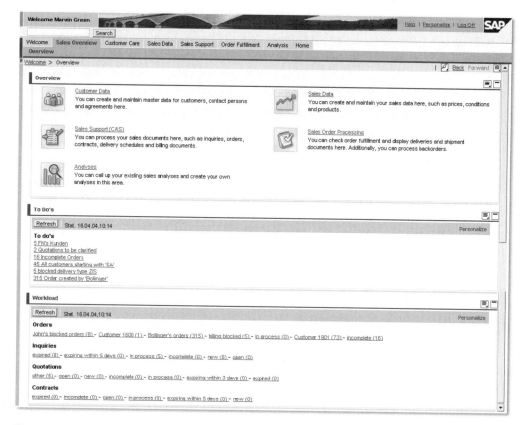

Figure 2.23 Internal Sales Representative Home Page

The new Internal Sales Representative role (ISR) in mySAP ERP, illustrated in Figure 2.23, provides a single point of access to all information and applications that internal sales representatives require, making it easy to perform the following activities:

▶ Answer inquiries from customers and prospects to ensure customer satisfaction

▶ Maintain and update customer master data and additional sales data

▶ Prepare and process inquiries, quotations, sales orders, and sales contracts

▶ Ensure efficient order management and fulfillment

▶ Provide information regarding order processes and logistics

▶ Monitor billing process

▶ Prepare reports and analyses for sales managers

Role-based Capabilities in Financials and Analytics

Business unit
analyst role Business unit analysts typically monitor key financial and operational figures for their business units and report these figures to senior management. They often have significant planning responsibilities, including examining their units' organizational structure and requesting changes from cost accountants as required, creating guidelines for unit planning, initiating the planning process, monitoring the response from line managers, and changing the plans accordingly. In addition, business unit analysts handle inquiries from line managers regarding planning as well as individual postings. Responding to these queries typically requires analytics to better understand the situation, as well as the ability to repost to the general ledger or request adjustments to existing postings. Business unit analysts also support fast close processes for accounting, monitor figures for operational processes, report anomalies to the back office, and sign off on the figures for their business units when postings are complete.

The new business unit analyst role within mySAP ERP provides the following functions:

▶ **Monitoring**
mySAP ERP provides a number of monitors that track aggregate key figures for a business unit, as well as identify budget overruns, postings that exceed a given threshold, and unusual postings.

▶ **Reporting**
Hierarchical reports within mySAP ERP help business unit analysts visualize the relationships between profit centers, cost centers, and orders in the business unit, and help analysts to navigate through large numbers of items, such as information for multiple cost centers.

Fixed-asset
accountant role Fixed-asset accountants create fixed assets within the accounting system, enter asset values, and monitor all transactions relating to fixed assets from acquisition to disposal. The fixed-asset accountant role within mySAP ERP aids these employees by supporting the following functions:

▶ **Period-closing transaction support**
mySAP ERP provides a single point of access for common period-closing transactions, making it easy for fixed-asset accountants to close capital spending orders and projects, post depreciation, reconcile the fixed-asset accounts with the general ledger, and create asset history sheets.

▶ **Record management**

mySAP ERP helps fixed-asset accountants to create asset master records, post asset values, compile asset value reviews, and monitor asset balances and depreciation. In addition, they can control and initiate mass changes, such as the simultaneous retirement or transfer of multiple assets.

▶ **Lifecycle evaluation**

mySAP ERP provides tools and information (such as asset history sheets and transaction lists) that help organizations evaluate the status of fixed assets during the complete asset lifecycle.

3 mySAP ERP for Midsize Businesses and Industry-Specific Needs

Companies and institutions with industry-specific needs and midsize businesses require specific capabilities from ERP software. This chapter shows how mySAP ERP addresses these requirements.

First, this chapter will highlight the industry solutions of SAP. We'll look at specific requirements within the automotive, banking, and consumer products industry, as well as mySAP ERP's industry-specific business benefits for the public sector and the retail industry. Then, we will examine Packaged Solutions. Packaged Solutions provide predefined capabilities, which are tailored to meet the requirements of midsize businesses.

3.1 Industry-Specific Business Benefits with mySAP ERP—Some Selected Examples

When we look at actual industries, the following question may arise: "How can an ERP solution, enriched with industry-specific functionality, solve industry-specific pain points and challenges?" Of course, topics such as business insight, productivity and flexibility are important for any industry, but there are also specific challenges that affect each industry.

SAP has a long and successful history of supporting businesses with enterprise software solutions, and has worked with a strong industry focus for 30 years. Today, organizations in the services, manufacturing, and public sectors use SAP's Enterprise Resource Planning (ERP) software to improve efficiency and achieve bottom-line benefits. The solution sets are based on an in-depth knowledge of the processes that drive each industry, which is why there is no such thing as a generic industry solution from SAP. Each SAP solution is tailored to meet the requirements of specific standards, processes, and challenges of every industry. SAP offers comprehensive industry portfolios covering 28 distinct industries that supplement mySAP Business Suite. mySAP ERP comes with extensive configuration capabilities to support diverse requirements of customers in a variety of industries.

SAP has always supported specific industry needs

This chapter examines some of these industry lines and will highlight the value of a capable Enterprise Management within these industries. The examples don't describe the delivery streams or availability of the indus-

ERP in Industries

try-specific functionality for mySAP ERP. We'll address this topic in Section 4.2, where we'll see what the architecture of a capable ERP solution, enriched with industry-specific capabilities, looks like. Instead, the examples in this chapter will show the business benefits that are available with an Enterprise Management solution within these industries. The examples comprise only a high-level description of the business benefits and the new and enhanced capabilities with mySAP ERP.[1] We have already provided you with a more detailed view of the generic and cross-industry scenario in Chapter 2.

3.1.1 Enterprise Management and Support in the Automotive Industry

ERP in the Automotive industry

Businesses in the automotive industry face increasing pressure to improve efficiency, reduce costs, and identify and respond to changing demands quickly. To improve brand value and gain market share, automotive Original Equipment Manufacturers (OEMs) are faced with the challenge to deliver high-quality products that meet the requirements of increasingly sophisticated customers. Ever-increasing competition further drives the need for innovation and speed. To address these challenges, businesses throughout the automotive value chain—from OEMs, suppliers, and third parties to dealerships—will benefit from improved brand management through identification of new market segments, rapid product development cycles that accelerate time to market, adaptive manufacturing processes, and others.

SAP for Automotive

Along with the SAP for Automotive set of solutions, mySAP ERP supports the critical business processes of automotive companies, and provides tools and best practices to help improve these processes. With mySAP ERP, organizations benefit from a scalable, flexible solution that can expand and adapt as requirements change over time.

By implementing Enterprise Management capabilities, OEMs and automotive suppliers can, for example, benefit in the manufacturing and procurement area. In addition, companies profit from variant configuration modelling, in the areas of vehicle management, warranty management, program and project management, operational and financial analytics, and enterprise asset management.

---

1 To get a more detailed view on the specific industries, we recommend that you visit the SAP homepage, *www.sap.com*.

Let's take a more detailed view of the additional benefits within the manufacturing and procurement area. With support for all automotive manufacturing strategies for example, mySAP ERP helps enterprises manage the full range of manufacturing activities—from planning to execution and analysis—in a single, end-to-end system. mySAP ERP delivers all elements of a customer-oriented manufacturing management system. By combining information from a variety of business processes (including planning, cost accounting, human capital management, materials management, warehouse management, plant maintenance, and quality management), mySAP ERP supports the development and execution of efficient production plans and ensures that accurate, comprehensive information is available at any time.

Manufacturing and Procurement

By using mySAP ERP with the SAP Just-in-Time Process for Suppliers application, businesses in the automotive industry can leverage just-in-time processes to improve responsiveness and reduce the complexity of obtaining automotive components and subcomponents. The solution supports inbound calls based on sales and forecasted orders, as well as outbound calls for replenishment based on Kanban methodology. Therefore, OEMs and automotive suppliers can develop effective supply chain processes that address changing demands throughout the value chain, improve efficiencies, and reduce manufacturing time and costs.

Just-in-Time Processes

mySAP ERP is designed to address the enterprise planning and management requirements of automotive OEMs, automotive suppliers, and automotive sales and service companies. New and enhanced capabilities that come with mySAP ERP for the automotive industry include internal and external collaboration, usability enhancements through role-based access, self services, and guided procedures, regulatory compliance and corporate governance, inventory management and traceability, and Radio Frequency Identification (RFID). With mySAP ERP and the SAP for Automotive set of solutions, businesses can drive innovation by developing superior insights, accelerate growth by identifying and responding to new product and expansion opportunities, and increase customer satisfaction, loyalty, and revenues by bringing superior products to market.

New and enhanced capabilities with mySAP ERP

3.1.2 Enterprise Management and Support in the Banking Industry

The importance of ERP in the banking industry continues to grow. Today banks face shrinking margins, tougher competition, and rapid change. Meanwhile, new legal and regulatory requirements such as the Basel II

ERP in the Banking Industry

Capital Accord and new International Accounting Standards (IAS) demand greater transparency and information that is more accurate and timelier. Due to the increased significance of such external factors, banks are striving for more transparent, higher-quality information—as well as enhanced efficiency in business processes that can help cut costs. Also, increasingly more banks recognize that they can ease their efforts through standard ERP applications, which rapidly replace custom-built software.

The most competitive banks in this environment are more customer-centric, efficient, and flexible. They have greater control over their costs and have boosted profitability. To achieve these goals, banks must evaluate any IT investment on its ability to provide a fast return and reduce operating costs. Effective investments must also support new business models and help banks optimize the Internet and mobile technology. Increasingly, banks require streamlined business processes and IT structures that are less complex; have an easy integration of new functions and processes that don't damage the underlying technology or previous investments, personalized data tools; and provide solutions that employees can access anywhere at any time.

Meeting these demands puts new pressures on the systems that banks use for ERP. In addition to increasing efficiency, today's ERP solutions must improve integration between business processes and technology for seamless transparency between ERP systems and other corporate applications. ERP solutions must also provide readily available, yet secure access to all internal organizational functions and processes for every bank employee, customer, vendor, and partner.

New and enhanced capabilities with mySAP ERP mySAP ERP combines proven, robust ERP software with extended functions that banks can use enterprise-wide to improve the management of corporate assets and critical business processes. Banks can transform their ERP system into a truly collaborative environment that the entire organization—as well as authorized customers and partners—can access. mySAP ERP offers all the key features banks need to address their most critical business tasks, including business analytics; human capital management functions that help to maximize workforce profitability; features for managing support operations that help to streamline logistics functions and project management; and features for managing corporate services for travel, facilities, incentives, and commissions.

A major capability for banks is the financial and management accounting that comes with mySAP ERP. This process helps banks to control corporate finance functions—with extended capabilities for fast closing and reporting—as well as support for rigorous corporate-governance mandates, such as Sarbanes-Oxley, that require complete transparency across the institution.

The financial capabilities within mySAP ERP help banks to monitor all financial accounting transactions in real time and simplify the processing of incoming and outgoing payments for improved cash flow. mySAP ERP combines planning, reporting, and analysis of competitive measures in one process to provide a more informed business analysis.

mySAP ERP ensures that banks can manage their enterprise business requirements and processes both today and in the future. It makes enterprise processes more transparent than is possible with SAP R/3. With greater transparency, banks can make better decisions and gain a competitive advantage.

3.1.3 Enterprise Management and Support in the Consumer Products Industry

Similar to the Automotive and the Banking Industry and, in general, to all other industries, consumer goods manufacturers face a series of challenges in today's low-inflation, slow-growth economic environment, too. Not only are many consumers spending less, but also their buying patterns are shifting and their needs and behaviours are more difficult to predict than in the past. Meanwhile, with the ability to wield tremendous buying power, retailers are demanding steady service improvements from their suppliers. And, as the popularity of retailers` private brands grows with improvements in quality and packaging, the market share for consumer products erodes further.

ERP in the Consumer Products industry

In addition to facing the general challenges shared by the entire consumer products industry, businesses in certain segments must confront obstacles like increasing national and international laws and regulations, changing fashion trends in the apparel and footwear segment, increasing safety regulations and increasing price competition in the home and personal care segment, and others.

Internal challenges common to all consumer products companies include management complexity, organizational fragmentation, and rigid cost structures and asset bases, as well as inflexible IT infrastructure that make it difficult to modify business processes in order to take advantage of new opportunities. Forward-looking consumer products companies will benefit from technologies that leverage and extend existing investments to create a flexible, adaptable business ecosystem.

mySAP ERP offers comprehensive features that help consumer products companies address challenges in key business areas, including financials, analytics, operations, and human capital management.

Now, we'll look at some specific key business areas. When it comes to transportation, mySAP ERP helps businesses meet shipping requirements and manage the multiple processes and reports required by foreign trade. Flexible options for consolidating deliveries into shipments include rule-based automation, manual consolidation, and collaborative order combination through the Internet. Support for collaborative tendering lets businesses tender directly into the transportation service provider's system. Consequently, organizations can integrate information from partners into their business processes and improve control of transportation plans, increase invoice accuracy, and reduce overall transportation costs.

Customer service is another business area where consumer products companies can benefit from mySAP ERP. mySAP ERP supports the complete customer service cycle, including post-sales support, ongoing support services, billing, and revenue recognition. mySAP ERP supports planned services by maintaining and managing all data pertaining to ongoing, scheduled, and anticipated service requirements. As a result, enterprises benefit from greater visibility regarding resource demand, which leads to more accurate forecasting and planning, as well as enhanced customer satisfaction.

Support for mobile technologies, lifecycle data management, improved recipe and trial management, direct store delivery, and support for RFID are just some of the new and enhanced capabilities designed to streamline processes for all businesses in the consumer products industry. In addition, there are new and enhanced capabilities for the different segments. For the food industry, for example, mySAP ERP offers a catch weight management solution that makes it easier to track weight and price variations and accurately assess the value of product orders and shipments. Support for beverage sales returns or monitoring the status of empties throughout sales and distribution are some examples of enhanced features specifically tailored for the beverage industry. Furthermore, mySAP ERP makes it easy to identify and substitute acceptable products to increase order fulfilment, a capability called *material substitution*, which is designed especially for the apparel and footwear industry.

For businesses in the consumer products industry, success depends on the ability to identify and adapt to market changes, to reduce operating costs without sacrificing quality, and to deliver exceptional customer service. Based on industry-standard best practices, mySAP ERP supports consumer products manufacturers with enterprise-wide information access and decision support, while allowing broad flexibility to respond rapidly to market changes and opportunities.

3.1.4 Enterprise Management and Support in the Public Sector

Organizations working in the public sector face pressures on many fronts. As citizen and business demand for around-the-clock access to information and services continues to increase, funding required to meet core functions is decreasing. Shrinking federal, state, and local budgets have also resulted in fewer grants, as well as less funding for existing grants. Consequently, funding from tax revenues has become more critical for covering payrolls and capital expenditures, making it increasingly important that organizations have insight into revenue forecasts. At the same time, there is a growing need for collaborative agency and program planning to reduce redundancy or the overlap of services, as well as for tools that increase employee efficiency and effectiveness. To address these challenges, public organizations will benefit from technology solutions that enable improved transparency and accountability, IT integration, resource optimization, enhanced collaboration, and increased information security.

ERP in the Public Sector

mySAP ERP offers an integrated system for financials, human capital management and payroll, operations, purchasing and logistics, grants management, and maintenance management. Capabilities tailored for public organizations to reduce costs, increase efficiency and effectiveness, facilitate collaboration, and improve decision-making are, for example, improved procurement processes, financial and management accounting, financial supply chain management, corporate governance, grants management, tax and revenue management, and workforce management.

Grants Management is one of the capabilities that is used primarily in the public sector environment. Together with the SAP Grants Management application, mySAP ERP helps organizations manage sponsored programs, such as grants, contracts, and cooperative agreements, from pre-award administration to post-award management and reporting. Key functions help organizations plan revenues and expenses that pertain to the management of grants, define internal and external budget funding sources, check the availability of funds on the budget item level, carry out control postings, calculate indirect and overhead costs, and more. And because the solution aligns an organization's financial structure with the

New and enhanced capabilities with mySAP ERP

financial and administrative requirements of the sponsor, organizations no longer need to compromise their organizational structures or financial reporting to meet sponsor requirements.

With self services and roles, a consolidated financial reporting, guided procedures, enterprise asset management, and collaboration capabilities, mySAP ERP offers new and enhanced features and processes that improve operations in the public sector.

By automating processes and providing enhanced insight into finances, mySAP ERP enables organizations to lower procurement costs and increase constituent satisfaction through around-the-clock online services. Public sector institutions can rely on mySAP ERP and SAP solutions to provide sustainable technology solutions that mitigate both project and financial risk and improve performance throughout their organizations.

3.1.5 Enterprise Management and Support in the Retail Industry

ERP in the Retail industry

While the retail industry encompasses a multitude of businesses, such as drug and grocery, do-it-yourself, convenience, fashion, and wholesale and department stores, all such businesses face similar challenges. Most battle increased competition, both nationally and globally—a comparable situation to the aforementioned examples in the automotive industry, banking industry, and consumer products industry. Retailers who currently operate only in the United States, for example, must deal with new competition from overseas vendors pushing into the U. S. market—and, at the same time, establish an international presence themselves. The impending elimination of trade quotas, which, over time, will eliminate "made in USA" protections, will further intensify global pressures. And due to price wars, retailers are investing heavily in loyalty programs, unique shopping experiences, and other differentiating strategies, as well as privately labelling goods and cutting out wholesalers.

Complicating this difficult economic environment is the trend toward greater consumer power and choice. Many customers are highly educated and demanding, often learning about products via television and the Internet before making a shopping decision. Customer buying criteria has also changed dramatically, making it harder for retailers to build consumer loyalty and predict spending patterns. The same customer, for example, may shop regularly both at large discount hypermarkets as well as at designer stores. Today's consumers also demand convenience and entertainment—a shopping experience that is tailored to their individual needs. As a result, many retailers are shifting away from traditional retail store models and toward hybrid stores, such as gas-and-grocery-store operations. Even general merchandise giants are successfully entering the grocery market. This trend is forcing many retailers to move into mass merchandise and compete on efficiency and price, or to offer higher-value brand-name products.

Retailers have to find ways to maximize ROI through short-term improvements and long-term initiatives in order to reduce costs and increase revenues. They have to work more effectively with distribution and supply systems required to manage a great variety of products, sales channels, suppliers, and stores. In addition, retailers can benefit from capitalizing on new market opportunities and leveraging new technology to optimize inventory management and simplify reporting.

mySAP ERP is a key element of SAP solutions for the retail industry, with business process support for best practices that help retailers streamline supply chains, merchandise management, store operations, and corporate management. The solution can be tailored to address the unique operating requirements of large and small companies in all segments of the retail industry. The solution offers capabilities that help organizations in the retail industry reduce costs, increase efficiency and effectiveness for all activities including merchandising, facilitate supply chain collaboration, meet new data and reporting requirements, and improve decision-making for all business processes.

SAP for Retail

The key functional areas—analytics, financial management and controls, supply chain optimization, multisite workforce deployment, and store operations—are specifically tailored to this industry and leverage the benefits of IT within the retail industry. For example, let's take a look at supply chain optimization.

mySAP ERP improves procurement processes by facilitating plan-driven and ad-hoc purchasing, complete inventory management, and intelligent reporting on all procurement activities. In addition to enabling traditional processes such as requisitioning, purchase order management, and invoice verification, it also supports innovative processes such as the use of self-service requisitions for maintenance, repair, and operations material and services, as well as process variant optimization. The solution supports all major areas of inventory management and warehousing, such as

New and enhanced capabilities with mySAP ERP

inbound and outbound processing, cross-docking,[2] specific strategies for warehouse optimization, and flexible valuation concepts. In addition to providing supplier relationship management tools, mySAP ERP also supports supplier selection and qualification, contract negotiations, bid invitations, and vendor evaluation. Supply chain planning, global trade management, and transportation management are just some examples of industry-specific functionality that can be added to provide additional features of direct benefit to retailers.

With new and enhanced capabilities like, for example, global data synchronization, collaboration with partners and suppliers, order processing using RFID, and self services and roles, mySAP ERP offers comprehensive support for all areas of retail operations—including finance, workforce management, store operations, logistics, and supply chain optimisation—to help the organizations meet and exceed their business goals.

Best practices for each industry Generally speaking, each mySAP ERP industry solution is tailored to the specific standards, processes, and challenges of the particular industry involved ensuring that the solution fits the way in which real enterprises meet the requirements of a business. Consequently, mySAP ERP delivers rich functionality and productivity-building tools throughout organizations— thereby enabling worldwide industry leaders to adopt best practices developed by SAP.

3.2 mySAP ERP for Midsize and Growing Companies

To accomplish the exponential growth in ERP applications that is expected from the segment of midsize businesses (see also Section 1.1), dedicated offerings are required to consider the specific needs of this customer segment. To provide this requirement, SAP offers midsize companies the best-in-class path to implement the scope of mySAP ERP step-by-step. The offering ranges from core enterprise resource planning processes to industry-specific scenarios. Customers profit from greater planning reliability, rapid implementation, lower costs, and less risk.

---

2 Cross docking means to take a finished good from the manufacturing plant and deliver it directly to the customer with little or no handling in between. Cross docking reduces handling and storage of inventory. The step of filling a warehouse with inventory before shipping it out is virtually eliminated. Simply stated, cross-docking means receiving goods at one door and shipping out these goods through the other door almost immediately, without putting them in storage.

3.2.1 Requirements Towards an ERP System

With mySAP ERP, SAP has introduced a solution for strategic and operational management of an organization that far exceeds the traditional meaning of enterprise resource planning. Most enterprises that use mySAP ERP for decision-making are midsize companies that must differentiate themselves from the competition and want to achieve distinctly more flexible business processes as well as operational excellence.

Few would be surprised to learn that these midsize companies see themselves as facing challenges similar to those that large enterprises encounter, including:

Facing today's challenges and restrictions

► Gaining transparency of their business

► Meeting specific reporting requirements

► Compliance with new laws and regulations (e. g., Sarbanes-Oxley, Basel II, IAS/IFRS)

► Increasing efficiency of operational processes and optimized use of resources

► Realizing a holistic solution with integrated business solutions and avoidance of media breaks

► Leveraging IT as support for and driver of new processes and innovations enabling swift adoption to ever-changing market requirements

Nonetheless, midsize companies operate within a completely different context, with specific restrictions and requirements that must be addressed:

► They strive for extremely rapid ROI because their financial leeway is far more limited than that of large companies.

► They need investment reliability regarding the future scalability and flexibility of the IT solution.

► They tend to have small IT teams, and business departments (like controlling and logistics) that can provide only limited involvement in IT projects.

► They are cautious regarding the costs of an IT project and need to minimize the related risks and potential impact on cash flow.

► They generally prefer predefined projects with clearly defined scope and benefits.

3.2.2 Packaged Solutions

To respond to these challenges, SAP introduced a modular approach to mySAP ERP, its market-leading ERP solution. According to this approach, customers receive the complete scope of mySAP ERP, however, it is implemented in several smaller steps according to the specific customer requirements, rather than implementing mySAP ERP in its entirety at once (see Figure 3.1).

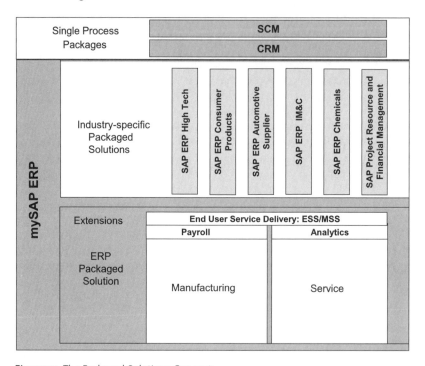

Figure 3.1 The Packaged Solutions Concept

Process scope   The SAP ERP Packaged Solution is a basic ERP package for production industries and service companies. The package, which is built on mySAP ERP, forms the foundation of SAP's modular approach. It provides essential core scenarios from financial management and logistics—such as implementation of procure-to-pay and order-to-cash. Furthermore, it encompasses financial accounting, controlling (cost center accounting, profit center accounting, and profitability analysis), sales (order management and distribution), materials management (procurement), production planning and control (make-to-order, make-to-stock, or repetitive environments), and some areas of human resources. Companies can easily enhance this base solution, for example, with an enterprise portal or additional processes for human resources (recruiting or payroll). Figure 3.2 outlines the scope of this solution.

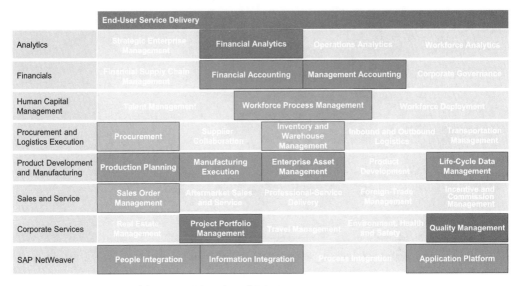

Figure 3.2 Process Scope of the Basic ERP Packaged Solution

Unlike other suppliers whose products require the complete replacement of legacy systems in one fell swoop, with mySAP ERP, SAP offers a step-by-step approach to implementation. Because mySAP ERP is powered by the SAP NetWeaver platform, companies can enhance it easily and protect their existing investments. The implementation approach is similar to the scenario whereby computer suppliers offer customers a basic computer with a specific processor and some service data at a predefined price. Customers then determine whether they want to add a DVD reader or burner—once again at a predefined price.

Step-by-step implementation

In addition to the basic package for core ERP functionality, SAP also offers ERP-based Packaged Solutions that handle the special needs of a specific industry, such as the SAP ERP Packaged Solutions for consumer products (e.g., food and beverage), industrial manufacturing, or construction industries. The contents of the base package depend on the customer's requirements of the solution. A customer decides on the starting scope and determines which scenarios and functionality will be required in the future.

Extend as you grow

As we already outlined, the Packaged Solution is not a limited version of the software. Rather, it offers a specific approach to implementation, according to the unique business needs of midsize and growing companies (see Figure 3.3).

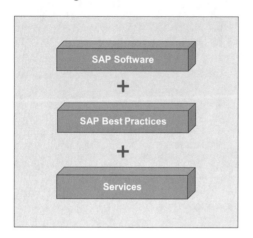

Figure 3.3 The Key Elements of Packaged Solutions

First, our world-leading ERP solution, mySAP ERP, forms the basis of the Packaged Solutions.

A predefined scope for the implementation of a customer-specific business solution requires a high level of expert knowledge about business processes and system configuration. At SAP, this expertise is bundled into the SAP Best Practices family of offerings, which contains the solution and industry knowledge of thousands of SAP customers and their implementation projects. SAP Best Practices provides detailed documentation, immediately accessible system configuration (customizing information), test data and catalogs, training materials, and end-user documentation for the scenarios, processes, and functionalities mapped with SAP Best Practices. This knowledge is the basis of every Packaged Solution.

In addition to process and industry knowledge, the Packaged Services offered by SAP Field Services, or the respective implementation offerings of SAP partners, are essential parts of Packaged Solutions. Through this, customers know the process and functional scope, the implementation time, and the cost of the package. The basic offerings of these special services in the context of Packaged Solutions are:

▶ Project management

▶ Delta requirements workshop

- ▶ Implementation of the predefined scope
- ▶ Technical installation of the solution
- ▶ Training of key users
- ▶ End-user documentation
- ▶ Predefined test catalog and entry sheets for data migration
- ▶ Support during the start of production

Beyond this basic offering and its corresponding implementation services, customers can order additional Packaged Services à la carte. These services help realize functional enhancements or simply provide services that are not offered with the basic package. For example, if customers want to enhance the base solution with industry-specific logistics functions, SAP NetWeaver Business Intelligence (BI), or a payroll or portal solution, they can add these functions and implement them step-by-step with a predefined scope, price, and implementation time during the initial project or, if they prefer, later on in a consecutive project phase. Additional services also include solution hosting, project financing, end-user training, change management, customer-specific reports or interfaces, data archiving, or post-implementation support (see Figure 3.4).

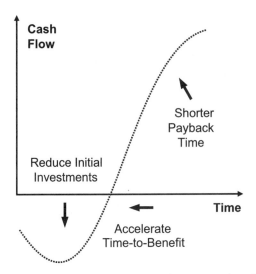

Figure 3.4 Realizing Monetary Advantages with Packaged Solutions

Customer Example

As an actual example, Avex Production was one of the first customers convinced of the Packaged Solution concept. Avex Production manufactures electronic components in Slovakia, near the border with Poland. The company serves five major customers—and more than 3,000 in all—across Europe, Asia, and the Americas. Because these customers demand that suppliers like Avex demonstrate speed, flexibility, tight cost control, and quality management, the company turned to the mySAP ERP solution as part of a packaged offering. SAP Consulting came on board to ensure that the solution was successful. In addition to the mySAP ERP software, the packaged offering included SAP best practices and an implementation methodology designed specifically for growing organizations. Using the SAP Best Practices Baseline Package offering, which is available in country-specific versions, SAP Consulting helped Avex realize a faster return on investment and reduced implementation time and costs.

Among the key requirements of Avex was gaining insight into key figures on the cost and efficiency of its production, as well as real-time access to the most important financial key performance indicators. Avex decided that the goal of the ERP Packaged Solution was to realize a completely integrated ERP solution with predefined scope, cost, and implementation schedule. This approach also helped by ensuring that there was only minimal disruption to the day-to-day business. After Avex succeeded completing a project in only three months with 60 % lower costs than a traditional project would have incurred, the company went live with its solution in the spring of 2005.

"SAP offered the best capability, a competitive price, global credibility, references, and an integrated solution with the opportunity for enhancement and growth," says Jan Orsuliak, Managing Director at Avex Production. "SAP Consulting implemented the solution with virtually no issues, allowing us to get up and running quickly with minimal disruption."

"We now have production costs under control and have eliminated losses from setting prices based on inaccurate cost calculations," Orsuliak says. "We have also become much more flexible through the availability of timely, accurate information. Instead of a formal monthly closing that was difficult to manage, we have our numbers immediately, in real time."

That has had an effect on the bottom line. "We expect to more than double profits from this year to next year," Orsuliak says. "By enabling us to manage and control costs, mySAP ERP is helping us to achieve these results."

3.2.3 SAP Financing

As small and midsize firms find it increasingly difficult to finance larger IT investments, SAP is now offering an alternative way to reap the benefits of next generation IT solutions. Financing an SAP project, including all related infrastructure and services, can start at 30,000 Euro (36,000 USD) or even less, thereby affording you with greater financial flexibility for other strategic business areas. Now, for the first time, you can finance integrated IT solutions through SAP Financing in a globally available all-inclusive offer that provides manageable, well-defined monthly payments. By doing this, SAP Financing offers a long-term alternative to lump-sum payments and unpredictable follow-up costs.

The result is that access to IT solutions—previously available to only larger corporations—is made possible by financing with monthly payments that are affordable and predictable, and processing that is fast and easy. The financing service covers all the major costs associated with your SAP investment. With SAP Financing, monthly payments are predictable for up to seven years.

These payments are all-inclusive, incorporating:

▶ SAP software

▶ Related hardware

▶ Third-party software from the SAP price list

▶ Services for customization, installation, and training

▶ Internal project costs

▶ Software maintenance costs up to one year during implementation

SAP Financing can save money and time, managing both the financing package and the IT solution in one easy step. In addition to turning an upfront investment for SAP solutions into affordable periodical payments, SAP Financing enables you to see all the associated costs.

Financing an IT project with SAP Financing is low-risk and completely tailored to meet your needs. With the help of your SAP consultant or SAP reseller contact, you can find a solution that addresses your needs and ensure that the proposed project and costs meet the requirements of the chosen business strategy. This SAP contact can then help you choose the cost structure and payment option that are most attractive for you. To optimize your return on investment (ROI), you can only start your payments when the IT project is deemed productive (i.e., up to 12 months after the project begins).

Breaking down your overall IT costs into manageable monthly payments provides many benefits. You gain instant access to and competitive advantage from a leading IT infrastructure that can help you to streamline your business and processes immediately. In addition, you free up capital expenditures that were previously dedicated to IT investments, and redirect resources into additional areas that will help your business compete such as innovation or expansion into new markets. By using SAP Financing to spread out your costs over time, you can also preserve existing credit lines and improve cash flow. In many instances, you can take advantage of the benefits of making regular payments rather than having to make a large, one-time investment.

Your choice of SAP solution will be supported by in-depth research and careful comparison of various options. Once you have decided on a solution, the financing approval procedure is relatively short. SAP Financing offers rapid assessment and approval through e-Finance capabilities and dedicated local financing contacts, which can take only minutes over the Web.[3]

---

3 See *www.sap.com/sapfinancing* for more details.

4 SAP NetWeaver and ESA—Architecture Facilitating the Change

As an open integration and application platform,
SAP NetWeaver enables IT to be an agent of transformation,
by aligning IT with the business objectives of your enterprise.

Changing business models, growing competition and globalization, tighter regulation, and increasing merger and acquisition activity are collectively accelerating the pace of business change. More than ever, success depends on IT's ability to adapt to evolving business needs quickly. CIOs need a robust, cost-effective way to leverage and extend a heterogeneous collection of enterprise applications to support new requirements and enable innovation. It is increasingly costly and inefficient to stitch together new business processes that span disparate applications or cross-organizational boundaries, or that require analytics and collaboration. For IT organizations to enable business agility, they must ensure that enterprise applications are not only high-performance business engines driving efficiencies, but also that they become flexible building blocks of future business systems. A clear blueprint for evolving existing architectures is required.

Flexible building blocks

SAP's answer is *Enterprise Services Architecture* (ESA), an open architecture for adaptive business solutions, enabled by the SAP NetWeaver platform. Building on the benefits of Web services, it delivers on the promise of *Service-Oriented Architecture* (SOA), enabling both flexibility and business efficiency without increasing costs. With ESA, companies have a cost-effective blueprint for composing innovative new applications by extending existing systems, while maintaining a level of flexibility that makes future process changes cost-effective.

Open architecture

4.1 mySAP ERP Powered by SAP NetWeaver

The SAP NetWeaver platform—which powers mySAP ERP and the mySAP Business Suite family of business solutions, SAP xApps packaged composite applications, and partner solutions—provides organizations with the robust, flexible infrastructure needed to support effective enterprise-wide change and innovation. Figure 4.1 illustrates how the SAP NetWeaver platform is the foundation for all SAP solutions and how mySAP ERP is the core of mySAP Business Suite.

As enterprises evolve toward an adaptive application environment, an Enterprise Resource Planning (ERP) solution based on an SOA allows organizations to draw on existing core ERP business processes for planning, execution, collaboration, and coordination. Equally critical, an ERP solution allows these processes to:

▶ Extend both enterprise-wide and beyond corporate boundaries

▶ Be closely integrated

▶ Be seamlessly connected to essential enterprise applications, such as customer relationship management and product lifecycle management systems

This extensive integration, which links both internal and partner systems, is a prerequisite for providing the necessary, real-time information to support visibility, velocity, and variability.

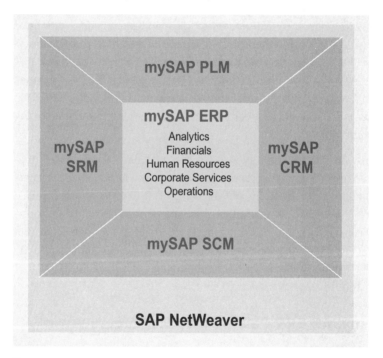

Figure 4.1 mySAP Business Suite

The implications for ERP software cannot be underestimated. For example, originally, businesses implemented ERP software primarily to improve the efficiency of their back-office business operations. Contrary to this ERP model, the 2004 version of mySAP ERP allows companies to leverage these efficiencies throughout the extended enterprise by enabling all authorized users to access mySAP ERP for daily tasks. Enabling this extendibility required uniting the SAP NetWeaver platform with the SAP R/3 solution—a significant evolution of the software. By combining the enterprise portals and business intelligence capabilities of SAP NetWeaver with the advanced business applications of SAP R/3, mySAP ERP 2004 dramatically increases efficiency in the administrative and operative environment, right to end-user desktops.

These strategic developments are designed to help enterprises increase business value in order to realize a faster return on investment (ROI). The services-oriented architecture provides greater flexibility, seamless business integration, and an increased capacity for innovation across the enterprise—all of which represent significant competitive advantages. In addition, tighter integration capabilities enable more streamlined business processes, as well as better integration with third parties for more effective information exchange and greater transparency between organizations. Furthermore, the extendibility increases overall efficiency by making information available to anyone, anywhere, anytime.

4.2 Architecture of mySAP ERP

The following section will describe the architecture of mySAP ERP and clarify the relationship between mySAP ERP and SAP NetWeaver.

4.2.1 General Architecture

To fully understand the architecture of mySAP ERP and its relation to SAP NetWeaver, let's look at its evolution through history, which is depicted in Figure 4.2. From the very beginning, when SAP R/3 was released in 1992, application functionality was clearly separated from the technology: There was an application layer, which was on top of the basis layer. With R/3 Enterprise, introduced in 1999, the basis layer was replaced by the SAP Web Application Server (SAP Web AS), which comprised all capabilities of SAP Basis enhanced by additional web capabilities. On the application side, Extension Sets introduced new features and functions via the Add-on concept, set on top of the SAP R/3 Enterprise core. By following a concept of strict modularization and encapsulation, the system was kept lean and efforts required for an upgrade were minimized.

From SAP Basis to SAP Web AS

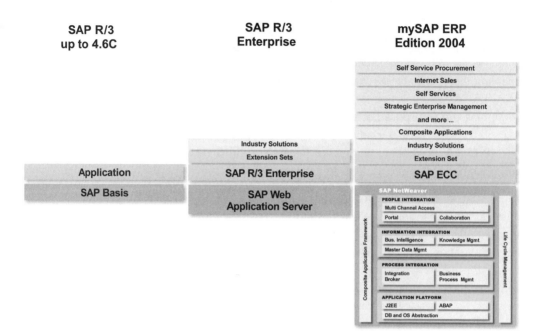

SAP R/3
up to 4.6C

SAP R/3
Enterprise

mySAP ERP
Edition 2004

Figure 4.2 Historical Evolution from SAP R/3 to mySAP ERP

After a very successful Ramp-Up, mySAP ERP Edition 2004 began mass shipment in Q1/2005. As described in the previous chapters of this book, which addressed functional and business aspects, compared with earlier releases, mySAP ERP extended its reach across functional and organizational boundaries considerably. From a technology perspective, this significantly increased requirements for integration on all levels, be it a people, information, process, or application integration level.

SAP ECC 5.0   Consequently, mySAP ERP was designed and built to take full benefit from SAP NetWeaver and its integration capabilities. On the application side, the successful concepts of modularization and encapsulation further evolved by moving towards ESA including the use of Web services. On the application side, the replacement of SAP R/3 Enterprise by SAP ECC 5.0 (ECC = ERP Central Component) can be considered as one great enhancement. For example, compared to SAP R/3 Enterprise SAP ECC 5.0 shows significant improvements in the area of usability. Furthermore, the integration to the composite components is even tighter with SAP ECC 5.0. In addition, new functionality was developed and integrated into SAP ECC 5.0, such as the New General Ledger. Last but not least, a big step was taken to enable our customers to achieve a lower Total Cost of Ownership (TCO) by technically integrating components which, during earlier releases, had to be implemented separately: SAP Business Information Warehouse (SAP BW), SAP Strategic Enterprise Management (SAP SEM), and Internet Transaction Server (ITS) technically moved into SAP ECC. Naturally, these components can still be implemented separately if necessary.

4.2.2 Architecture of Industry Solutions as Part of mySAP ERP

After we have highlighted the generic architecture of mySAP ERP, we must describe the link to industry-specific capabilities. In general, an industry solution consists of cross-industry functions from the ERP core, plus industry-specific functions from one or more industry-specific components, which are delivered with or on top of the core. In some cases, industry solutions also include functions from other cross-industry components in the mySAP Business Suite, such as SAP Customer Relationship Management (CRM), SAP Supply Chain Management (SCM), and so on. To understand the availability of industry solutions, it's important to know their components and the resulting dependencies in terms of the delivery stream and schedule.

Currently, industry-specific functionality is made available along three major delivery streams:

Three main delivery streams

▶ **Core**
Industry-specific functionality is delivered as part of SAP R/3 Enterprise Core (or SAP ECC Core).

▶ **Extension Set/Enterprise Extension**
Industry-specific functionality is delivered as part of SAP R/3 Enterprise Extension Set (or SAP ECC Extension Set).

▶ **Add-on**
Industry-specific functionality is delivered as part of an Add-on to SAP R/3 Enterprise or SAP ECC.

With mySAP ERP 2004, special industry solutions are shipped either within SAP ECC, or as an Extension Set or Add-on. Industry solutions delivered as part of the core or as an extension are available at the same time that SAP R/3 Enterprise or SAP ECC is available. Add-ons are available at a later date than the delivery of the core component and the Extension Sets.

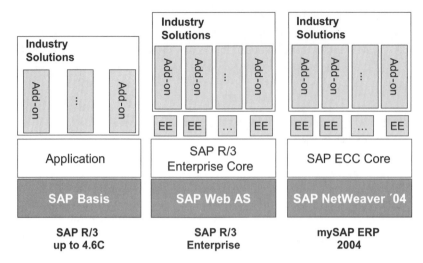

Figure 4.3 mySAP ERP Architecture—Evolution of Industry Solutions

Figure 4.3 depicts the evolution of SAP's industry solutions up to mySAP ERP Edition 2004. With SAP R/3 releases up to 4.6C, industry-specific functionality is delivered as an Add-on on top of the application layer. Due to the three-layer-architecture of the latest release of SAP R/3—SAP R/3 Enterprise—industry-specific functionality is either in the core, in the extension set or, as with former SAP R/3 releases, delivered as an Add-on. These delivery streams continue with SAP ECC since this release follows the three-layer-architecture concept.

Available for mySAP ERP 2004	
A	SAP for Aerospace and Defense
n/a	SAP for Apparel and Footwear*
A	SAP for Automotive
E	SAP for Banking
E	SAP for Beverages
C	SAP for Chemicals
C	SAP for Consumer Products
E	SAP for Defense and Security
A	SAP for Engineering, Construction & Operations
	SAP for Financial Service Providers
C	SAP for Global Trade Management
A	SAP for High Tech
C	SAP for Industrial Machinery & Components
A	SAP for Mill Products
C	SAP for Pharmaceuticals
	SAP for Professional Services
A	SAP for Public Sector
E	SAP for Public Sector - Management
C	SAP for Retail
	SAP for Service Providers
E	SAP for Utilities - FERC 2.0

* Available only in mySAP ERP 2004—not planned for mySAP 2005

Figure 4.4 Industry Availability with mySAP ERP 2004; A = Add-on, E = Extension, C = Core.

Figure 4.4 shows the different delivery streams that are used for each industry solution within mySAP ERP 2004. Apparently some industry-specific functionality is not delivered with mySAP ERP. Particularly SAP for Healthcare, SAP for Higher Education & Research (Campus Management), SAP for Insurance, SAP for Media, SAP for Mining, SAP for Oil & Gas, SAP for Public Sector (PSCD), SAP for Telecommunications, and SAP for Utilities are not available with mySAP ERP 2004. Customers who need one or more of these industry-specific functionalities should upgrade to SAP R/3 Enterprise or wait for mySAP ERP 2005, since these industry solutions will be available with SAP ECC 6.0, the successor of SAP ECC 5.0 (see also Section 7.1.7).

4.3   Understanding Integration Challenges

Before we delve into how the different SAP NetWeaver components are solving the integration challenges on all levels impacted, we must understand what exactly are the potential sources of complexity.

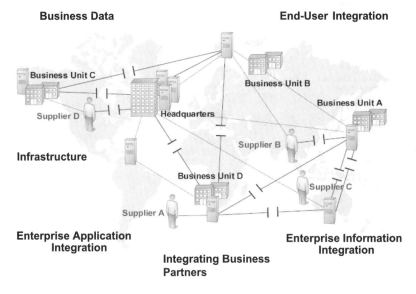

Figure 4.5 Integration Challenges in Today's Business Environment

We'll start with the high-level business perspective. As you can see in Figure 4.5, today's businesses are running global processes, connecting their individual users and unique sources of information to their end-to-end process across the globe. While this alone is a challenge, it is becoming even more complex when you look at the speed with which business requirements are changing—they are truly dynamic. The straightforward result is that, as experience shows, a conventional infrastructure that is based on multiple systems and platforms is often difficult to manage and lacks the flexibility and scalability needed to respond fast enough to new business requirements.

Back to the original question: Where is the integration challenge? The answer is: Today's IT infrastructures need to be able to integrate users, information, and end-to-end business processes without losing the flexibility and scalability needed to adapt to the changing business requirements.

Now let's look at this from the bottom-up, that is, view mySAP ERP 2004 from a technical perspective. As you can see in Figure 4.6, mySAP ERP 2004 comprises a multitude of functional components. These, in a tightly interwoven way, need to be technically integrated in order to support the business processes that depend on their smooth cooperation.

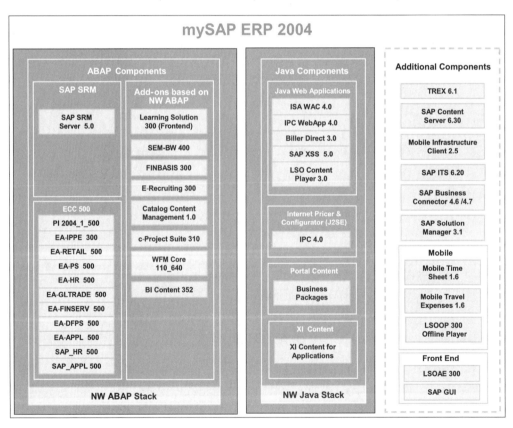

Figure 4.6 mySAP ERP 2004 from a Technical Perspective

4.4   SAP NetWeaver in Detail

SAP NetWeaver is the optimal way to integrate all systems running SAP or non-SAP software. It is pre-integrated with business applications, which reduces the need for custom integration. Based on industry standards, SAP NetWeaver can be extended with commonly used development tools such as Java 2 Enterprise Edition (J2EE), Microsoft .NET, and IBM WebSphere (see Figure 4.7).

It allows you to flexibly and quickly change business processes and strategies. Because it allows you to capture end-to-end business processes and, simultaneously, decouple those processes from underlying IT systems, you can dynamically add, remove, or change steps in a business process. Once you have the infrastructure in place, you can easily extend those processes to new communities inside and outside your organization, while leveraging existing investments. Since SAP NetWeaver takes a holistic approach to integration, it allows you to drive new business strategies that range from the outsourcing of non-strategic assets to the integrating or consolidating of IT following a merger or acquisition. For example, when outsourcing certain functions, you can shift the execution of specific activities in and out of the company, while retaining control of the overall business process.

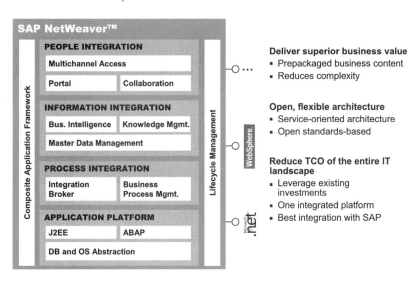

Figure 4.7 SAP NetWeaver Integration and Application Platform

4.4.1 Benefits of SAP NetWeaver

SAP NetWeaver offers unique benefits throughout the enterprise, including the following:

Benefits to C-Level Executives

For executives charged with continuously driving change and innovation to grow the business, SAP NetWeaver facilitates enterprise-wide business process evolution while reducing risks and containing costs. SAP NetWeaver provides the flexibility, visibility, and control to effectively execute, measure, and refine corporate strategies. For businesses, it also facilitates the outsourcing of selected functions; the centralizing, decentralizing, or consolidation of operations; and the integration of IT after acquisitions and mergers.

Benefits to Line of Business Managers

Line-of-Business (LOB) managers need to solve specific business risk issues and deliver rapid Return On Investment (ROI). Consequently, they benefit from tools that enable them to develop industry-specific business processes, drive innovation throughout their units, and quantify and analyze results. With SAP NetWeaver, businesses can easily develop extensible best practices, leveraging existing skills to augment current practices or compose new practices to meet their needs. SAP NetWeaver ensures a free flow of accurate information throughout the supply chain and product lifecycle, both within and outside the organization.

Benefits to IT Executives

For IT executives who must align IT initiatives with business objectives, SAP NetWeaver provides a technology platform that enables a flexible, end-to-end business process lifecycle while leveraging existing IT investments. Its architecture, based on open standards, supports both current requirements and future expansion, and it significantly reduces the complexity of the IT landscape, systems integration and consulting costs, and the risks associated with changing systems that are already operating. SAP NetWeaver improves development by enabling businesses to compose new business practices using a Service-Oriented Architecture (SOA) based on Web services, Java, and other industry standards.

4.4.2 SAP NetWeaver Building Blocks and Their Value in mySAP ERP

SAP NetWeaver—People Integration

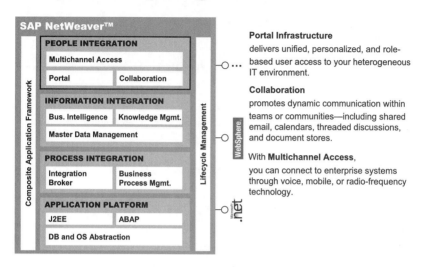

Figure 4.8 SAP NetWeaver—People Integration

People Integration aligns the right functionality and the right information with the right people. On the people level, end users will settle for nothing less than a seamless user experience. Users don't care and should not have to care about growing system diversity. They have the right to expect boundless collaboration functionality, and complete access to all the information they need in their role, regardless of its origin.

Portal Infrastructure is one of the key components enabling people integration via SAP NetWeaver (see Figure 4.9). SAP Enterprise Portal provides a unified, role-based, secure and web-based interface to all information, applications and services. To run the portal, you need a standard browser on the desktop; no additional software components are required. As part of SAP Enterprise Portal, the portal infrastructure provides secure access to structured data coming from any kind of business application, such as data warehouses, databases, and SAP or non-SAP applications.

Portal Infrastructure

While intranet capabilities and information-based aggregation still are relevant in gathering and organizing the data, portals have made it possible to advance interactions with users, customers, and partners in important ways. A portal enables a business to organize and provide data efficiently. For example, a component sales team might use the sheer variety of information provided by a portal to persuade a customer to adopt a new component in the customer's design for future products. That customer expects the business to maintain updated information about future designs and to innovate by creating new products to fit those designs.

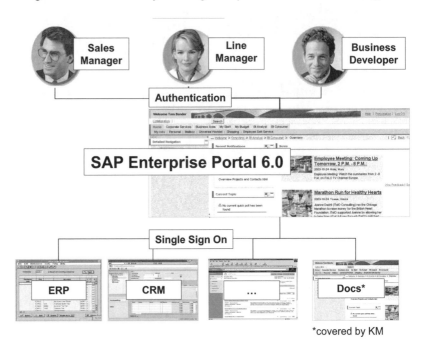

Figure 4.9 Portal Infrastructure

Business suppliers and partners play vital roles in the ongoing process to collect and disseminate key customer and product knowledge. In short, information is king in meeting these expectations. An advanced portal makes the information accessible, relevant, and, perhaps most important, helps customers with ongoing challenges to change their organizations in ways that can best incorporate new products and new technologies.

Improved accessibility to application services and the integration of those underlying sources of information are integral to providing efficient access to the different kinds of information required by various users within the extended enterprise. Within the portal, these users can be notified proactively, alerted to relevant events, and guided through a proactive resolution path (see Figure 4.10).

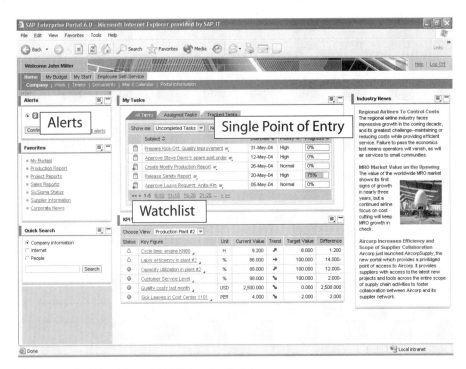

Figure 4.10 End User View of SAP Enterprise Portal

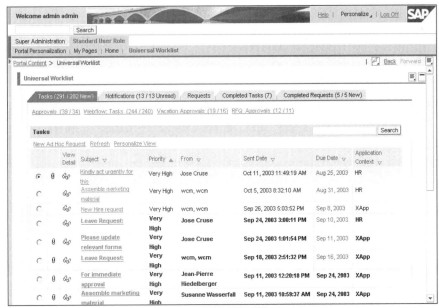

ONE list for MANY backend components, e.g., SRM, CRM, R/3, ...

Figure 4.11 Central Inbox on SAP Enterprise Portal

When we analyze the typical work patterns of different users today, we can separate information sources into four categories: applications and legacy databases, business intelligence, unstructured documents, and Web services and content. To work seamlessly within these information source streams—and to better identify key data and insights amid the massive data constantly being accumulated—an abstraction layer is used to correlate and understand the data and logic received from these sources. Another role of this abstraction layer is to understand users, their profile, their authority, and the requirements that they must meet in order to perform a function or respond to a request. This layer must also be able to present data and logic in effective ways whenever a user requests information, or when the business needs to push information to users based on ongoing business events.

Creating a seamless navigation experience across multiple applications, while retaining the context of the navigation, can only be achieved by creating a unified world of data and metadata, application components, and best business practices. This shared collaboration knowledge is accomplished by abstracting fundamental business objects and the relationships between them across multiple applications. Portal Infrastructure delivers user-centric collaboration through unification, one of the two application integration hubs. This integration allows data and relationships to be accessed and traversed through the virtual metadata layer.

Collaboration *Collaboration* promotes dynamic communication within teams or communities—including shared email, calendars, threaded discussions, and document stores (see Figure 4.12). Real-time collaboration tools including online meetings, chat, instant messaging, and application sharing, and drive dynamic communication through permanent and ad-hoc groups and communities are used. Employees can instantly interact and exchange knowledge, and information resources can be accessed and shared in an issue-related, cost-saving team environment.

Collaboration is of great strategic concern to any organization seeking to enable continuous business innovation and maintain advantage in a competitive economic environment. With the right mix of collaborative capabilities, companies can optimize processes, boost efficiency, trim costs, and improve the flexibility required to quickly respond to changes in the marketplace.

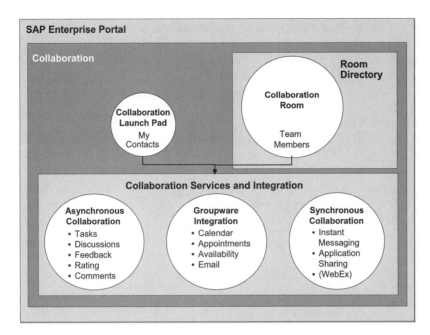

Figure 4.12 Collaboration Capabilities Accessible via SAP Enterprise Portal

For large, distributed organizations, the need for sophisticated collaboration capabilities is palpable. To successfully compete in the global economy, these companies need flexible ways to team up, interact, and exchange information with portal users in various locations and in different time zones around the world. For small and midsize companies, the need is no less urgent. Organizations of every size are searching for ways to manage information overload, deal with the vagaries of distributed information storage, and overcome the obstacles of distance.

From the end user's perspective, the collaboration capabilities of SAP NetWeaver can be divided into two distinct areas: asynchronous and synchronous collaboration (see Figure 4.13). On the asynchronous side, the primary focus is on collaboration rooms—virtual workspaces that can be easily created by the end user via predefined templates. Any portal-based application and all types of structured and unstructured portal content can be part of a collaboration room, enabling teams to access and share all project-related tools, services, and information in a single, shared virtual environment. Asynchronous collaboration also involves task lists and ad-hoc workflow capabilities, which are explained in more detail below.

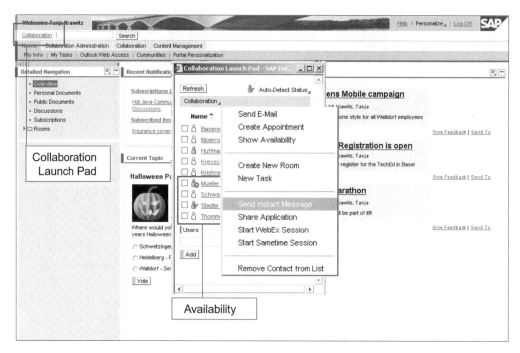

Figure 4.13 End User's View of Embedded Collaboration in SAP Enterprise Portal

On the synchronous side, the focus is on application sharing and instant messaging. This functionality enables teams and work groups to share information, ideas, and work in a highly productive manner. With the ability to instantly communicate and share ideas, teams can quickly resolve problems without the need for time-consuming, face-to-face meetings. A simple launch pad provides immediate, centralized access to contacts and collaborative services, and displays team members' online availability in real time.

From a more technical perspective, another significant capability is third-party integration. Because all collaboration capabilities are based on an open platform, they can be quickly integrated with third-party systems to protect an organization's existing investments and enable users to work with familiar tools. For example, collaboration rooms can easily incorporate groupware solutions such as Microsoft Exchange and Lotus Domino. This enables users to conveniently display their calendars and access current overviews of their daily schedules. Third-party synchronous collaboration tools such as WebEx can also be integrated, enabling portal users to effectively work with non-portal users.

Collaboration rooms are structured virtual work environments with pre-defined content and services that are tailored for groups of users to support their daily business processes. For example, take an event management team put in charge of organizing a convention. Numerous people are involved in the project and they come from multiple departments including Event Planning, IT, Catering, Marketing, and Product Management.

Asynchronous Collaboration– Collaboration Rooms

The common virtual work environment for this project is a collaboration room, in which each project member has access to the information and services they need to make the event a success. The event staff has access to a document repository, business intelligence reports on food and beverage distributors, a task/workflow list for delegating tasks, and a calendar to set up project meetings. While the marketing and product management team members have access to their own document repositories, they share the calendar and task/workflow list with the event staff. And although the IT team continues to have exclusive access to specific systems, which only it is authorized to use, common access to the calendar and task/workflow list is shared with all other teams.

With SAP Enterprise Portal, collaboration rooms are designed to manage all the complex access rights associated with the distributed, cross-functional nature of the project. The idea is to enable groups to work closely together in a way that maintains the integrity of access permissions and security for all information and applications. It also provides the necessary flexibility for room owners to add or remove structured content and create room relations to other rooms as needed.

SAP Real-Time Collaboration (RTC) enables end users to communicate via interactive online meetings and exchange information and knowledge. Services available through SAP real-time collaboration include online awareness, and instant messaging/chat and application sharing, all of which are explained in more detail below.

Synchronous Collaboration– SAP real-time Collaboration

The *Awareness* service acts as an online status detector, indicating whether a user is logged on to the portal and available for ad-hoc collaboration activities such as instant messaging or application sharing. A self-explanatory icon is used to indicate the user's online status.

Automatic identification of a user's online status is based on a polling mechanism used for communication between the client component and the Real-Time Messaging Framework (RTMF) on the portal server. The RTMF is a portal service responsible for handling all real-time collaboration messages exchanged between the client and the portal server. Although this mechanism constantly updates an end user's online status, it is the end users who ultimately determine whether they want to be detected. Status options include the following:

▶ **Auto-Detect**
Automatically displays the end user's online status to other portal users.

▶ **Do Not Disturb**
Tells other portal users that the end user is online but unavailable for collaborative activities.

▶ **Suppress Status**
Reveals nothing about the end user's online status. Other portal users cannot tell whether the end user is online.

Instant Messaging   The *Instant Messaging* service enables portal users to communicate with one another in real time via text messages and is accessible through the collaboration launch pad, from a collaboration room member list, or from within an application sharing session (discussed below). To send a message, the user selects a name from his/her contact list and selects the `Send Instant Message` option from the corresponding drop-down menu. Only contacts that are currently online and available for collaborative activity can receive messages. Online availability status for instant messaging is managed by the same polling mechanism discussed above in the context of the awareness service.

With SAP Real-Time Collaboration (RTC), users can conduct multiple instant messaging sessions simultaneously and even use the instant messaging service in combination with the RTC application sharing service. Users can also send a single instant message to multiple users at the same time. If more than one recipient responds, the session instantly transforms itself into a chat-like event. In such a situation, the session window displays each text message entered by chat participants immediately and logs the messages in chronological order. For easy identification, each message is preceded by the sender's name. At any time during the session, existing participants can leave or new participants can join in a fluid fashion, without disrupting the collaborative activity.

Multichannel   With *Multichannel Access*, you can connect to enterprise systems through Access   voice, mobile, or Radio-Frequency Identification (RFID) technology. The vision of mobile enterprise has finally become a reality as companies have realized that Multichannel Access is essential to cut costs and increase employee productivity. SAP NetWeaver multichannel capabilities allow end-users to interact with business processes via various access methods (e. g., text, voice), various devices (e. g., PDA, phone, Laptop, PC, RFID) and different network connections (e.g., online, offline). As a result, processes and information can be extended to a wide variety of employees and partners, and managers can access the aggregated data and tools they need to make informed decisions from almost any location (see Figure 4.14).

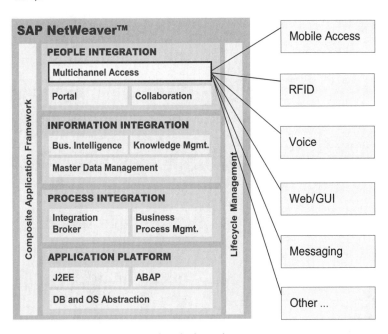

Figure 4.14 SAP NetWeaver and Multichannel Access

The key elements of Multichannel Access are NetWeaver Mobile, SAP Auto-ID Infrastructure, Message Interfaces (SMS, Fax, Email) and web-based GUI.

▶ NetWeaver Mobile comprises various technical architectures used for enabling end-to-end mobile business solutions targeting specific user roles and device platforms.

▶ SAP Auto-ID Infrastructure connects RFID data directly from auto-ID data-capture sources, such as RFID readers, and integrates high-volume data directly into enterprise applications in real time.

▶ SAP Voice Application Framework is a technology that will be integrated into future releases of SAP NetWeaver. It is not part of the SAP NetWeaver '04 delivery.

▶ Web-based GUI enables end users to gain access to their enterprise business via a browser.

▶ SAP NetWeaver provides standardized interfaces to link third-party communication management applications with business applications. It enables the integration of phone, Fax, SMS, or email.

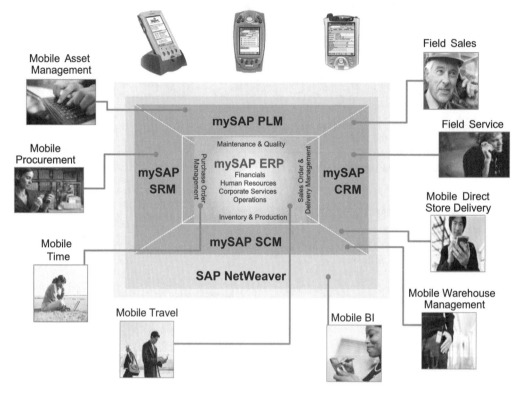

Figure 4.15 mySAP Mobile Business

SAP NetWeaver—Information Integration

Users need to have constant access to consistent information, regardless of where it is stored. Information integration solves this challenge. It provides your company with both structured and unstructured information that is consistent and accessible (see Figure 4.16).

SAP Business Intelligence

SAP Business Intelligence (SAP BI) provides best-of-breed functionality, plus industry-specific features and best practices based on three decades of SAP experience. Timely access to relevant information has always been critical to business success. Now, with the widespread use of the Internet, wired and wireless data collection technologies such as Radio Frequency Identification (RFID), and the subsequent increase in new data sources, it is even more important. As a result, companies have amassed huge amounts of data in an effort to understand their business, improve performance, and build stronger relationships with employees, customers, and partners.

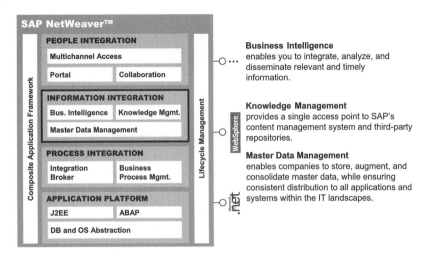

Figure 4.16 SAP NetWeaver—Information Integration

But it's difficult to exploit that data—to make sense of it and put it to work across the enterprise. As many companies have learned, data is scattered throughout the organization in a variety of systems, and many companies have little more than a piecemeal approach to collating, organizing, and interpreting their data. They struggle with fragmented tools and fragmented data, and end up with a fragmented, incomplete view of their business. With SAP BI, SAP offers a better approach that provides us with the complete picture of a business. It orchestrates a powerful business intelligence platform, a comprehensive set of tools, planning and simulation capabilities, and data-warehousing functionality—all delivered through sophisticated and user-centric enterprise portal technology to provide a coherent, comprehensive solution. This means that you can use SAP BI to integrate data from across the enterprise and beyond, and then you can transform it into practical, timely business information to drive sound decision-making, targeted action, and solid business results.

With SAP BI, you can have an accurate, complete, up-to-the-minute view of your entire business—information you can use to act and compete. For example, SAP BI gives you powerful tools so you can create and deploy graphical, interactive reports and applications quickly and easily. It supports ad-hoc queries and distributes responses to the desktop, web client, mobile devices, or email.

Consistent view of enterprise daten SAP BI provides a data warehouse software component that ensures an integrated, consistent view of your enterprise data, as well as a suite of tools to analyze data from both internal and external sources (see Figure 4.17). That means you can combine information from any source (SAP solutions and non-SAP systems), and you can link traditional business environments with e-business operations.

Figure 4.17 The Full View of SAP Business Intelligence

SAP BI provides tools, such as query, reporting, and multidimensional analysis, to support collaborative decision-making. Users can access data on detail or summary levels, and they can analyze and share business information using a web browser. Users can create their own reporting environments, graphically represent data, and visualize relationships between business information and spatial information to produce geographical analyses. SAP BI visually represents data analysis in a variety of formats, including grids, graphs, maps, and more.

Industry-strength business planning and simulation capabilities are fully integrated into the SAP BI component. Therefore, the "single version of truth" does not end with reporting and analysis, but also extends to the domain of planning and business simulations. For example, you can develop your own planning applications or activate existing functions for financial budgeting or promotion planning. As an example within mySAP ERP, Strategic Enterprise Management (SEM) leverages SAP BI for analysis and planning purposes (see Figure 4.18).

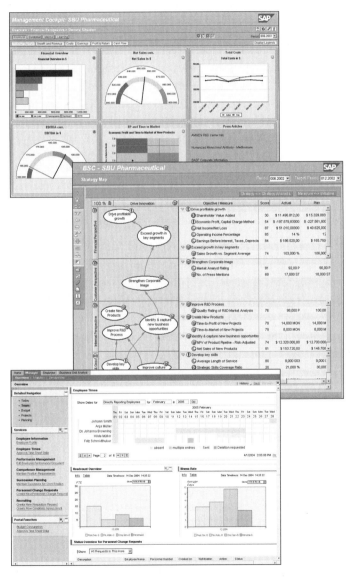

Figure 4.18 Planning and Simulation with mySAP ERP SEM Leveraging SAP BI

SAP BI lets you combine structured information (such as reports from daily business transactions) and unstructured information (such as email and corporate documents), as well as data from external sources, all through your enterprise portal. You can securely deliver that information to executives, knowledge workers, and business partners around the world through a portal. Furthermore, the portal's enterprise unification technology allows you to access information from various sources and work across applications simply by dragging and grouping business object icons with related applications on the user interface.

SAP BI helps you identify, manage, and share information assets. It allows decision-makers to collaborate on reports and analyses for additional insight and action. For example, an analyst can add commentary to key figures in a budget report, thereby accelerating the budget approval process. Moreover, integrated broadcasting technology enables reports to be scheduled and distributed automatically to extended audiences, within and beyond the corporate firewall.

The analytical and data modeling tools of SAP BI can help decision-makers visually represent objectives and model scenarios to identify optimal strategies. They can monitor progress toward goals as well as the performance of key indicators by using external and internal benchmarks.

Knowledge Management

Knowledge Management (KM) is the umbrella term for the management of unstructured information, that is, all kinds of documents. The business challenge is to transform unstructured information into organizational knowledge by structuring and classifying it in such a way that it becomes accessible and relevant to the enterprise's knowledge workers. Because today's enterprises are increasingly distributed in their operations—often global in scope—there is an urgent need to create a central point of access within the enterprise to manage information and translate it into knowledge for success.

The amount of information in organizations is increasing exponentially, and much of it is unstructured—documents on department file servers, web pages on subsidiary web servers, email, groupware, and slide presentations, to name just a few examples. These unstructured and often unmanaged resources contain mission-critical knowledge that companies need in order to maximize business advantage. The challenge is to transform that information into organizational knowledge—to bring it into the context of critical business processes.

The knowledge management capabilities of the SAP NetWeaver platform address this important challenge by structuring and classifying the entire spectrum of unstructured content, making it accessible to users and available for improving decision-making (see Figure 4.19). SAP Enterprise Portal provides you with a configurable set of connectors, repositories, and services, including a full-featured search engine that makes all unstructured information accessible to users. Moreover, integration of such features with other capabilities of SAP NetWeaver creates a role-driven network of information, collaboration, analytics, and alert options across your organization.

Figure 4.19 Knowledge Management User Interfaces

Creating strategic resources from unstructured information

The knowledge management capabilities of SAP NetWeaver help you manage all facets of unstructured information—from collaborative authoring and publishing to advanced search and navigation features—with extraordinary ease and efficiency. These capabilities include:

▶ Functions for effectively creating and working with information in documents

▶ A powerful search and classification engine

▶ Adaptability through an open set of extensions

▶ Role-based access and full integration with the SAP NetWeaver integration and application platform

Because users naturally store information in a variety of locations, all these "places" or "document repositories" should be combined within one "virtual view." The knowledge management capabilities of SAP NetWeaver provide this virtual view, which ensures the accessibility of all documents to all authorized users and provides critical information services.

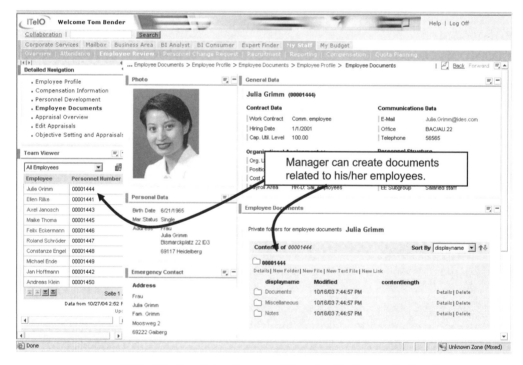

Figure 4.20 Knowledge Mangement Embedded in Manager Self Service

The knowledge management capabilities of SAP NetWeaver support the entire document lifecycle. Standard user interfaces provide all the basic functions required for working with documents—authoring, publishing, classifying, versioning, publishing workflows, and more. Automatic classification services sort documents into the appropriate channels, and subscription mechanisms push the new content to target audiences. To complete the cycle, readers can provide feedback to authors and use the rating function. Template-based authoring and publishing using multiple channels make life easy for occasional authors, while administrators can utilize an extensive framework for detailed configurations and additions to the system. From a mySAP ERP perspective, Manager Self Service (MSS) is a good example of how mySAP ERP is leveraging the embedded use of KM (see Figure 4.20).

What good is information if users can't find it? To resolve this fundamental issue, the knowledge management capabilities of SAP NetWeaver come with a search and classification engine. This fully equipped and integrated engine provides knowledge workers with tremendous power and flexibility for finding what they need, when they need it. With the search and classification engine, users can do the following:

Powerful search and classification functions

▶ Search across multiple content repositories and discover related documents anywhere in the system

▶ Retrieve originals or highlighted HTML versions of nearly 200 file formats

▶ Navigate through logical hierarchies—commonly known as taxonomies—populated by automatic classification

▶ Associate information in documents with individuals and identify content experts

▶ Use fuzzy and linguistic search methods in nearly 30 languages (see Figure 4.21)

▶ Benefit from dynamically ranked search results and document summarization

Because Knowledge Management (KM) is a tightly integrated capability of SAP NetWeaver, searching is not restricted to unstructured information and can be extended to structured business content. These search and classification mechanisms have already been applied to other SAP solutions and will continue to be extended to provide powerful search functions across a wide range of critical business information.

Figure 4.21 Powerful TREX Search Capabilities

Today, companies around the world in industries ranging from mill products to media services are facing similar problems—they are unable to
assimilate, harmonize, and distribute enterprise data vital to business
decisions that impact the entire enterprise. Every day, in every industry,
key decisions are being made using industry-specific business processes.
However, managers are not receiving the appropriate information from
these processes that they need to leverage the harmonized data from different systems. Either the systems are highly inefficient due to numerous
integration points, or they are simply not integrated. As enterprise applications continue to become more complex and generate escalating
amounts of information, managers are finding it increasingly difficult to
access the information they need quickly to make decisions that maximize profitability, customer satisfaction, and efficiency.

According to the Grocery Manufacturer's Association of America, "Inaccurate and time-consuming product information exchanges between
CPG manufacturers and their retail trading partners add significant costs
and create inefficiencies throughout the supply chain. An estimated 25
billion USD to 50 billion USD in extra costs due to these problems could
be greatly reduced through industry-wide data synchronization. Due to
the impact that unsynchronized data can have on trading partner operations and relationships, synchronization is a critical initial step toward
efficient electronic commerce and advanced applications such as collaborative planning forecasting and replenishment, scan-based trading, and

collaborative supply chain management." In other studies, in the financial services sector, it has been estimated that up to 30% of brokerage transactions fail due to the lack of harmonized master data.

SAP Master Data Management (SAP MDM) supports unified data storage across company branches in a heterogeneous IT landscape. It permits common use of master data from systems that were originally different, and ensures that the data is consistent across system boundaries, irrespective of the system location or vendor. SAP MDM is not disruptive. You can implement comprehensive master data management without ripping out or altering existing systems, or incurring the downtime that often results when implementing enterprise-wide software. SAP MDM is implemented on a step-by-step evolutionary basis that minimizes disruptions to your existing infrastructure.

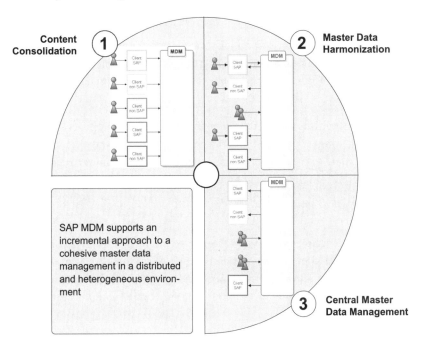

Figure 4.22 The Key Capabilities of SAP Master Data Management

Key capabilities delivered by SAP MDM, as depicted in Figure 4.22, are:

SAP MDM consolidates master data objects from different systems. Typically, this information is transferred to a business information warehouse from which users can access data for integrated, company-wide analyses, reporting, and decision-making. Given this capability, managers can produce, analyze, disseminate, and update such vital information as accurate

Content consolidation

global spending analyses, centralized supplier product catalogs, or the number of unique customers or business suppliers the company has at any point in time.

Master data harmonization For enterprises operating large, distributed IT landscapes on a global scale, it is essential to harmonize consolidated master data through consistent maintenance and distribution. SAP MDM harmonizes master data to provide central management of global attributes, which ensures that all systems receive the same master data during distribution. It allows you to control data at the local level so that individual systems receive only the data they need, when they need it.

SAP MDM also ensures the controlled distribution of all local changes. Highly structured control mechanisms determine the data objects that belong together in a business sense, the target systems for distribution, and the time and scope of data distribution.

Business partner administration, centralized provisioning of product masters, and the definition and administration of nonvariable parts are just a few examples of the master data harmonization capability at work.

Central master data management In addition to content consolidation and master data harmonization, SAP MDM offers central master data management, which supports the maintenance of complete object definitions, including dependencies, in a centralized server. Centralization means one-stop data maintenance—local systems rarely need to be maintained. Instead, active status management procedures update each individual client system with a copy of master data.

For global companies that want to ensure brand identity and consistent product specifications, central maintenance of master data is invaluable. For example, a centralized data pool can supply global managers with consistent control over information relating to their important global accounts. The same data pool can supply updated product data to multiple locations around the world for the management of production, assembly, sales, and distribution.

Open and highly scalable, SAP MDM helps companies reduce data maintenance costs and the amount of inconsistent and outdated master data, which significantly reduces TCO. But SAP MDM goes well beyond simple cost reduction. It also positively impacts a company's top and bottom lines, ensuring cross-system data consistency in a way that greatly accelerates business process execution and promotes increased collaboration. Furthermore, by providing homogenized data for use in enterprise-wide business analytics, SAP MDM ultimately improves corporate decision-making, increasing a company's ability to succeed in today's highly competitive business environment.

SAP NetWeaver—Process Integration

Today's IT landscapes are increasingly complex and difficult to integrate. You need a solution that makes new levels of collaboration and connectivity possible among all the systems and applications within your enterprise and across your entire value chain. In addition to integrating these heterogeneous system environments, you want to leverage your existing legacy systems—in today's environment, a "rip and replace" solution is not feasible. You also want your implementation to support the goal of standardizing on a services-based architecture.

In short, you need a powerful Integration Broker who can solve the integration challenges discussed in Section 4.3. But, integration alone is useless if you don't have the necessary tools and environment available to model and drive your processes in today's dynamic environment. Fortunately, SAP Exchange Infrastructure (XI) Business Process Management can meet this need (see Figure 4.23).

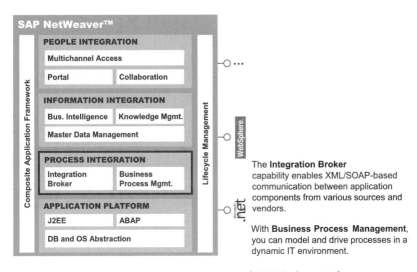

Figure 4.23 SAP NetWeaver Process Integration with SAP Exchange Infrastructure

SAP Exchange Infrastructure (SAP XI) is a powerful integration broker that works well within your IT landscape and with its various connectivity, format, and protocol requirements. A component of the SAP NetWeaver platform, SAP XI runs on the SAP Web Application Server.

SAP XI—The integration broker

SAP XI reduces integration and maintenance costs of IT systems by providing a common, central repository for interfaces. It supports cross-component business process management (BPM) within the same solution. And, it offers an integrated toolset to help organizations build their own integration scenarios by defining the appropriate messaging interfaces, mappings, and routing rules. SAP XI is based on a native web infrastructure that leverages open standards and supports multiple communication approaches, including central hubs and peer-to-peer connections. It protects your technology investment by seamlessly integrating all existing components from both SAP and third-party vendors without any disruption. SAP XI optimizes SAP's extensive knowledge of business processes, including the need to capture and share collaborative knowledge during the entire software lifecycle.

How SAP XI meets integration needs Figure 4.24 shows you typical challenges to be met in order to integrate and consolidate today's IT landscapes:

▶ Individual, point-to-point integration connections are in use, based on a wide variety of technologies that had been available at the time of implementation.

▶ Different integration approaches are taken per business purpose (A2A, B2B, BPM, Industry Standards, ...).

▶ As an attempt to overcome exisiting integration needs, a patchwork of integration solutions has been applied.

▶ There is no centralized knowledge or management of integration aspects available.

▶ We see a grown infrastructure, which is not adaptable and, thus, expensive to maintain.

▶ High costs are associated with the integration and upgrade of application components.

In the following, we will show how SAP XI reduces integration complexity by providing an open integration platform that drives collaborative business processes at sustainable costs (see Figure 4.25).

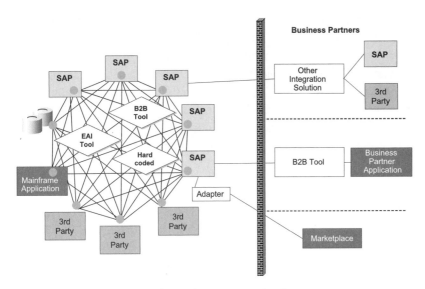

Figure 4.24 Today's Grown and Complex Integration Landscapes

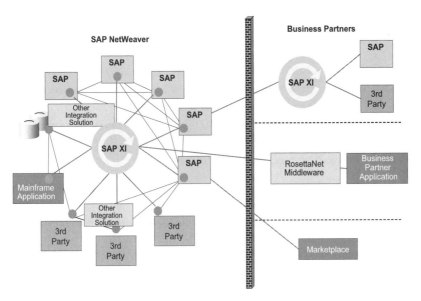

Figure 4.25 Ingration with SAP Exchange Infrastructure

SAP XI lets you integrate collaborative processes across multiple applications both within and beyond the boundaries of the enterprise. Processes are integrated using standards-based XML messaging. All related information is described using Web services standards.

Standards-based process integration

Integration knowledge management	SAP XI features a central integration repository and an integration directory that store all your shared collaboration knowledge across all components throughout a solution's lifecycle—from design through configuration and deployment. Integration definitions are separately maintained in the integration repository, away from functional application coding. This means that you can upgrade functional coding without affecting the repository definitions. The repository contains shared collaboration knowledge from SAP, your partners, and third-party vendors.
Prepackaged integration content	Business content from various sources is available for SAP XI. All mySAP Business Suite solutions and SAP NetWeaver components quickly deliver predefined business content such as data types, messages types, interface description, business scenarios, and process patterns. Furthermore, SAP offers business packages that are complete solutions for business problems. Business applications, technical infrastructure, and business content are delivered to match industry standards and all three items are tuned to work as one. Companies can leverage these collective capabilities to get a head start in integration projects. The SAP XI integration repository is open to third-party and custom content, allowing the component to serve as the centralized instance for all integration content.
Cross-component BPM	SAP XI allows you to model cross-component business processes and scenarios. This, in turn, enables you to drive and control complex business processes across business applications and enterprise boundaries. SAP XI covers the full process lifecycle, including design, automation, execution, and monitoring. The collaboration knowledge in SAP XI allows you to describe integration processes from a top-down, high-level perspective, rather than your having to hardcode them into attached components.
Heterogeneous landscape connectivity	SAP XI helps you integrate heterogeneous applications. You can integrate business applications running on SAP Web AS by using SAP XI messaging proxies, without the need for additional adapters. SAP XI can also directly call an application that offers a Web services interface. And, with its Java 2 platform, Enterprise Edition (J2EE) Connector Architecture (JCA)-based adapter framework, SAP XI enables you to integrate virtually any application or system, including packaged applications and those requiring a particular protocol, by using the appropriate adapter from SAP or a certified partner.
B2B integration	SAP XI stores your collaboration partner profiles in its integration directory, allowing you to communicate with your partners based on these data. Support for industry-standard protocols, such as those used for

RosettaNet, UCCnet, or CIDX, is provided via adapters and corresponding mappings.

SAP XI handles the Web service calls you send or receive in an advanced manner, and can provide value-added services. SAP XI can also evaluate Web service calls based on the content and definitions that you have placed in the integration directory. SAP XI selects the appropriate definition and sends it on as a Web service, or transforms the Web service call into the format and protocol that the receiving destination expects.

Web service management

To run your collaborative business processes, SAP XI features a robust and high-performance integration server. SAP and its partner supply all the adapters you need to access other applications, files, and databases, and to connect via using various protocols and industry standards.

Collaborative business processes with SAP XI

The integration directory manages all the information relevant to a specific customer IT environment and it uses this dedicated shared-collaboration knowledge to drive the core of the SAP XI execution environment—the integration engine of SAP XI. The integration engine provides a runtime infrastructure for secure XML-based communication between the instances of the various components, as well as for mapping and routing.

Integration engine and integration directory

For both B2B transactions and communications along your value chain, you have extensive individual and special requirements that affect execution and security. Individual agreements between you and your business partners must be managed centrally so that they can be made available across your entire landscape. The SAP XI integration directory performs this job. Agreements regarding connectivity, security, and other essential operations that take place between you and your business partners are kept in the integration directory. Alternatively, at design time, integration knowledge—such as business scenarios or interface descriptions—is maintained in the integration repository. Together, the integration directory and the integration repository allow you to manage all your integration tasks and scenarios in a single location.

Security and partner agreements

The Business Process Engine (BPE) is tightly connected with the integration engine and fully integrated into the integration server. During message flow between heterogeneous systems, the engine utilizes all the shared collaboration knowledge required to execute a business process. An easy-to-use graphical modeler gives you access to the message types and interfaces involved in a process. It lets you define the series and sequence of steps and actions required to run the process. During execu-

Business Process Engine

tion, the BPE also correlates and links related messages based on a unique, user-defined identifier.

SAP XI provides open integration technologies that drive collaborative business processes, reducing one of your major IT infrastructure problems, namely, complexity. SAP XI also offers the following benefits to you and your organization.

Lower TCO   SAP XI reduces the cost of integration and lets you reuse existing components such as your investments in Electronic Data Interchange (EDI). SAP XI protects your investment by seamlessly integrating components from both SAP and third-party vendors.

Process-centric integration   With SAP XI, you can integrate business processes within and across organizational and technical boundaries. The component makes optimal use of SAP's extensive knowledge of business processes, including capturing and sharing collaborative knowledge during the entire software lifecycle. The process-centric information model in SAP XI is based on Web services: It follows the principles of Enterprise Services Architecture, the SAP blueprint for services-based, enterprise-scale business solutions that offer the increased levels of adaptability, flexibility, and openness required to reduce total cost of ownership.

Process automation   SAP XI orchestrates message flow the way you define it for each of your individual business processes. You can automate processes according to your unique needs across heterogeneous systems and beyond enterprise boundaries.

Integration scenarios   You can build your own integration scenarios using the integrated toolset in SAP XI. The toolset defines the appropriate messaging interfaces, mappings, and routing rules necessary to connect application components or create collaborative processes that involve business partners.

Open standards   Because SAP XI is based on a native web infrastructure that leverages open standards, it allows you to use current industry standards and has the built-in flexibility to support future standards.

Integration   By making SAP XI one of your essential IT technologies, you are able to deal with the challenge of integrating your IT landscape. Through its powerful integration capabilities, SAP XI enables a new level of adaptive business solutions while enabling process-centric collaboration across your entire value chain.

Business Process Management   Business Process Management (BPM) focuses on driving processes within and across different applications. It allows companies to design and model processes in order to execute them in an automated fashion. Critical business processes can therefore be streamlined, managed, and optimized on the fly after they have been analyzed, both from a technical and business perspective.

BPM covers the full process lifecycle: design, automation, execution, monitoring, analysis and optimization. It orchestrates the message choreography between systems and business partners using stateful interactions. It supports the deployment of processes that span the value chain, eradicating the point-to-point integration problem, independent of different technical infrastructures. In this way, process management is similar in appearance to Enterprise Application Integration (EAI); however, BPM exceeds the integration of data flow on a technical messaging layer. Rather, it is about managing process flow control across and within systems and, at the same time, across an entire process instance that might also include business partners.

Machine-to-machine communication and human interaction, planned or spontaneous, are important differentiators between the different flavors of process management.

Cross-Component Business Process Management handles processes where the message flow between different business applications is dependent on several messages, or on time and business actions, or reactions. Interdependencies can be defined using an internal state derived from the content of incoming messages. Messages belonging to one process instance are identified by correlations as common denominators on the basis of message content (e.g., a Purchase Order, an ASN, a Confirmation, and an Invoice in a procurement process via the Order ID in combination with the business partner ID and the company code).

Managing processes across business systems

SAP XI is the component within SAP NetWeaver, empowering cross-component process management. SAP NetWeaver thus offers an Integration Broker and a BPM solution for process integration rather than a standalone BPM system apart from the message-oriented middleware (see Figure 4.26).

A graphical process editor is an integral part of SAP XI's Integration Builder. Business Processes are Integration Repository and Integration Directory objects and are integrated with Business Scenarios and all other repository (and directory) objects. The delivery and usage of process templates is supported. These templates act as business process blueprints and patterns and need to be implemented and deployed by the customer. At runtime, business processes are executed by the Business Process Engine (BPE), an integral part of SAP XI's Integration Server. For the execution of message relevant process steps (e.g., send, transform), the BPE relies on services offered by the Integration Engine. SAP XI provides technical process monitoring capabilities either from a message view (XML message monitoring) or a process view (process runtime log). Navigation from message to process monitoring is supported. In addition, integration to the Runtime Workbench of SAP XI and to SAP Computing Center Management System (CCMS) is also supported. SAP XI supports Business Process Execution Language for Web services (BPEL4WS), but is also receptive to other open standards via a pluggable interface where standard formats can be imported and exported.

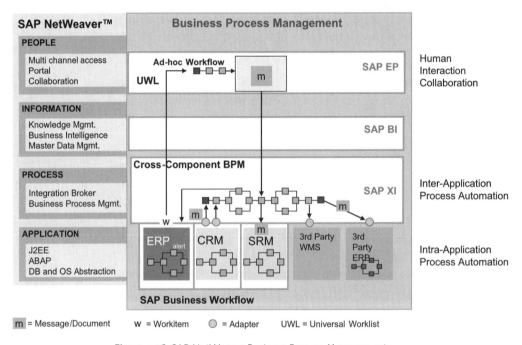

Figure 4.26 SAP NetWeaver Business Process Management

SAP NetWeaver—Application Platform

The SAP Web Application Server (Web AS) (see Figure 4.27) is the technical platform for SAP NetWeaver, providing the complete infrastructure to develop, deploy, and run all SAP NetWeaver components, the mySAP Business Suite, customer-developed applications, and third-party Java 2 Enterprise Edition (J2EE) 1.3 compliant applications. The SAP Web AS brings together the benefits of a proven, scalable and reliable infrastructure with the interoperability and flexibility of Web Service infrastructure. SAP Web

AS supports the proven ABAP technology and the open source Internet-driven technologies—Java and J2EE—offering best-in-class, comprehensive security solutions that protect data and ensure the confidentiality of business transactions.

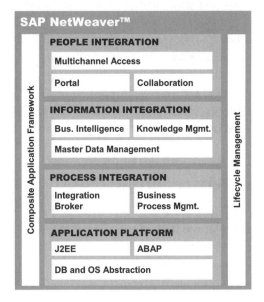

SAP Web Application Server

- J2EE 1.3-compliant Java server and ABAP server side by side
- Zero Footprint UI (Browser)
- Model driven UI, patterns
- Highly scalable and reliable advanced caching
- OS and DB abstraction layer

Support for
Adaptive Computing
Infrastructure

Figure 4.27 The SAP Web Application Server

One of the key differentiators of the SAP Web AS is that it contains both an ABAP personality and a Java personality. These are often referred to as the ABAP stack and the Java (or J2EE2) stack; or the ABAP Engine and the J2EE Engine. Both the ABAP stack and the Java stack exist in a single, unified system. This has many advantages. First, a customer's existing investment in software and skills is preserved. For example, the users, developers, and administrators will all be familiar with the ABAP stack. There are certainly new features and enhancements, but this happens with every release. To begin using the SAP Web AS (and components based on it), users won't have to be completely retrained; they'll just have to understand the deltas from their prior release. But now, they will have business-strength access to the Java Engine. The SAP Web AS also embraces native web technologies while providing all the benefits of SAP's knowledge and experience through an evolutionary, standards-based approach. With the SAP Web AS, SAP delivers a homogeneous infrastructure for Java-based and ABAP-based applications. All existing business objects and interfaces can be used with both the Java environment and the ABAP environment. This approach gives companies a single infrastructure that leverages both environments. This helps to reduce deployment costs since a separate web server is now no longer necessary to begin web enabling business processes. The customer is also not forced to begin using Java until he or she is ready. This allows customers to get training in Java at their own pace, be it aggressively or conservatively. Furthermore, all of the application server benefits that SAP applications are recognized for in the ABAP world are now being ushered into the Java world by SAP: reliability standards such as high availability, scalability, and security, and benefits that help lower TCO such as software lifecycle management, simple design, deployment strategies, and ease of administration. Finally, SAP supports openness by offering DB/OS platform independence for Java applications, support of Web services and participation in open Java standards.

4.5   ESA—Enterprise Services Architecture

Enterprise Services Architecture (ESA) is the SAP blueprint for service-based, enterprise-scale business solutions that offer the increased adaptability, flexibility, and openness needed to reduce total cost of ownership. ESA combines SAP experience in enterprise applications with the flexibility of Web services and other open standards. New applications can be created on top of existing enterprise applications and are served by Enterprise Services Architecture to increase the value of current systems and automate new processes (see Figure 4.28).

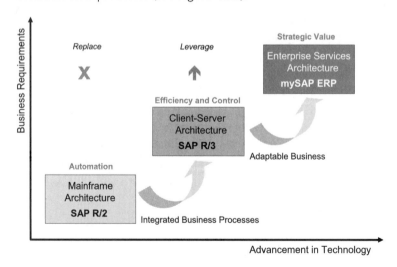

Figure 4.28 Evolution of Enterprise Services Architecture

ESA goes beyond traditional Enterprise Application Integration (EAI) to provide a unified set of business processes and information that supports the increased agility required by the rapid pace of business and technological change. Organizations can determine the speed at which innovations are created and adopted, make outsourcing more manageable, extend business processes to include partners, and offer products to new customers in a more seamless way.

4.5.1 EAI Provides Only a Partial Answer

For IT organizations to enable business change, they must find a cost-effective blueprint to evolve existing architectures towards greater flexibility across heterogeneous landscapes. In the mid-1990s, these constraints gave rise to EAI, which attempted to stitch together business scenarios using specific application-to-application (A2A) interfaces designed for performance and reliability. But EAI has not produced an integration architecture that is cost-effective in the long run, and it has proven to have its own problems. More recently, Web services have held out great promise, but their true power remains to be tapped.

While EAI tools can successfully link individual applications, they require that programmers understand in detail how each of the applications linked together work internally to create a tightly coupled integration. Programmers then have to maintain these links over the useful life of the applications. Creating and maintaining these hardwired links is expensive and resource intensive. Every process change triggers expensive and complex programming and testing.

Furthermore, reusing functionality developed in these distributed environments becomes very difficult. All too often EAI becomes a high-cost path, with companies spending five times as much in services and support as they do on EAI tools. This complexity and cost stands in the way of "IT enabling" business change.

Any answer to the challenges of enabling flexible processes spanning heterogeneous landscapes must emphasize long-term adaptability and cost reduction. Furthermore, it must leverage the same infrastructure, whether the integration methods are between applications within a department, across enterprise boundaries, or some combination of the above.

4.5.2 Web Services Begin to Address IT Challenges

Addressing Issues of Heterogeneity and Reuse

A Web service represents a self-contained, self-describing piece of application functionality that can be found and accessed by other applications using open standards. A Web service is self-contained, because the application using the Web service does not have to depend on anything other than the service itself. A Web service is self-describing, because all the information on how to use the service can be obtained from the service itself. The descriptions are centrally stored and accessible—through mechanisms that are based on Web standards—to all applications that would like to invoke the service. In summary, Web services answer the need for a standardized and vendor-agnostic way to cope with heterogeneity and to create interoperability and compatibility among various applications.

Instead of requiring programmers to establish and maintain links between applications, Web services are loosely coupled, making connections simpler and more flexible and allowing application architects to more easily find and understand services offered by other cooperative applications. Applications can access a Web service across a network using mechanisms based on Web standards.

Web services provide a standards-based way for an application to expose granular functionality such as "delete order," which would remove an order from one particular system. To do this, Web services use highly standardized interfaces to hide how the underlying functionality is implemented. In this way, Web services begin to answer the following challenges faced by IT organizations:

▶ Heterogeneity

The ability to communicate with other applications using standards-based mechanisms simplifies connectivity across heterogeneous landscapes. Web services can easily be used by applications that require them, as standardized catalogs of services are developed. Similarly, the abstraction of functionality provided by Web services is very useful in heterogeneous environments, because it conceals the differences between systems on a technical level. Since Web services hide implementation details of the underlying applications, a developer "using" Web services to build a new solution needs no prerequisite knowledge of the structure of the applications that deliver the service. Moreover, the developer can rest assured that his or her solution using the Web service will not be impacted if the underlying applications change.

▶ **Reuse**

Web services also provide preliminary answers to issues regarding flexibility and reuse. Changes can be made in the underlying implementation or in the program calling the Web service, as long as the behavior of the Web service stays the same. This continuity of behavior provides the basis for combining and reusing Web services without creating a spaghetti-like maze of unmanaged complexity.

Enhancement Needed to Support Enterprise Scenarios

Today, Web services are largely being used to expose functionality delivered by single applications. An example could be a Web service to delete an order in one particular system—a task that might be a single step in a larger process.

However, Web services are too granular to be efficient building blocks for enterprise business scenarios. The process of canceling an order illustrates this point. From a business perspective, the directive to cancel an order encompasses several cross-functional and cross-application activities, including sending a confirmation to the customer, removing the order from the production plan, releasing materials allocated to the order, notifying the invoicing department, and changing the order status to "inactive" or deleting it from various systems. Each of these activities may be a Web service offered from different systems. The ability to build a complex end-to-end solution to cancel an order would be a very powerful enterprise-level business service. Clearly, efficiently developing new business solutions that leverage existing applications calls for business-level building blocks that aggregate the benefits of multiple Web services.

4.5.3 Enterprise Services Architecture Extends Web Services Benefits

Realizing this need, SAP has defined Enterprise Services Architecture (ESA). ESA takes Web services standards and services-oriented architecture principles and extends them to meet the needs of enterprise business solutions. It helps IT organizations leverage existing systems to build and deploy flexible solutions that support end-to-end business scenarios across heterogeneous landscapes. ESA addresses the business issue that most companies are facing—extending existing IT assets to support business change and innovation, while lowering total cost of ownership.

What is Enterprise Services Architecture?

Enterprise Services Architecture is SAP's open architecture for adaptive business solutions. The fundamental premise of ESA is the abstraction of business activities or events, modeled as enterprise services, from the actual functionality of enterprise applications. Aggregating Web services into business-level enterprise services provides more meaningful building blocks for automating enterprise-scale business scenarios (see Figure 4.29). Enterprise services allow IT organizations to efficiently develop composite applications, defined as applications that compose functionality and information from existing systems to support new business processes or scenarios. All enterprise services communicate by using Web services standards, can be described in a central repository, and are created and managed by tools provided by SAP NetWeaver. The order-to-cash business scenario illustrates the benefits of Enterprise Services Architecture.

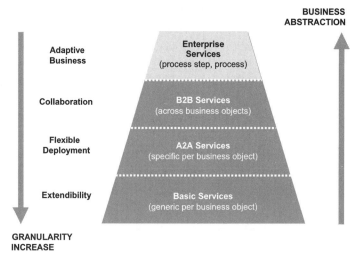

Figure 4.29 Enterprise Services

As Figure 4.30 shows, order-to-cash involves multiple applications—customer-facing applications, such as Customer Relationship Management (CRM), supplier-facing applications, such as Supply Chain Management (SCM), and Enterprise Resource Planning (ERP) systems where the order resides, and where all transactions and fulfillment entities are stored. In the typical order-to-cash scenario, employees act as human integrators, sitting in front of many different applications, transferring information from one to the next by copying and pasting and retyping information, making process-flow decisions as needed. The applications, when they are communicating, are hardwired via brittle connections that are expensive to maintain.

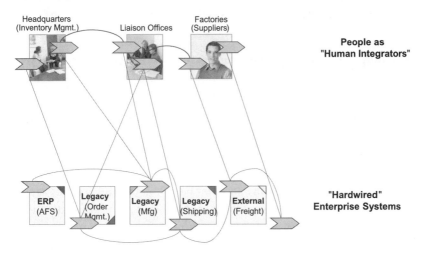

Figure 4.30 Extended Order-to-Cash Process

Order-to-Cash Scenario with Enterprise Services Architecture

With Enterprise Services Architecture, a composite application can use enterprise services to automate the flow of information from application to application. Each user in the business scenario has a role-based interface that provides exactly the information and functionality required to meet their goals. The process is defined, controlled, implemented, and managed at a business level, with SAP NetWeaver providing the environment to construct enterprise services to control the flow of information from one enterprise application to the next (see Figure 4.31).

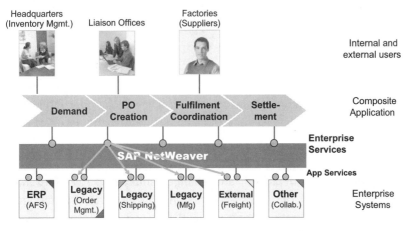

Figure 4.31 Order-to-Cash Scenario with Enterprise Services Architecture

Key Characteristics of Enterprise Services Architecture

The following key characteristics of Enterprise Services Architecture are integral to implementing business scenarios like the order-to-cash scenario:

▶ **Enterprise Services Architecture extends the benefits of Web services** to enterprise business scenarios by aggregating existing systems functionality into business-level enterprise services.

▶ **Enterprise services are modeled from an "outside-in" perspective.** While the core set of enterprise services identified by a company may be substantially enabled by legacy or enterprise applications (including those from SAP), they are not defined or constrained by SAP, or any other vendor's applications. In other words, Enterprise Services Architecture defines or models services "outside-in" for any application that is based on business events relevant to enterprise business processes, not necessarily on an existing application or implementation. SAP will evolve its applications to support enterprise services that are designed for each business domain or industry that it currently addresses.

▶ **Enterprise Services Architecture offers a blueprint for enterprise-wide business process evolution with complete investment protection.** Enterprise Services Architecture is a blueprint for a customer's entire IT landscape, as well as an application architecture for SAP. Leveraging its breadth and depth of industry knowledge, SAP is defining an inventory of enterprise services that promote reuse of functionality across SAP solutions and third-party solutions. SAP expects that customers will independently select a core set of enterprise services needed to support their key business scenarios. They will then match these with enterprise services available from SAP, develop custom enterprise services where needed, and build flexible business solutions by leveraging existing IT systems.

▶ **Enabled by SAP NetWeaver, Enterprise Services Architecture offers a gradual path to flexible, service-centric system landscapes.** Enterprise Services Architecture allows for a gradual and nondisruptive transition of existing applications and architecture to higher levels of flexibility and value.

▶ **Enterprise Services Architecture allows new business processes to be developed, deployed, and changed independently of existing applications.** "Consumers" of enterprise services are isolated from changes in applications that "provide" the service. Enterprise Services Architecture leverages an abstraction layer between the way an enterprise service is used, and the way the corresponding functionality is implemented within an enterprise application. This abstraction allows composite applications or custom user interfaces using the service, or its so-called "consumers," to be decoupled from the applications "providing" the service. As a result of the decoupling, IT can leverage the rich functionality and best practices of enterprise applications to support new, innovative business solutions, and still grow these solutions independently of changes in the underlying applications.

4.5.4 Enabling Enterprise Services Architecture with SAP NetWeaver

SAP has designed SAP NetWeaver to support the integration and application platform needs of enterprise architectures, while enabling standards-based interoperability with other platforms that may be part of the landscape. SAP NetWeaver enables the *development*, *deployment*, and *administration* of enterprise services. SAP NetWeaver can help customers "service-enable" their system landscapes by supporting communication based on Web services standards. With SAP NetWeaver, customers can leverage services that are part of enterprise suites like mySAP Business Suite, as well as create custom services as needed.

In addition to providing tools for creating and managing enterprise services, SAP NetWeaver also supports the design, implementation, and execution of applications that use those services, like composite applications and custom UIs. SAP has developed a framework for quick and easy assembly of composite applications in a repeatable fashion. SAP NetWeaver provides a unified application development platform that contains the tools, methodologies, rules, user interface patterns, and services that allow SAP, its partners, and customers to build composite applications, either as products for sale or custom applications for use by one company.

4.5.5 What Enterprise Services Architecture Means for Customers

With Enterprise Services Architecture, the traditional challenges of system landscapes no longer stand in the way of IT support for business initiatives. Enabled by SAP NetWeaver, Enterprise Services Architecture helps customers manage heterogeneity of systems landscapes. This allows the underlying application components that supply the functionality represented by the enterprise service to be altered, without impacting applications "using" the service. Furthermore, Enterprise Services Architecture enables customers to see their existing systems not merely as powerful business engines for today, but also as the building blocks of future business processes.

Enterprise Services Architecture intrinsically supports an incremental development process. Its use of abstraction makes it relatively easy to combine and recombine functionality from different applications as needed, and without having to pull solutions apart and start over. This quality is mirrored in SAP NetWeaver, which supports an upgrade path that begins with a portal interface for Web services, and leads to an evolving array of services and composite applications of ever-greater complexity and scope.

Whether called upon to free up capital by reducing TCO, enable business change, or support innovation, IT organizations can now leverage and extend IT assets to reach these goals.

5 Transition and Upgrade to mySAP ERP

To increase the business value of existing ERP landscapes and to benefit from the offered scenarios, customers must answer at least three questions before they can entertain using an Enterprise Services Architecture: "Which contract do I need to license?" "Which release level should I use?" and "Which components do I install?" This chapter provides valuable insight into the most important criteria that can help you make that decision.

After highlighting the enhanced business benefits of mySAP ERP and looking at the underlying technology, customers may ask, what should they consider when they think about making a transition to mySAP ERP. In general, there are three important perspectives that must be considered: the license view, the upgrade view, and the implementation view. Based on the current situation, one, two, or all of these perspectives are important to a customer.

An evolution, not a revolution

As we already described earlier in this book, a move to mySAP ERP is an evolutionary step and not a disruptive one, like the move from mainframe to client-server. From the first release of mySAP ERP, SAP offered an Enterprise Resource Planning (ERP) solution that provides all the pieces required to support a state-of-the-art ERP business: technical capabilities like the Portal Infrastructure, Exchange Infrastructure (SAP XI), and Business Information Warehouse (SAP BW), as well as applications and functions for additional business value, such as Strategic Enterprise Management (SAP SEM), Employee Self Services (ESS) and Manager Self Services (MSS), and more.

From a technical point of view, mySAP ERP offers a very different approach compared to what customers may remember from early SAP R/3 installations—this point is key to the reason for the transition to mySAP ERP. This time, it is not about implementing all the technology and functionality in one single installation. Rather, mySAP ERP has been designed to take an incremental approach. It includes SAP components that can be deployed step-by-step, at the customer's own pace, to utilize mySAP ERP, and to widen the functional scope of clients' operational and strategic business processes while leveraging existing assets. SAP Business

Deploy as you go

Information Warehouse (SAP BW), along with analytics from SAP SEM or SAP Enterprise Portal (SAP EP), is just one example of what customers can get when they move to mySAP ERP.

Consequently, when it comes to upgrades and implementation, customers don't have to install all of the components at once. In many cases, in fact, this process may not require them to immediately upgrade their current SAP R/3 instance. It really comes down to looking at the current needs from three different perspectives—licensing, upgrades, and implementation—to determine where customers will gain the highest business value from mySAP ERP.

5.1   Dimensions to Know

Three important dimensions

mySAP ERP is a mySAP solution that can be licensed by existing and new customers. Once you have a mySAP ERP (or mySAP Business Suite) license, you can consider your upgrade or implementation options (see Figure 5.1). For all companies, these next two steps—the upgrade of their current SAP R/3 installation and the implementation of other mySAP ERP components—can follow a flexible timeline based on the company's particular set of business objectives. SAP is committed to support clients in finding the best path forward for their company.

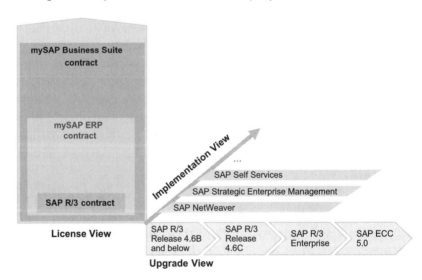

Figure 5.1 Dimensions to Know

5.1.1 License View

Which contract do I need to license?

Customers currently on an SAP R/3 contract can choose to move either to a mySAP ERP license or a mySAP Business Suite license, which includes mySAP ERP along with mySAP Supply Chain Management (mySAP SCM), mySAP Customer Relationship Management (mySAP CRM), and so on.[1] The decision to license mySAP ERP or mySAP Business Suite is customer-specific and relates to the individual business needs and requirements. Section 2.1 has already emphasized that mySAP ERP is a part of mySAP Business Suite. Figure 5.2 shows the functional differences between these two SAP solutions. These differences are mainly based on the areas of Customer Relationship Management (CRM), Supply Chain Management (SCM), and Supplier Relationship Management (SRM) where mySAP ERP focuses on execution capabilities; planning capabilities, however, are covered by mySAP Business Suite.

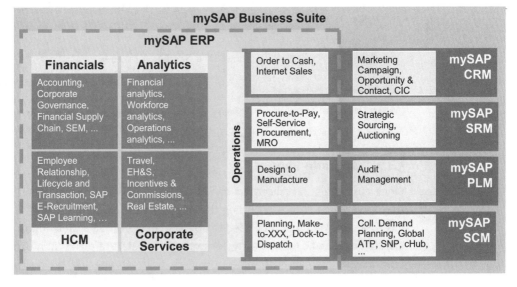

Figure 5.2 mySAP ERP versus mySAP Business Suite

Why should customers update their license? For SAP customers, irrespective of which SAP R/3 release they have in productive use, the move to mySAP ERP is recommended so that they can leverage the full SAP NetWeaver integration and application platform, enhanced applications, and new planning and analytical capabilities in their ERP environment. In addition, these customers will receive a conversion credit for their previ-

---

1 For customers already on a mySAP Business Suite license, no further licensing conversions are required.

ous investments. Figure 5.3 distinguishes these capabilities by showing the Bill of Materials (BOM) for mySAP ERP 2004. This particular BOM contains the shipment package of mySAP ERP 2004. As cited in Figure 5.3, an additional pricing may apply to different areas.

ABAP Components:
- ECC 5.0 (incl. ECC Core, Extension Set, PI, PI_BASIS, and ST-PI)
- FINBASIS 3.0
- E-Recruiting 3.0
- SEM-BW 4.0
- SRM Server 5.0
- Learning Solution 3.0 (Frontend)
- Catalog Content Management 1.0 (SAP Catalog)
- cProject Suite 3.1
- WFM Core 1.10_640

Java Components:
- Self Services 5.0 (XSS incl. ESS and MSS)
- Biller Direct 3.0
- Internet Sales (ISA) 4.0
- Learning Solution 3.0 (Content Player)
- IPC 4.0 (for ISA and for SRM)

Mobile Components:
- Mobile Time and Travel 1.6
- Mobile Sales for HH 2.0
- Mobile Direct Store Delivery 2.0
- Mobile Asset Management 2.5

SAP NetWeaver:
- Web AS 6.40 (ABAP, Java, integrated ITS, IGS)
- BI 3.5 (ABAP and Java Integration Functionality)
- Exchange Infrastructure (XI) 3.0
- Mobile Infrastructure 2.5
- Enterprise Portal 6.0 (incl. Portal Platform, Content Management and Collaboration)
- TREX 6.1

Frontend Components:
- SAPGUI
- BW, KW Frontend Components
- Learning Solution 3.0 (Offline Player, Authoring Environment)

Further Components:
- BI Content 3.52
- Business Packages for EP 6.0 (Portal Content) for selected processes
- XI Content for selected processes
- Business Connector
- Solution Manager 3.10

(Additional pricing may apply to different areas)

Figure 5.3 mySAP ERP 2004 — Bill of Materials

5.1.2 Upgrade View

Which release level should I go for? Once customers have licensed mySAP ERP (or mySAP Business Suite), they have some choice regarding the upgrade of their current SAP R/3 environment. Whether they need to upgrade their SAP R/3 system immediately (for specific functionality, for example), or start to plan that move now, customers can determine how they want to upgrade their systems — that is, whether they want to move to SAP R/3 Enterprise or to the new SAP ERP Central Component (SAP ECC) 5.0 as the technical successor to SAP R/3 in the ERP environment.

Customers must consider that SAP ECC 5.0 and all future releases are only available with a mySAP contract. If customers rely on their existing SAP R/3 license, they can only upgrade to release levels up to SAP R/3 Enterprise.

With an SAP upgrade, each customer faces different strategic and operational challenges. The need for assistance with an upgrade depends on the complexity of the existing SAP solution, the scope of the upgrade project, and the customer's experience with SAP upgrades. We'll take a look at several transition and upgrade services offered by SAP in Section 5.3.

5.1.3 Implementation View

The mySAP ERP architecture allows you to select from among all the components and features delivered by mySAP ERP—for example, SAP SEM, self-services, or the complete SAP NetWeaver technology platform. This freedom to choose which components you want to install allows companies to implement portions of mySAP ERP incrementally, based on their current system environment, and planned IT projects, short- and long-term business needs, as well as where they see the greatest returns to be gained. The transition to mySAP ERP therefore includes the implementation of its various components and capabilities. Here, it becomes clear that mySAP ERP's benefits, functions, and features are not contained in just one single SAP component. For example, while SAP ECC 5.0 is one piece of mySAP ERP 2004 and offers a lot of ERP functionality, a customer might have additional requirements in other areas of mySAP ERP—the Portal Infrastructure, Exchange Infrastructure, or Information Infrastructure—or, in application areas like Internet Sales, Self-Service Procurement, and others. All these features are not part of SAP ECC 5.0, but are available with the mySAP ERP solution, and customers can start by selecting these offerings that bring the greatest immediate benefit. In short, customers can implement their most business-critical mySAP ERP components.

Which components do I install?

5.1.4 Release and Maintenance Strategy with mySAP ERP

In addition to the three different views, licensing, upgrade, and implementation, customers should note the release and maintenance strategy with mySAP ERP. This strategy will determine you are making the right decision, especially when it comes to converting the existing license or upgrading the existing system landscape.

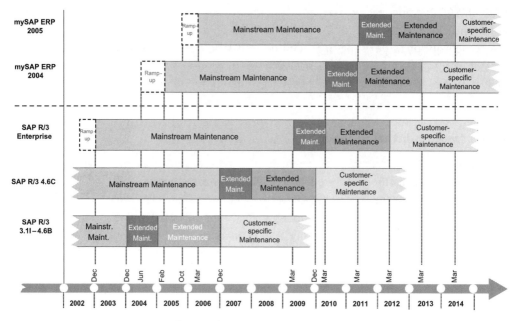

Figure 5.4 Release and Maintenance Strategy with mySAP ERP

<table>
<tr><td>SAP's 5-1-2 strategy</td><td>Now let's take a more detailed look at the release and maintenance strategy with mySAP ERP. SAP's maintenance strategy follows a 5-1-2 principle. This 5-1-2 strategy ensures a consistent maintenance message across the SAP portfolio. It provides SAP's customers with a commitment to long-term, reliable use of their SAP solutions and affords them the flexibility required to identify a suitable path forward.</td></tr>
</table>

What does 5-1-2 mean? The 5-1-2 maintenance strategy defines maintenance phases for a solution edition: Five years of mainstream maintenance at a standard maintenance fee; one year of extended maintenance at the standard maintenance fee, plus an additional 2 %; and two years of extended maintenance at the standard maintenance fee, plus an additional 4 %.

Mainstream maintenance describes the main phase of the Software Component Lifecycle, in which customers fully benefit from all features and commitments from SAP Standard Support.[2]

Maintenance never ends Toward the end of mainstream maintenance, customers have three options:

---

2 See also *www.sap.com/services/support/standard.epx* for detailed information on SAP Standard Support.

▶ **Upgrade**
Typically SAP recommends an upgrade before customers reach the end of the mainstream maintenance phase. The delivery of new releases of the licensed software, as well as upgrade tools, is included in the maintenance contract.[3]

▶ **Extended maintenance**
SAP offers extended maintenance for some releases (at extra cost, but with all the benefits of the mainstream maintenance phase).

▶ **Customer-specific maintenance**
If customers don't opt for an upgrade or for extended maintenance, they enter customer-specific maintenance automatically. During this phase, SAP still provides most of the features of SAP Standard Support, but some restrictions apply.

Mainstream and extended maintenance include all industry Add-ons. If there are several releases of an industry Add-on for the same underlying release, only the latest Add-on release will be supported until the end of mainstream maintenance and during extended maintenance of the underlying release. Mainstream and extended maintenance include legal changes for existing functionality for Human Capital Management (HCM), as well as for financials and logistics for country versions shipped by SAP, and also for industry Add-ons, wherever applicable.

Mainstream and extended maintenance

Toward the end of the mainstream maintenance period for a release, SAP decides whether to offer extended maintenance for this release for an additional maintenance fee. Customers must order extended maintenance for their releases; otherwise, they will automatically enter the customer-specific maintenance mode. Ordering extended maintenance allows customers to continue running their installations since they will receive all of the services and support offerings that are familiar to them from the mainstream maintenance period.

An example: Customers running on SAP R/3 4.6B or releases below should upgrade as soon as possible, because these releases are already out of mainstream maintenance. See Figure 5.4 and Figure 5.5 for a clarification of the release and maintenance strategy with mySAP ERP. As we can see SAP R/3 4.6B or releases below are out of mainstream maintenance since the beginning of 2004. Although customers can decide to extend the maintenance for these releases with an additional mainte-

---

3 Visit the SAP Customer Services Network *(www.sap.com/services/solutionupgrades .epx)* to learn more about the possible transition options and SAP's offerings to efficiently support the upgrade.

nance fee, the recommendation is for them to upgrade these releases as soon as possible.

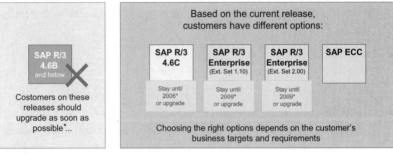

Figure 5.5 Different Upgrade Options

Customer-specific maintenance
SAP follows the motto "support never ends" so that each customer can decide to enter a customer-specific maintenance mode once the mainstream or extended maintenance phase is complete. In that case, customers should note that some restriction will apply to the scope of the maintenance. Within the customer-specific maintenance mode, customers will receive no support packages and legal changes. Besides that, there will be limited technology upgrades and only a customer-specific problem resolution that covers a resolution of problems, for example, only in case of known solutions or workarounds. During customer-specific maintenance, the customer continues to pay the standard maintenance fee. Customer-specific maintenance does not have to be ordered explicitly, but begins automatically.

Continuous improvement through SAP's maintenance
What do customers get for their maintenance fee? SAP products and maintenance are designed for continuous improvement. SAP has provided, and moreover will provide, the next SAP software release—including upgrade software and a migration package for the next SAP software generation within the maintenance contract. In addition, customers can benefit from technology upgrades to keep their end-to-end technology stack up to date, as well as from an existing infrastructure to manage specific customer codes. The SAP maintenance contract is the basis for continuous improvement. Customers will receive best business practices and state-of-the-art technology enabling quality management, problem resolution, and knowledge transfer. As a result, clients can ensure technical robustness, minimize the business impact associated with malfunctions and downtime, and learn from best practices how to manage total cost of ownership and innovation.

The decision when and where to upgrade the existing system landscape—and where to start—is a customer-specific arbitration and depends on the customer's business targets and requirements. In the following section, we'll provide you with some deployment options based on these criteria.

5.2 Customer Scenarios and Deployment Options

In this section, we'll look at the different scenarios that customers might encounter. A transition path for a customer depends mainly on two dimensions—the current release level and the current license contract—both influenced by the decision regarding which additional components a customer wants to benefit from most and therefore must implement.

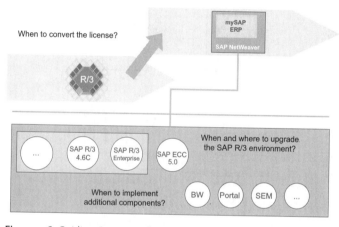

Figure 5.6 Guiding Questions for a Transition to mySAP ERP

The following scenarios are based on different as-is states. Given these scenarios, there will be distinct business situations followed by specific transition recommendations or paths. By following these paths, customers can derive specific value out of the solution, for example if a customer needs specific analytic capabilities, he or she can implement BW. However, you must keep in mind that an upgrade to SAP ECC 5.0 is possible only if customers already have a mySAP solution license. To represent all possible scenarios, Figure 5.7 illustrates the potential as-is state and the possible and recommended transition paths. The columns in each scenario describe the current release level of a customer, whereas the rows reflect the current contract type. The possible transition paths are identified with an arrow. At the end of the transition, there are statuses to which customers can plan to transition. These statuses and the appropriate transition paths will be described for each scenario.

Different options lead to the same place

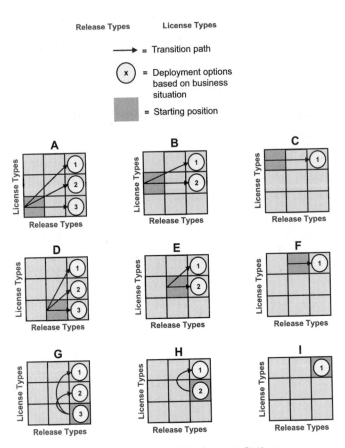

Figure 5.7 Customer Scenarios and Deployment Options

Customer Scenario A

SAP R/3
License/Imple-
mentation of
Release 4.6B
or below The first scenario comprises customers who are currently on a SAP R/3 contract and run a SAP R/3 4.6B release or below. As was mentioned before, we recommend that customers upgrade these releases as soon as possible since mainstream maintenance has already ended. In addition, by looking at the business requirements, we can point out three diverse business situations:

▶ Customers require capabilities beyond ERP

In that situation, it would be advisable to upgrade to SAP R/3 Enterprise or SAP ECC 5.0 and convert the license to mySAP Business Suite. By upgrading the release level and converting the license, clients now have the full value of the latest releases and the full value of the mySAP Business Suite scope. In addition, there will be a continued maintenance for the implemented release level.

- Business requires deeper and broader ERP functionality or customer wants to deploy long-term SAP strategy incrementally, starting with mySAP ERP, and then moving to mySAP Business Suite

  Here SAP also suggests an upgrade to SAP R/3 Enterprise or SAP ECC 5.0. The license should be converted to mySAP ERP. Besides the upgrade values mentioned in the first point, clients would benefit from the full value of mySAP ERP in this case.

- Business wants to continue to leverage SAP R/3; no short-term plans to extend further

  Through an upgrade to the latest SAP R/3 release, SAP R/3 Enterprise, customers ensure a continued maintenance.

Customer Scenario B

This scenario is based on the assumption that although customers still run on SAP R/3 4.6B or below, they have already converted their license to mySAP ERP. This scenario constitutes two main business situations:

mySAP ERP License/Implementation of Release 4.6B or below

- Business requires capabilities beyond ERP

  This situation mirrors the first point in customer scenario A. Once again, customers have to upgrade to SAP R/3 Enterprise or SAP ECC 5.0 and convert their license to mySAP Business Suite. The value of that transition was mentioned before.

- Business requires deeper and broader ERP functionality

  Besides the full value of the existing mySAP ERP, contract customers should upgrade to SAP R/3 Enterprise or SAP ECC 5.0 to get the most value out of the latest technical releases.

Customer Scenario C

Scenario C once again assumes a release level of SAP R/3 4.6B or below, but the current contract type is mySAP Business Suite.

mySAP Business Suite License/Implementation of Release 4.6B or below

- Business requires deeper and broader ERP functionality

  Since customers already have the full value of mySAP Business Suite, they should expand their ERP capabilities through upgrading to SAP R/3 Enterprise or SAP ECC 5.0.

Customer Scenario D

This scenario shows those customers who are currently on a SAP R/3 contract and on a SAP R/3 4.6C Release. As described in the previous chapter, customers in this scenario benefit from a longer mainstream mainte-

SAP R/3 License/Implementation of Release 4.6C

nance than do the clients in scenarios A through C. The business situations can look like the following:

▶ Business requires capabilities beyond ERP

In this case, customers can decide either to stay on their current SAP 4.6C Release—since this is still under mainstream maintenance until the end of 2006—or upgrade to SAP R/3 Enterprise or SAP ECC 5.0 to ensure a longer mainstream maintenance, and benefit from the full value of the latest releases. To get capabilities beyond ERP they nevertheless have to convert their license to mySAP Business Suite.

▶ Business requires deeper and broader ERP functionality, or customer wants to deploy long-term SAP strategy incrementally, starting with mySAP ERP, then moving to mySAP Business Suite

Once again, customers can either decide to stay on the current release or upgrade to SAP R/3 Enterprise or SAP ECC 5.0. We've already mentioned the benefits of an upgrade. To follow a long-term SAP strategy and to deepen the ERP functionality, clients must convert their license to mySAP ERP.

▶ Business wants to continue to leverage SAP R/3; no short-term plans to extend further

Here customers can stay on their current release, or upgrade to SAP R/3 Enterprise or SAP ECC 5.0 if they want to leverage the full value of these releases.

Customer Scenario E

mySAP ERP License/Implementation of Release 4.6C

Scenario E describes customers who are currently running on a SAP R/3 4.6C Release and already profit from the value of a mySAP ERP contract. As with scenario B, here, too, we can identify two possible deployment options based on different business situations:

▶ Business requires capabilities beyond ERP

Besides the recommendation to convert the license to mySAP Business Suite, customers could decide to stay on their current release or to upgrade to SAP R/3 Enterprise or SAP ECC 5.0. This depends once again on the ERP functionality required and is therefore a customer-individual decision. Through the conversion to mySAP Business Suite, customers can now benefit from the full value of this solution and, if they decide to upgrade their release level, they can also benefit from the full value of SAP R/3 Enterprise or SAP ECC 5.0 and a continuous and longer maintenance for these releases.

- Business requires deeper and broader ERP functionality

  Once again, the requirement of deeper and broader ERP functionality can be solved by an upgrade to SAP R/3 Enterprise or SAP ECC 5.0.

Customer Scenario F

This scenario compares customers on SAP R/3 4.6C and a mySAP Business Suite contract. Because these customers already have the maximum solution set from a license point of view, there is only one business situation that they can employ to leverage their IT landscape.

mySAP Business Suite License/ Implementation of Release 4.6C

- Business requires additional capabilities

  Through an upgrade to SAP R/3 Enterprise or SAP ECC 5.0, customers can get a higher value out of their existing mySAP Business Suite license. From a maintenance point of view, they could also stay on their current release level since mainstream maintenance for SAP R/3 4.6C is still ongoing.

Customer Scenario G

Clients, who are in this situation, are already on the latest release level that is available with a SAP R/3 contract, SAP R/3 Enterprise. Therefore, this situation differs from the upcoming scenarios (H through I) that demonstrate business situations for customers who might already be running SAP ECC 5.0. As already mentioned, the use of SAP ECC 5.0 is possible only if customers have a licensed mySAP contract.

SAP R/3 License/Implementation of Release 4.7

- Business requires capabilities beyond ERP

  In addition to a license conversion to mySAP Business Suite, customers can consider an upgrade to SAP ECC 5.0 (if they convert their license to a mySAP solution).

- Business requires deeper and broader ERP functionality or customer wants to deploy long-term SAP strategy incrementally starting with mySAP ERP, then moving to mySAP Business Suite

  In this case, clients thinking about an additional upgrade to SAP ECC 5.0 should convert their license to mySAP ERP. By doing this conversion, they can leverage the full value of the mySAP ERP offering.

- Business wants to continue to leverage SAP R/3; no short-term plans to extend further

  Since SAP R/3 Enterprise is still under mainstream maintenance until 2009, customers can freeze additional IT investments in this business situation.

Customer Scenario H

This scenario targets customers who already have a mySAP ERP contract and are using a SAP R/3 Enterprise or SAP ECC 5.0 release type. If customers have SAP R/3 Enterprise, they can, once again, consider an upgrade to SAP ECC 5.0; however, this is a customer-individual decision based on the specific needs and business processes that should be solved and supported (this is valid for all business situations in scenarios H through I):

▶ Business requires capabilities beyond ERP

Once again, we recommend that you convert to mySAP Business Suite to have the full value of this solution set.

▶ Business requires deeper and broader ERP functionality

If customers are already using SAP ECC 5.0, there is no action required; otherwise, clients can consider an upgrade to that release.

Customer Scenario I

The last scenario depicts the "final transition stage" that any customer undergoes. Holding a mySAP Business Suite license and running on SAP R/3 Enterprise or SAP ECC 5.0 allows only one more business situation:

▶ Business requires additional capabilities

Of course, customers on SAP R/3 Enterprise can upgrade to SAP ECC 5.0. In addition, customers can leverage value by implementing additional capabilities that are part of the license agreement.

The scenarios A through I describe situations where customers gain value via upgrading their IT environment and licensing the right product. These value enhancements can be further intensified by using the right strategy when implementing additional capabilities and components.

The following examples provide you with more ideas of what kind of options—in which particular business situations—can be considered to be valid. There is no "one size fits all" recommendation. Each option solves different business pain points and can act as the most valuable path for a specific customer. Customers should consider that some release levels mentioned are only available with a specific license type as already discussed in this chapter. SAP ECC, for example, is only available within a mySAP solution contract; SAP BW 3.5 is only available with mySAP ERP, mySAP Business Suite, and/or SAP NetWeaver. The type of license, however, is not relevant in the following examples. Instead, the focus should be on the different upgrade and implementation options and the resulting implications for each customer. You should note that these options are only examples for an entire range of customer-specific options that are available.

Figure 5.8 shows the options of a customer who is currently only running SAP R/3 4.6C. This scenario is based on the hypothesis that the customer wants to benefit from Business Information Warehouse (BW) capabilities provided by mySAP ERP.

Example: Implementation of Release SAP R/3 4.6C

In this case, we'll discuss three options. Option A symbolizes a more conservative approach. This option mirrors the strategy mentioned in previous business situations—business wants to continue to leverage SAP R/3; no short-term plans to extend further. In this situation, the client should implement SAP BW 3.5 in parallel and stay on the current SAP R/3 4.6C Release. Besides the immediate start of the SAP BW 3.5 implementation, the customer has no additional costs by upgrading the SAP R/3 environment. Nevertheless, if the customer wants to benefit from mainstream maintenance, an upgrade of SAP R/3 4.6C is still required by the end of 2006.

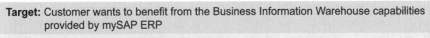

Target: Customer wants to benefit from the Business Information Warehouse capabilities provided by mySAP ERP

Today: Customer operates SAP R/3 4.6C only

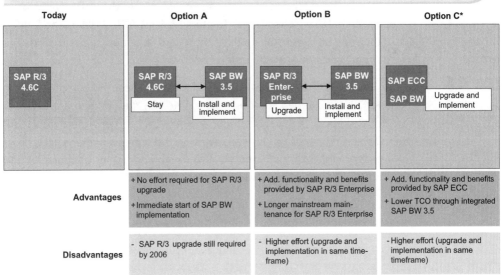

Figure 5.8 Example of a Deployment Option—Customer on SAP R/3 4.6C

In Option B, the customer upgrades the environment to SAP R/3 Enterprise and, concurrently, installs SAP BW 3.5. By doing so, the customer can benefit from the additional value of this release level and thereby ensure a longer mainstream maintenance. The most apparent disadvantage of this option is the effort required to perform an upgrade and an implementation at the same time.

This disadvantage also holds true for Option C, where an upgrade to SAP ECC 5.0 and an implementation of an integrated SAP BW 3.5 occur simultaneously. By running SAP ECC 5.0 and SAP BW 3.5 on the same instance, the customer can lower TCO while leveraging value via SAP ECC 5.0 capabilities.

Example: Implementation of Release SAP R/3 4.0B and SAP BW 3.0B

Another example is shown in Figure 5.9. Here we have a customer currently using SAP R/3 4.0B and SAP BW 3.0B. The options resulting from this scenario are exemplary for customers running on SAP R/3 4.6B or for earlier releases and older components, like SAP BW 3.0B. This example assumes that the customer wants to benefit from Business Information Warehouse capabilities provided by mySAP ERP.

In Option A, the customer decides to upgrade the existing SAP R/3 environment to SAP R/3 Enterprise, but, simultaneously, stay on the older SAP BW 3.0B Release. The customer should consider that SAP BW 3.0B—similar to SAP R/3 4.0B—is already out of mainstream maintenance, and therefore, the extended maintenance phase causes the customer to incur an additional maintenance fee. The functionality in SAP BW is also limited to this release level. Of course, the client can now benefit from the extended value of SAP R/3 Enterprise.

Option B assumes that the customer has already licensed one of the mentioned and presumed solutions so that he can now implement SAP BW 3.5. In addition, the customer upgrades the SAP R/3 environment to SAP ECC 5.0. Compared to Option A, Option B requires a higher effort; however, it provides an increased value through additional functionality and an ensured longer mainstream maintenance period.

In Option C, the customer implements SAP ECC 5.0 and SAP BW in an integrated form to reduce TCO. Compared to Option B, Option C ensures a lower TCO and more functionality via upgrading to the latest available release.

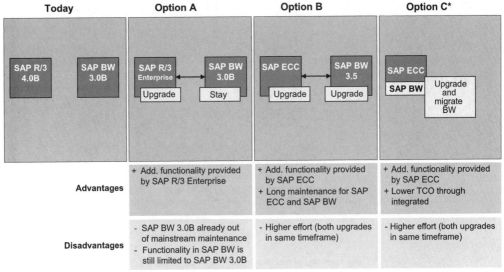

Target: Customer wants to benefit from the Business Information Warehouse capabilities provided by mySAP ERP

Today: Customer operates SAP R/3 4.0B and SAP BW 3.0B

	Today	Option A	Option B	Option C*
Advantages		+ Add. functionality provided by SAP R/3 Enterprise	+ Add. functionality provided by SAP ECC + Long maintenance for SAP ECC and SAP BW	+ Add. functionality provided by SAP ECC + Lower TCO through integrated
Disadvantages		- SAP BW 3.0B already out of mainstream maintenance - Functionality in SAP BW is still limited to SAP BW 3.0B	- Higher effort (both upgrades in same timeframe)	- Higher effort (both upgrades in same timeframe)

* These are examples only. More options might be available to the individual customer.

Figure 5.9 Example of a Deployment Option—Customer on SAP R/3 4.0B and SAP BW 3.0B

A similar example is described in Figure 5.10. Again, the customer faces the situation whereby the existing SAP R/3 environment is already out of mainstream maintenance. Instead of a SAP BW system, the customer has a SAP Internet Transaction Server (ITS)[4] in place. The customer needs both Business Warehouse capabilities and Self-Services provided by mySAP ERP. First, the customer should upgrade the existing SAP R/3 environment to SAP R/3 Enterprise or SAP ECC 5.0.

Example: Implementation of Release SAP R/3 3.1I and SAP ITS

Option A assumes that the customer upgrades to SAP R/3 Enterprise. In addition, he implements a SAP BW 3.5 and maybe upgrades the SAP ITS environment. Throughout this project, the customer ensures a longer mainstream maintenance for the SAP R/3 and SAP BW releases. In addition, the client benefits from enhanced functionality provided by SAP R/3 Enterprise. Since the customer now has a broader implementation scope, the TCO of the existing system landscape can increase.

---

4 The SAP Internet Transaction Server converts SAP screens into HTML format making it possible to access SAP systems with user-friendly Web technology.

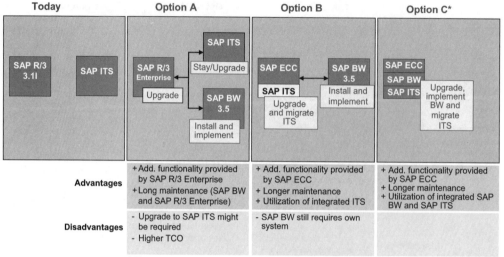

Target: Customer wants to benefit from the Self Services and the Business Information Warehouse capabilities provided by mySAP ERP

Today: Customer operates SAP R/3 3.1I and SAP ITS

Today	Option A	Option B	Option C*
	Advantages	+ Add. functionality provided by SAP R/3 Enterprise + Long maintenance (SAP BW and SAP R/3 Enterprise)	+ Add. functionality provided by SAP ECC + Longer maintenance + Utilization of integrated ITS	+ Add. functionality provided by SAP ECC + Longer maintenance + Utilization of integrated SAP BW and SAP ITS
	Disadvantages	- Upgrade to SAP ITS might be required - Higher TCO	- SAP BW still requires own system	

* These are examples only. More options might be available to the individual customer.

Figure 5.10 Example of a Deployment Option—Customer on SAP R/3 3.1I and SAP ITS

Another option, Option B, depicts an integrated SAP ITS. Although the SAP BW system still requires its own system, the customer can now use an integrated SAP ITS.

Lastly, Option C shows an integrated SAP BW and an integrated SAP ITS. The advantages of this situation have been described before.

Example: Implementation of SAP R/3 4.7, SAP ITS and SAP BW 3.5 A more complex example is characterized in Figure 5.11. The customer currently operates SAP R/3 Enterprise, SAP ITS, and SAP BW 3.5. In addition, the client has a third-party system in place. The customer requires Self Services, Business Information Warehouse, portal, and integration capabilities provided by mySAP ERP.

Option A shows a situation whereby SAP Exchange Infrastructure (XI) and SAP Enterprise Portal (EP) are implemented. The integration of the existing systems can now be handled via the implemented SAP XI, whereas a user-centric environment can be installed via SAP EP. The one disadvantage here is the inflated size of the system landscape.

If the customer decides to upgrade to SAP ECC 5.0 and to go for an integrated ITS, he can also implement an integration platform and a user-centric environment as shown in Option B.

Compared to Option B, Option C originates from an integrated SAP BW. The advantage here, compared to Option B, is a system reduction through a higher integration of SAP BW and SAP ITS.

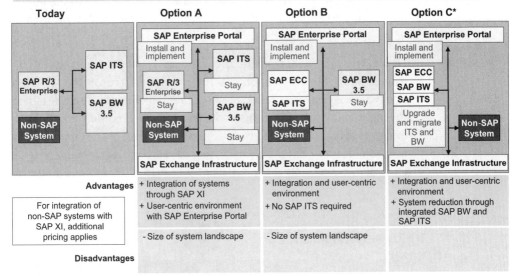

Target: Customer wants to benefit from Self Services, Business Information Warehouse, portal, and integration capabilities provided by mySAP ERP

Today: Customer operates SAP R/3 Enterprise, SAP ITS and SAP BW 3.5

* These are examples only. More options might be possible to the individual customer.

Figure 5.11 Example of a Deployment Option—Customer on SAP R/3 Enterprise, SAP ITS, and SAP BW 3.5

5.3   Transition and Upgrade Services

Along with a transition and an upgrade, come technical and functional enhancements, which may be one reason—or one motivating factor—for customers to upgrade. Yet, because these two steps are not a daily occurrence, there can be different challenges surrounding a transition and an upgrade respectively. According to the challenges posed by an upgrade, SAP has a broad and flexible portfolio with offerings, along all lines of services—including Active Global Support, SAP Consulting, Education, Custom Development and others—in place. Since SAP has introduced the 5-1-2 maintenance strategy for all solutions that are based on SAP NetWeaver, SAP customers have maximum flexibility in planning their SAP transition.

5.3.1 General Needs and Challenges Surrounding Transition and Upgrade Projects

SAP offers a broad and flexible service portfolio

If we look at actual scenarios, we can see that, on average, a project life-cycle consists of four phases: discovery, evaluation, implementation, and operations. Customers have to align their IT strategy with the SAP release strategy, before they can define their specific transition and upgrade strategy to be implemented in the project plan. When it comes to the implementation and operations of a solution, the goal of a customer is to minimize project costs and risks.

Figure 5.12 represents potential challenges of an SAP upgrade. Challenges during the preparation of an upgrade are listed on the left-hand side, whereas challenges during the execution of an upgrade are listed on the right-hand side. Of course, challenges vary according to the customer-specific situation and the affected target group. For example, a system administrator has problems finding all relevant upgrade notes, while a decision-maker must have sufficient information to approve the budget.

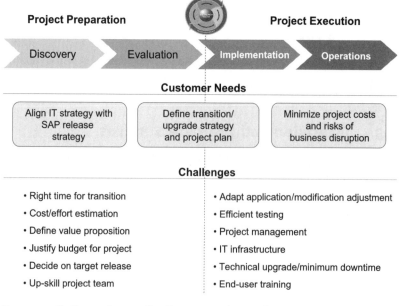

Figure 5.12 Challenges Surrounding Transition and Upgrade Projects

If we take a closer look at the left-hand side of Figure 5.12, there are two aspects that seem to be more critical than the others—the right time for a transition or upgrade and the cost and effort estimation. There are also two main features of an execution of an upgrade—the application and modification adjustment and the testing.[5]

Four phases of transition and upgrade projects

Based on these challenges and because each customer situation is different, depending on the current landscape and the experiences of upgrades, SAP offers a standardized but flexibly adaptable portfolio of upgrade offerings.

5.3.2 SAP Transition and Upgrade Offerings

As illustrated before, customers can face challenges during the preparation and the execution of an upgrade. We'll see how these challenges highlight SAP's Transition and Upgrade Offerings for both phases of an upgrade. Customers should consider that the availability and the pricing of the SAP services might vary depending on regional or local needs.

Preparing a project

If we look at the preparation of an upgrade, we can identify important challenges like the right timing for a transition, the decision for the target release, the cost and effort estimation, the staffing of the project team, and others. To meet these challenges, SAP defined focus areas to facilitate and help customers work through these decisions. Figure 5.13 shows the most relevant challenges in preparing a transition or an upgrade. Customers need strategic advice on a transition to mySAP ERP, and its definition of a value proposition and a business case respectively. Three focus areas, scope, costs and impact, depend on each other. Contingent on the scope, for example, the costs may be higher, and therefore, the impact on the existing solution can vary. Finally, customers have to ensure that the project team has sufficient skills.

Preparing a transition or an upgrade

---

5 Based on SAP Upgrade Survey 2004/2005 (SAP AG) with a total number of participants of 673 (in 2004) and 453 (in 2005) respectively. The survey has been conducted with customers (92 %) as well as with partners (8 %).

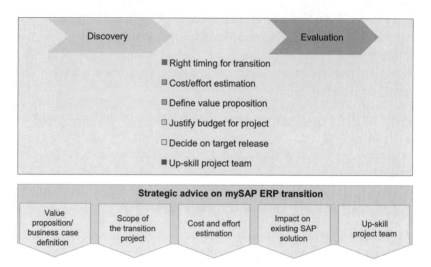

Figure 5.13 Challenges in Preparing a Transition and Upgrade Project

Figure 5.14 and Table 5.1 give an overview of all advanced services necessary to master the key challenges in the preparation of a SAP transition or upgrade. This list of services represents the offerings of all SAP lines of services.

When we take a closer look at the value proposition, we have three services with different scalability. A mySAP ERP Discovery Workshop gives customers a high level insight into mySAP ERP. SAP Accelerated Value Assessment for mySAP ERP provides at least two days of onsite service to analyze the added value of mySAP ERP in specific customer context. An even more customer-specific approach is provided by the SAP Value Assessment, which can determine a detailed value proposition and business case definition for a SAP transition.

As previously mentioned, the next three focus areas are related to each other. SAP Consulting offers specific evaluation workshops, for example, for E-Recruiting. For customers doing business in a global environment, the SAP Globalization Workshop provides information about how SAP software can reflect specific globalization needs. As a trend of today's IT, business-hosting services allow flexible outsourcing, for example.

To ensure the right project team, a SAP Upgrade Methodology Workshop may provide customers with an understanding of SAP standard methodology for an upgrade project.

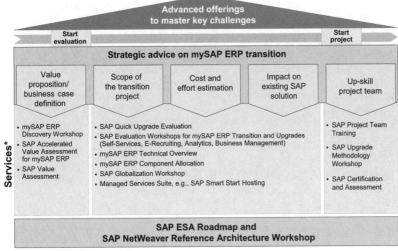

Figure 5.14 SAP Offerings for Preparing a Transition and Upgrade Project

Offering	Target Group	Context of Use (Phase)	Short Description
mySAP ERP Discovery Workshop	CEO; CIO; Project manager	Value proposition and business case definition (Upgrade Evaluation)	One day onsite workshop to understand mySAP ERP proposition: What is the general added value? What are the key mySAP ERP upgrade scenarios?
SAP Accelerated Value Assessment for mySAP ERP	CIO; CFO; Project manager; Process owners	Value proposition and business case definition (Upgrade Evaluation)	At least two days onsite service to analyze the additional value of mySAP ERP in specific customer context.
SAP Value Assessment	IT decision maker; Project manager	Value proposition and business case definition (Upgrade Evaluation)	At least 20 days service to work out the detailed value proposition and business case of a SAP transition.
SAP Quick Upgrade Evaluation	CIO; Project manager	Cost and risk estimation (Upgrade Evaluation)	Two day onsite service with focus on a high-level estimation of costs and effort related to an upgrade project.

Table 5.1 SAP Transition and Upgrade Services for Preparing a Transition or Upgrade Project

Offering	Target Group	Context of Use (Phase)	Short Description
mySAP ERP Evaluation Employee and Manager Self Services; mySAP ERP Evaluation Employee and Manager Self Services Technology Workshop	CIO; CFO; Project manager; Project team leads; SAP Administrators	Project scope and impact on existing SAP solution (Upgrade Evaluation)	One day onsite, knowledge transfer and technical assessment; Two days onsite, solution assessment for selected scenarios.
mySAP ERP Evaluation Analytics (BW) Workshop; mySAP ERP Evaluation Analytics (BW) Workshop Technology (upgrade/installation)	CIO; CFO; Project manager; Project team leads; SAP Administrators	Project scope and impact on existing SAP solution (Upgrade Evaluation)	One day onsite, knowledge transfer and technical assessment; Two days onsite, solution assessment for selected scenarios.
mySAP ERP Evaluation E-Recruiting Workshop; mySAP ERP Evaluation E-Recruiting Technology Workshop	CIO; CFO; Project manager; Project team leads; SAP Administrators	Project scope and impact on existing SAP solution (Upgrade Evaluation)	One day onsite, knowledge transfer and technical assessment; Two days onsite, solution assessment for selected scenarios.
mySAP ERP Evaluation Business Management SEM-BCS (for EC-CS or FI-LC Customers/for SEM-BCS Customers)	CIO; CFO; Project manager; Project team leads; SAP Administrators	Project scope and impact on existing SAP solution (Upgrade Evaluation)	One day onsite, knowledge transfer and technical assessment; Two days onsite, solution assessment for selected scenarios.
mySAP ERP Technical Overview	IT decision maker; Project manager; Project team leads; SAP Administrators	Impact on existing SAP solution (Upgrade Evaluation)	One day onsite service with focus on knowledge transfer for the project team and technical assessment of the specific upgrade situation.
mySAP ERP Component Allocation	CIO; Project manager; Technical project lead	Impact on existing SAP solution (Upgrade Evaluation)	Three days per mySAP ERP instance, designing ideal system landscape of a mySAP ERP solution for a SAP customer.

Table 5.1 SAP Transition and Upgrade Services for Preparing a Transition or Upgrade Project (cont.)

Offering	Target Group	Context of Use (Phase)	Short Description
SAP Globaliza-tion Workshop	IT manager; project manager; System architects	Project scope and impact on exist-ing SAP solution (Upgrade Evalua-tion)	One day onsite work-shop to find out how business can be done on a global scale with SAP solutions, including the benefits about Unicode.
Managed Ser-vices Suite: e.g., SAP Smart Host-ing	CIO; CEO; Project manager	Upgrade Evalua-tion, Implementa-tion, Operations	Holistic and long-term support in managing the system landscape infra-structure.
SAP Project Team Training	Project Manager, Project Team	Up-skilling of the project team (Upgrade Evalua-tion)	Flexible training (e.g., 1–5 day classroom or E-Learn-ing) to ensure appropriate skills and competencies of the project team early in the project.
SAP Upgrade Methodology Workshop	Project manager; Project team leads	Up-skilling of the project team (Upgrade Evalua-tion)	One day onsite service with focus on knowledge transfer on standard upgrade methodology and upgrade tools.
SAP Certification and Assessment	In-house con-sultants; System integration part-ners and end users	Up-skilling of the project team (Upgrade Evalua-tion)	Assessment to ensure qualified staff and mini-mize project risk via stan-dardized measurement of skills and competencies. Duration depending on certification and curricu-lum.
SAP ESA Road-map	CIO; CTO; Pro-cess owners	Upgrade Discov-ery and Evaluation	20 days onsite consulting for an analysis of optimi-zation potential by intro-ducing enterprise archi-tecture services.
SAP NetWeaver Reference Archi-tecture Work-shop	CIO, CTO	Upgrade Discov-ery and Evaluation	At least 10 days consult-ing with recommendation for a transition from today "as is" landscape to target landscape powered by SAP NetWeaver.

Table 5.1 SAP Transition and Upgrade Services for Preparing a Transition or Upgrade Project (cont.)

An upgrade or transition project is driven by the strategic direction of a customer's decision. This decision should be based on SAP's release and product strategy, for example, to an early adapter or follower of an ESA based software. With the ESA Roadmap, SAP can help the customer to define his or her own strategic roadmap—or SAP could help to discover what a reference architecture powered by SAP NetWeaver should look. These two services usually take up to a month.

Executing a Project

Executing a
transition or
an upgrade Once an upgrade project has been started, several challenges could apply. Setting up an efficient testing or the most valuable end-user training are only some examples. Again, in accordance with the challenges identified in Figure 5.15, SAP defined a project and risk management, including focus areas, such as IT infrastructure adjustment, technical deployment, application and modification adjustment, testing, and end-user training, to master potential challenges.

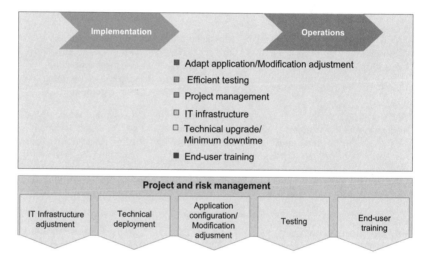

Figure 5.15 Challenges in Executing a Transition and Upgrade Project

Here again, SAP offers a broad variety of tools and services to support customers executing a transition or upgrade project as shown in Figure 5.16 and Table 5.2. Criteria that influence the need for adjusting IT infra-structures depend on the customer's current hardware consumption, for example disk space, and the objective to consolidate SAP systems as part of the upgrade project or switch technology (Unicode). Services such as SAP Data Management, SAP Unicode Workshop, and the SAP Cli-ent/Component Migration Service may help customers in this matter.

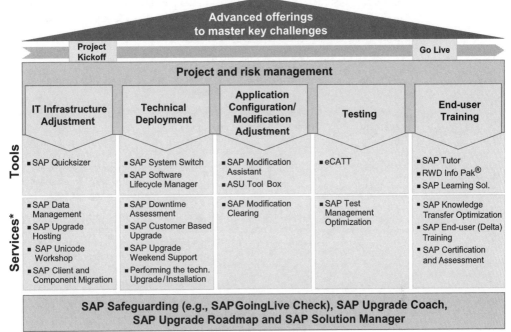

Figure 5.16 SAP Offerings for Executing a Transition and Upgrade Project

The proven System Switch Technology has significantly reduced downtime compared to previous SAP R/3 releases. Because an upgrade within an SAP solution that includes multiple SAP components is preferable, the SAP Lifecycle Manager is the optimal tool to validate the technical design of the upgrade environment. If the standard upgrade tools estimate an unaffordable downtime, the SAP Downtime Assessment and SAP Customer Based Upgrade may help to meet the required downtime window.

A key challenge—and also an objective—in an upgrade project is returning modification into SAP standard. The scalable approach of the SAP Modification Clearing Service allows customers to identify relevant SAP modifications and custom developments in a first step. Analyzing the possibility to return these modifications into SAP standard can help to implement changes in a more expedient and timely manner.

Efficient testing is necessary to minimize required versions and effort and to ensure an accurate go-live afterwards. The SAP Test Management Optimization can identify potential improvements and streamline test procedures.

Several tools such as SAP Tutor, and also flexible end-user training offerings and concepts, are available to ensure a seamless release upgrade for end users.[6]

Offering	Target Group	Context of Use (Phase)	Short Description
SAP Data Management	Technical project team; Process owners	IT infrastructure (Upgrade Implementation)	Usually a five day remote service that helps to minimize database growth prior to the technical upgrade; a service that also helps to establish an archiving concept.
Upgrade Hosting	Project manager; Technical project team	Sizing/IT infrastructure (Upgrade Implementation)	SAP Hosting provides upgrade hosting with a special offer to cover temporary hardware requirements during an upgrade.
SAP Unicode Workshop	Project manager; System Architects; IT Managers	IT infrastructure (Upgrade Implementation)	One day onsite workshop that helps to understand any unicode issues.
SAP Client Migration	CIO; Process Owners; Project manager; Project Lead; Technical Project Lead	IT infrastructure (Upgrade Implementation)	Helps to merge SAP systems to reduce hardware and server landscape.
SAP Component Migration	CIO; Process owner; Project manager; Technical project lead	IT infrastructure (Upgrade Implementation)	Helps to combine separated components in a single target system.
SAP Upgrade Weekend Support	Technical project team; System administrators	Technical Upgrade Procedure (Upgrade Implementation)	A named contact person during the technical upgrade process on a dedicated weekend or holiday.
SAP Downtime Assessment	Technical project team; System administrator	Technical Upgrade Procedure (Upgrade Implementation)	Estimate downtime versus affordable downtime and prepare Onsite Upgrade Support to reduce the downtime caused by the upgrade.

Table 5.2 SAP Transition and Upgrade Services for Executing a Transition or Upgrade Project[6]

---

6 Table 5.1 and Table 5.2 represent only a high-level description of SAP's services offering. More details can be viewed on SAP's Service Marketplace by using the quick links /upgrade-erp and /upgradeservices respectively.

Offering	Target Group	Context of Use (Phase)	Short Description
SAP Customer Based Upgrade (CBU)	Technical project team	Technical Upgrade Procedure (Upgrade Implementation)	A special SAP Service to reduce technical downtime during the upgrade beyond what can be achieved with the standard upgrade tools.
Performing the technical upgrade	System administrators; Technical project lead	Technical Upgrade Procedure (Upgrade Implementation)	Service to perform a technical upgrade.
SAP Modification Clearing	Application project team; CIO; CTO	Application/Modification adjustment (Upgrade Implementation)	Depending on the degree of modification, this service can help to accelerate the technical upgrade process and reduce the TCO by returning SAP modifications to standard during the upgrade.
SAP Test Management Optimization	Project manager; Project team	Testing (Upgrade Implementation)	SAP provides help and guidance to optimize your test procedure and administration. This service provides recommendations on how to improve your current test environment and how to effectively use latest SAP test technologies such as eCATT for test automation.
SAP Knowledge Transfer Optimization	Project manager; Project team; Training coordinator	End-user training (Upgrade Implementation)	More efficient up-skilling of affected end users by leveraging E-Learning concepts and simulation tools.
SAP End-User (Delta) Training	Process owners; Support Staff; Power-User; End-User	End-user training (Upgrade Implementation)	Training to reduce TCO by ensuring that all user types and support staff are optimally prepared for new environment at lowest cost.

Table 5.2 SAP Transition and Upgrade Services for Executing a Transition or Upgrade Project[6] (cont.)

Offering	Target Group	Context of Use (Phase)	Short Description
Upgrade Educational Services	Project team; Affected end users	End-user training (Upgrade Implementation)	To ensure that affected end users are sufficiently up-skilled, SAP provides a suite of delta classes and E-Learing offerings. Determine the specific training needs using the SAP Upgrade Course Finder. Online training (E-Learning) concepts using simulation tools such as SAP Tutor can help to significantly reduce an end-user training effort.
SAP Safeguarding for Upgrade	Entire project team	Master key pain points of an SAP upgrade project (Upgrade Implementation)	Once you have decided to upgrade, the Safeguarding for Upgrade program safeguards the upgrade project providing tailored offerings to successfully master critical pain points.
SAP Upgrade Coach	Project manager; Project team leads	Project and risk management (Upgrade Implementation)	SAP upgrade expert who provides project assistance and acts as named contact person for all upgrade related issues. The service is provided as a 10 day onsite engagement that includes the delivery of an upgrade assessment and multiple project reviews.

Table 5.2 SAP Transition and Upgrade Services for Executing a Transition or Upgrade Project[6] (cont.)

Through SAP Safeguarding, customers can analyze potential challenges at the beginning of a project and help to resolve critical issues. A service plan and recommendations of the SAP Going Live Functional Upgrade Check, for example, is an ideal opportunity for customers to get an SAP assessment on their upgrade situation. The SAP Upgrade Roadmap can be used as a guideline for an upgrade project. It includes links to SAP Best Practice documents and templates; for example, the upgrade guides and the master guide, to name two examples. Experienced customers can benefit from this service by using the SAP Upgrade Roadmap as a checklist of their project; inexperienced clients can leverage this tool and use it as a "bible."

The SAP Solution Manager is a requirement for the technical installation and upgrade to SAP ECC 5.0. This tool is a platform for the whole lifecycle of an SAP solution. SAP acknowledges that using the SAP Solution Manager is an initial investment for customers, but using it in one or multiple areas will quickly pay off. While the SAP Solution Manager includes all relevant information to manage a SAP solution, the SAP Software Lifecycle Manager complements the SAP Solution Manager for specific technical aspects. Leveraging information on business scenarios and the system landscape available in the SAP Solution Manager, the SAP Software Lifecycle Manager is able to validate the technical design in an upgrade project, for example.

SAP Solution Manager

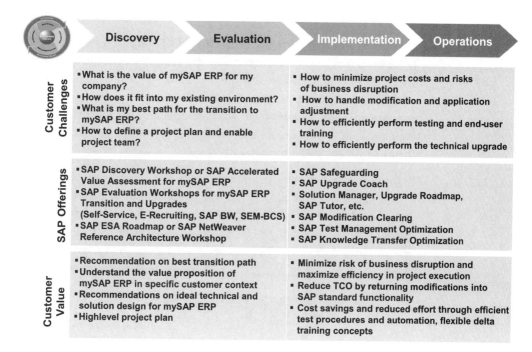

	Discovery / Evaluation	Implementation / Operations
Customer Challenges	▪ What is the value of mySAP ERP for my company? ▪ How does it fit into my existing environment? ▪ What is my best path for the transition to mySAP ERP? ▪ How to define a project plan and enable project team?	▪ How to minimize project costs and risks of business disruption ▪ How to handle modification and application adjustment ▪ How to efficiently perform testing and end-user training ▪ How to efficiently perform the technical upgrade
SAP Offerings	▪ SAP Discovery Workshop or SAP Accelerated Value Assessment for mySAP ERP ▪ SAP Evaluation Workshops for mySAP ERP Transition and Upgrades (Self-Service, E-Recruiting, SAP BW, SEM-BCS) ▪ SAP ESA Roadmap or SAP NetWeaver Reference Architecture Workshop	▪ SAP Safeguarding ▪ SAP Upgrade Coach ▪ Solution Manager, Upgrade Roadmap, SAP Tutor, etc. ▪ SAP Modification Clearing ▪ SAP Test Management Optimization ▪ SAP Knowledge Transfer Optimization
Customer Value	▪ Recommendation on best transition path ▪ Understand the value proposition of mySAP ERP in specific customer context ▪ Recommendations on ideal technical and solution design for mySAP ERP ▪ Highlevel project plan	▪ Minimize risk of business disruption and maximize efficiency in project execution ▪ Reduce TCO by returning modifications into SAP standard functionality ▪ Cost savings and reduced effort through efficient test procedures and automation, flexible delta training concepts

Figure 5.17 SAP Offerings for a Transition and Upgrade Project

Figure 5.17 summarizes SAP's offerings to conduct a transition and upgrade project. Besides the challenges and offerings that were already discussed, it also provides an overview of the main value drivers associated with the preparation and execution of an upgrade or transition. Value drivers like the different recommendations listed or a high-level project plan, for example, are only some of the benefits customers can gain through SAP's services while preparing a transition or upgrade project. In the area of executing a project, customers can profit from minimized risks, reduced costs and efforts, and flexible concepts.

5.4 Conclusion

As we have seen, there are different ways to move to mySAP ERP and to leverage the full value of this mySAP solution. There is no "one-path-fits-all" approach; it depends on the customer's current SAP landscape, upcoming IT projects, and short- and long-term business needs.

As a general rule, customers should have either the latest release of SAP R/3 or SAP ERP Central Component in order to ensure maximum compatibility with mySAP ERP. This means all customers with a release level of SAP R/3 4.6C or below should consider making a technical upgrade to SAP R/3 Enterprise or to SAP ECC 5.0.

Customers who are currently using SAP R/3 Enterprise can upgrade to SAP ECC 5.0, where they will see the benefits of its added features. They are also best-suited to evaluate the immediate benefit of implementing additional capabilities using SAP Enterprise Portal or other mySAP ERP components, and to determine which components are most suitable for their current business needs, and where and how they can best maximize their investment in the short-term.

Regardless of which path customers choose, they should plan to move to mySAP ERP—this will afford them the full spectrum of benefits of SAP NetWeaver and the entire set of offerings, now and in the future, made available from SAP for their ERP processes. Whatever path clients take, SAP will provide a comprehensive set of services to yield a fast return on investment.

6 Next Generation—Proof Points

During the mySAP ERP 2004 Ramp-Up, SAP has performed extensive analysis of Ramp-Up projects to determine to what extent mySAP ERP 2004 is meeting customer needs. To find out more about this Ramp-Up, as well as selected success stories from customers, who have already made the step to the next generation, read on.

6.1 mySAP ERP 2004 Ramp-Up

In this section, SAP's Ramp-Up concept will be introduced. During Ramp-Up, selected SAP customers have the opportunity to implement a new product or release before it's available to the general public. In the following sections, you'll learn about the Ramp-Up process and how SAP supports the participants.

6.1.1 Software Innovation with SAP Ramp-Up

The SAP Ramp-Up program is the safest way to implement new SAP software as soon as it becomes available. You gain all the advantages of being one of the first companies to adopt a new, leading-edge solution—and SAP ensures that you achieve a smooth, cost-effective implementation with an early return on your investment. That's because SAP supplies its customers with proactive SAP monitoring, support, and knowledge transfer from start to finish.

Start Early with the SAP Ramp-Up Program

SAP Ramp-Up is a lifecycle phase for every new SAP solution, including the mySAP Business Suite solutions, which begins as soon as the software is released to customers (see Figure 6.1 and Figure 6.2). When customers participate in the SAP Ramp-Up program, SAP ensures them a safe and cost-effective implementation of the new software by providing special coaching, support, and training before and during the project. SAP Ramp-Up includes:

▶ Implementation assessment

▶ Dedicated project monitoring and support

▶ Early training

Support during Ramp-Up

▶ Information sharing within the community of all SAP Ramp-Up projects

At the start of the project, SAP provides project assessment as needed, including feasibility checks and project scoping. Knowing in advance what the project will entail helps our customers to avoid problems later.

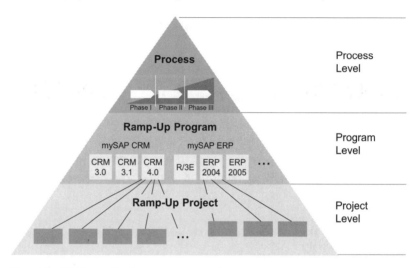

Figure 6.1 SAP Ramp-Up Overview

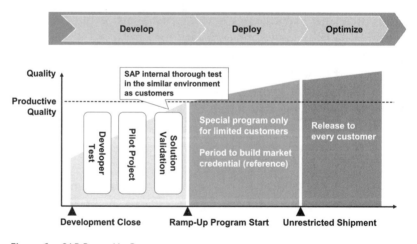

Figure 6.2 SAP Ramp-Up Process

SAP expert as single point of contact

During the project, a dedicated SAP expert serves as a single point of contact. This expert provides proactive risk identification, tracks all problems, and serves as the customer's advocate to ensure that he or she gets rapid bug fixes and problem resolution. This contact also authorizes SAP Safeguarding services for the implementation such as SAP GoingLive Check or SAP Solution Management Assessment.

The dedicated SAP expert is part of the SAP Ramp-Up back-office team, which works rapidly to resolve all issues. The back-office team is usually part of SAP's development organization, so the customer can quickly and easily give feedback on the software, request enhancements, and benefit from the knowledge of thousands of SAP developers (see Figure 6.3).

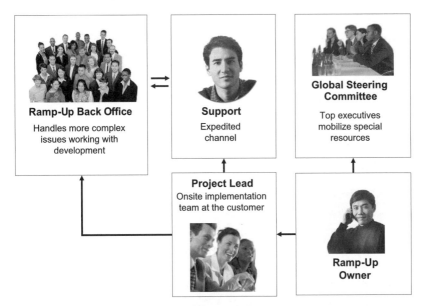

Figure 6.3 SAP Ensures the Early Success of Their SAP Ramp-Up Projects

With all this dedicated support and direct communication with SAP, Ramp-Up customers achieve a quick and easy implementation of the new solution in a well-coordinated team effort.

When a company participates in the SAP Ramp-Up program, it can benefit from early and new product training, and tools and information for its team, including third-party consultants working on the SAP implementation. This early training, the SAP Ramp-Up Knowledge Transfer training program, includes classroom training sessions and workshops, as well as E-Learning maps—a new online learning resource to help customers navigate through material at their own pace.

Knowledge transfer

Information Sharing Within the SAP Ramp-Up Community

Information sharing within the global SAP community of SAP Ramp-Up experts allows everyone to benefit from the experiences of others during SAP Ramp-Up projects. The exchange of feedback and implementation tips helps greatly to reduce customer's costs and to accelerate the implementation. For example, teams don't have to spend precious time and resources creating a workaround that has already been developed in another SAP Ramp-Up project.

A Head start on ROI

For those companies participating in the SAP Ramp-Up program, their employees are empowered early on with a leading-edge business solution. Their department becomes a strategic model for other business units in the company. Moreover, the company gains the competitive advantage of being one of the first in the industry to implement a new SAP solution.

Ramp-Up back office Ramp-Up customers are assured a safe, smooth implementation with continuous monitoring of the project's status and progress. Within SAP, project success is visible at the highest possible level, that is, up to the SAP executive board. Customers benefit from continuous knowledge transfer and a direct feedback path to SAP. They also benefit from the expert assistance of their dedicated SAP contact, along with all the support of the SAP Ramp-Up back-office team, to resolve issues quickly and effectively. Everyone works together to ensure success, saving time and money during implementation and accelerating return on investment.

Ramp-Up owner Best of all, as licensed users of the new SAP solution and SAP Ramp-Up participants, customers receive all the project review and proactive monitoring by the SAP Ramp-Up back office and the SAP Ramp-Up owner at no additional cost, which accelerates the payback even more. The SAP Ramp-Up owner, an SAP Ramp-Up team member, provides updates on available training and assistance when customers are interested in becoming an active reference.

Summary In short, SAP Ramp-Up is the optimal way to get a head start on implementing new SAP software and to achieve an early return on your investment:

▶ Accelerated payback due to reduced implementation time and reduced costs due to proactive support

- ► Safe, low-risk implementation due to SAP board executive management's attention to SAP Ramp-Up and continuous knowledge transfer
- ► All the advantages of being a first mover in your industry

Ramp-Up added Value

With the SAP Ramp-Up program, all parties involved receive significant benefits. All SAP customers are assured of receiving market-proven, reliable, and robust new solutions as early as possible. The SAP Ramp-Up program is a well coordinated, standardized introduction process that allows new SAP solutions to go to market sooner—with more new functionality and higher quality than ever before.

If your company participates in the SAP Ramp-Up program, you gain access to the newest technology with minimum risk and accelerated ROI. There is never a need to be apprehensive about adopting a new solution from SAP. And since SAP introduces all new solutions and major software releases through the SAP Ramp-Up program, it's easy to find out exactly how and when to become an early implementer of any new SAP solution.

All SAP solutions are designed to meet real-world needs and reflect the real-world experience of companies like yours. SAP field personnel and partners are armed with valuable practical knowledge, so they can help everyone right from the start.

The bottom line is that you get innovative new SAP solutions of the highest quality, faster than ever. You become productive quickly and realize tangible benefits rapidly with leading-edge SAP solutions—all while staying a step ahead of your competitors.

Only Excellent Quality Software Is Released to SAP Ramp-Up

Before we begin the SAP Ramp-Up program for a new SAP solution, we thoroughly test and validate the software at SAP with a truly innovative approach. Starting from scratch—just as your company will with the new software and the same documentation and training that your consultants will use—we select a team of SAP consultants to implement the software. This team provides feedback on its experiences to our application development and documentation groups. We wait to release the software to SAP Ramp-Up until this virtual customer team reports that the software is of high quality, easy to implement, and fully documented. In the validation phase, we also assess the solution on all database and operating-system combinations to ensure that it meets our high quality standards.

Testing of the software

Become an SAP Ramp-Up Participant

To find out how your company can apply to participate in the SAP Ramp-Up program, contact your local SAP representative or visit *http://service.sap.com/rampup*.

Participants in the SAP Ramp-Up program must obtain a license for the new SAP software, whether it is a completely new solution or a new release of an existing SAP solution. The proactive monitoring and project review by the SAP Ramp-Up back office and SAP Ramp-Up owner is provided at no additional charge.

6.1.2 mySAP ERP 2004 Ramp-Up proves Next-Generation ERP Success

Following the success of its Ramp-Up program, mySAP ERP 2004 shipped on February 28, 2005—the first time in SAP's Ramp-Up history that a solution was available for general shipment earlier than planned. An analysis of Ramp-Up customers shows that the majority is looking for next-generation ERP.

Next-generation ERP

mySAP ERP is the next-generation ERP solution from SAP, combining analytics, Human Capital Management (HCM), financials, operations, and corporate-services functionality. The successor to SAP's flagship ERP solution SAP R/3, mySAP ERP offers new functionality, increased productivity through new user interfaces and roles, integrated analytics in all business processes, and the flexibility necessary to create differentiated business processes.

SAP demonstrated the stability and viability of the solution in the months following the release-to-customer shipped on June 21, 2004. Global brand name companies such as General Mills and Siemens had been among those actively adopting and successfully implementing the solution.

Are Customers Asking for Next-generation ERP Functionality?

SAP has performed extensive analysis of Ramp-Up projects to determine to what extent mySAP ERP 2004 is meeting customer needs. The questions to be answered were: Are Ramp-Up customers really demanding next-generation ERP functionality? Are the scenarios that they're asking for leveraging the SAP NetWeaver's full capabilities? To find the answers, it's necessary to understand how to assess business scenarios in terms of their "business value" and "technical value," respectively.

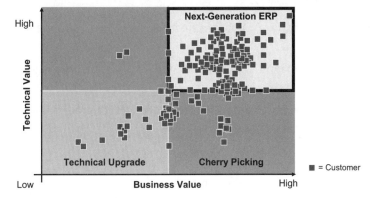

Figure 6.4 mySAP ERP 2004—a Proofpoint for Next-Generation ERP

Business scenarios for mySAP ERP 2004 are classified according to their technical and strategic business value. They're considered of high business value if they strongly leverage the key mySAP ERP pillars of productivity, adaptability, flexibility, business insight, and reduced TCO. Low business value scenarios involve standard ERP functionality.

High technical value scenarios benefit from SAP NetWeaver integration capabilities across all integration layers: user integration, information integration, process integration, and application integration. Low technical value scenarios are standalone components, for example, SAP Enterprise Central Component (SAP ECC) and SAP Business Intelligence (SAP BI).

Classifying Ramp-Up Projects

Each dot in Figure 6.4 represents a specific Ramp-Up project, which comprises several business scenarios implemented in this specific customer project.

Projects in the lower-left quadrant continue to use SAP standard functionality but have upgraded to current technology. An example is a customer who continues to run standard mySAP ERP Financials after having upgraded the SAP R/3 Enterprise system to SAP ECC. **Technical upgrades**

The so-called cherry pickers are projects that use strategic next-generation ERP business scenarios while remaining in an SAP R/3—now SAP ECC-centered—environment. An example is a customer implementing a new General Ledger, which, despite being highly strategic, lies entirely within SAP ECC. **Cherry pickers**

The upper-right quadrant represents those customers who use a broad set of next-generation ERP scenarios simultaneously. Many employ full SAP NetWeaver functionality:

▶ SAP Enterprise Portal (SAP EP) to ensure high user satisfaction and productivity

▶ SAP Business Information Warehouse (SAP BW) to ensure information integration across all data sources

▶ SAP Exchange Infrastructure (SAP XI) to ensure smooth process flow

Thus, true next-generation ERP projects rate high for both business and technical value.

As the graph indicates, most of the Ramp-Up projects lie in the next-generation ERP quadrant—clear proof that mySAP ERP 2004 meets the customer's expectations on both the business and the technical level.

6.2 Customer Successes

mySAP ERP represents the logical step for organizations into next-generation ERP, regardless of whether they implement the full scope at once or, more commonly, in a phased approach. SAP's continuous research and development, as well as services and support offerings, make mySAP ERP a safe choice for organizations of all sizes and industries.

The following customer reports represent a selection of leading organizations across the globe that have made the step to mySAP ERP. These reports address their objectives and approaches to transitioning to mySAP ERP, as well as the major benefits realized.

6.2.1 Boehringer-Ingelheim, Germany

Streamlined processes and reduced costs with mySAP ERP

At a glance

Industry	▶ Pharmaceuticals
Key Challenges	▶ Replacement of a multilevel, high-effort process with long cycle times
	▶ Consolidate to overcome use of different media
	▶ Integration of travel planning for online booking including access to external reservation systems
	▶ Integration of travel management with other internal processes

Solutions and Services	▶ mySAP ERP Travel Management including travel planning and travel expense management
Why SAP Solution	▶ Good experience with SAP as a reliable partner ▶ Integration into existing SAP landscape ▶ Comprehensive solution offering
Implementation Highlights	▶ Participation in SAP Ramp-Up for the new release of SAP Travel Management with mySAP ERP ▶ Project successful much sooner thanks to qualified advice and support from SAP Consulting during implementation ▶ Implementation within the timeline and budgeted costs
Key Benefits	▶ Integrated travel processing with a single interface ▶ Planning, booking, and accounting processes accelerated ▶ Greater transparency with information on status at all times ▶ Lower costs while performance improved ▶ Steady high rate of online bookings of over 80 percent
Implementation Partner	▶ SAP Consulting
Existing Environment	▶ SAP infrastructure with solutions for Finance, Controlling, Materials Management, Maintenance, Sales and Human Resources Management
Database	▶ Oracle
Operating System	▶ HP/UX
End users	▶ 800 secretaries/ca. 4,500 business travelers

How we think and act at Boehringer Ingelheim, a successful pharmaceutical company since 1885, is based on the Vision "Value through Innovation." Activities focus on the development of innovative medicinal products for human medicine and animal health.

The success of the corporate vision, which has been adopted and practiced throughout the company since 1994, is reflected in the balance sheet: Boehringer Ingelheim posted annual sales of 8.2 billion Euro (10 billion USD) in 2004.

Around 9,500 employees work at the two German sites in Ingelheim and Biberach. The company's international operations demand that almost half of the employees are prepared to travel frequently. Every year sees a total of around 36,000 business trips, incurring costs of approximately 25

36,000 business trips by desk staff every year

million Euro (30 million USD). Furthermore, planning business trips, reserving hotels, booking tickets, calculating expenses, and juggling costs all demand great effort in terms of processing. Telephone and videoconferences have not done much to improve matters. There has been a steady increase in the number of business trips, prompting those with responsibility at Boehringer Ingelheim to introduce innovative technologies that allow for more efficient processes. This, in turn, creates added value in Travel Management, in particular, IT support in travel planning and linking this with the established travel expenses accounting system.

Faster, stream-lined processes

The actual processes are multistage processes characterized by separate media, little transparency, and long processing times. This was particularly apparent in travel planning. Therefore, the target processes were defined with the following goals in mind: accelerating procedures, lowering costs, and streamlining planning processes.

Implementation of measures to achieve these goals began with the decision to support the new travel planning solution within mySAP ERP Travel Management. Due to the overall satisfaction with SAP as Boehringer Ingelheim's IT partner over many years, the corporate IT strategy was aimed at SAP solutions, and simple cost-effective integration in existing infrastructures tipped the balance. This was corroborated by the extended range of functions in mySAP ERP Travel Management for online bookings. In addition to the existing links to Global Distribution Systems such as Amadeus, mySAP ERP also offers interfaces with booking systems for hotels and rail travel.

"Thanks to the integrated processing from planning to accounting, SAP Travel Management allows for greater transparency and thus reduced throughput times. Considerable added value can be seen in the lower costs for processing travel. When faced with the need to cut the costs of business travel, we have had to make our employees aware of the problem," says Erwin Albinger, Travel Manager, Boehringer Ingelheim.

Online booking rate of over 80 percent

This has obviously been successful in Ingelheim and Biberach. We now have a steady rate of online bookings for air and rail travel, hotels and rental cars of over 80 percent. Furthermore, the remaining bookings also reach the Travel Agency via the workflow.

Excellent rate of acceptance

The 800 secretaries involved in organizing business travel have readily accepted the new system. The secretaries, who act as service providers for business travelers, can make use of the full online comfort of communicating directly with external travel partners and booking systems. By working with Travel Planning and Travel Expenses Accounting, they can handle the entire process decentrally from planning through booking, collecting receipts to accounting.

One advantage of this partnership is that this increases the employees' own sense of responsibility, which is one of the core values at Boehringer Ingelheim. Another advantage is that it also generates considerable financial benefits:

The new travel management process in Ingelheim and Biberach was started within 12 months. The new and comfortable electronic process has worked out considerably well. The number of online bookings has increased while the costs have begun to fall. Given that one or two additional developments were required for the process, this was indeed rapid implementation, only possible with the competent support of SAP Consulting. Implementation of the project was accelerated by efficient advice, whereby the rapid procurement of information—thanks to the interaction between SAP Consulting and SAP Development—had a positive effect.

This was particularly effective with respect to the cooperation of external providers such as AMADEUS, the railway, and HRS as the innovative links allowed a number of "friction-induced losses" to be avoided. These links are now extremely stable.

"By implementing mySAP ERP, Boehringer Ingelheim has achieved a reduction in process costs, a faster rate of processing, and more transparency. In light of these results, it is understandable why this company's opinion of SAP is positively unanimous: expectations wholly satisfied".

Expectations wholly satisfied

Andreas Brandt, SAP HR User Support, Boehringer Ingelheim

6.2.2 Carl Zeiss Optronics GmbH, Germany

Quick and easy upgrade to mySAP ERP 2004 with SAP Ramp-Up

At a glance

Industry	▶ High-Tech
Key Challenges	▶ Changing the system platform and databases in the course of the upgrade
	▶ Implementing a new workflow for logistics accounting

Project Objectives	▶ Transition from SAP R/3 to mySAP ERP
	▶ System landscape unification
	▶ Improved business processes
	▶ Closer integration of international service partners
Solutions and Services	▶ mySAP ERP 2004, SAP NetWeaver Business Intelligence (SAP NetWeaver BI), SAP NetWeaver Application Server (SAP NetWeaver AS),
	▶ SAP Ramp-Up, SAP GoingLive Check, SAP EarlyWatch Alert
Why SAP Solution	▶ Fast solution upgrade with SAP Ramp-Up
	▶ Lower total cost of ownership due to a uniform system platform
Implementation Highlights	▶ Changed to new server structures and database systems
	▶ Project completed 20 percent faster than planned
	▶ Project costs were 10 percent lower than planned
	▶ Simultaneously implemented a new workflow for logistics accounting
	▶ Replaced 50 percent of all modifications with standard functions
Key Benefits	▶ Created a future-oriented basis for high-performance, web-based processes by harnessing the interaction of mySAP ERP, SAP NetWeaver BI, and SAP NetWeaver AS
	▶ Fast and secure upgrade, on schedule and on budget, with SAP Ramp-Up
	▶ SAP Ramp-Up coach provided direct access to the appropriate contact people at SAP
	▶ Advance access to the newest functions of SAP's latest software solutions
Implementation Partner	▶ SAP Consulting
Existing Environment	▶ SAP R/3 4.6C, SAP Internet Transaction Server (SAP ITS)
Database	▶ Oracle
Hardware	▶ Sun
Operating System	▶ AIX

Due to the increasing demands of internationalized markets, Carl Zeiss GmbH of Oberkochen, Germany, needed to swiftly upgrade from SAP R/3 to mySAP ERP and facilitate the secure and efficient execution of cross-country and -company processes over the Internet.

A leading provider of optoelectronic sensory technology, Carl Zeiss Optronics GmbH develops, manufactures, and sells high-tech products such as thermal imaging devices, laser range finders, sighting systems, periscopes, stabilized sensor platforms, and optomechanical subsystems all over the world. For this wholly-owned subsidiary of Carl Zeiss AG, research and development are high priorities; its most important customers are systems companies and public contractors. Both a full-range supplier and a technology and program partner, Carl Zeiss Optronics is constantly expanding its international activities. The company is already active in more than 30 countries and employs more than 400 people. Its current focal points in sales are Europe, the Middle East, South Africa, and North America.

For its global business, Carl Zeiss Optronics needs high-performance systems and processes for integrating partner companies online and quickly sharing information on products and services. These partners include, in particular, service companies that handle onsite customer equipment maintenance. Shrinking technology cycles, constantly changing customer demands, and the need for all-around efficiency made it all the more essential for the company to take action. The transition from SAP R/3 to mySAP ER, which Carl Zeiss Optronics had already planned for in the medium term, gave the company a new purpose—building future-oriented and more efficient IT structures. "Our top priority during the upgrade project was improving cooperation among partners via web-based processes. In the future, we also want to systematically use SAP NetWeaver Business Intelligence (SAP NetWeaver BI) to map our company planning in just one system, thereby ensuring that all of our business processes are transparent," says Manfred Schmid, IT director and project lead at Carl Zeiss Optronics.

Integrating international partners online

Up to that point, the company's global service partners had accessed its SAP R/3 systems with relative difficulty using SAP Internet Transaction Server (SAP ITS). Today, this process is handled by SAP NetWeaver Application Server (SAP NetWeaver AS), which Carl Zeiss Optronics received along with mySAP ERP: All services activities related to, for example, providing maintenance of high-tech products to global customers are now based on web processes that run much more smoothly due to the interaction of mySAP ERP, SAP NetWeaver BI, and SAP NetWeaver AS.

Additional processes are set to follow. "Not least, this upgrade and the resulting uniform system platform also grant us the opportunity to reduce operating costs and the total cost of ownership of our IT landscape," adds Schmid.

SAP Ramp-Up sets the pace The time period allocated for upgrading to mySAP ERP 2004 left almost no room for error: The project was to be completed by the beginning of July 2005 at the latest. "We recognized the chance to put pressure on to act within the company, due to the specified go-live deadline in the ramp-up phase. That really helped us focus and drive activities within our organization more quickly," says Schmid. After HP, the external service provider responsible for system hosting, was brought on board in Jena, Germany, the project was ready to start at the beginning of 2005. With constant support from SAP Ramp-Up, the four-member team from Carl Zeiss Optronics carefully prepared for the upgrade: Possible alternative scenarios were investigated, milestones were defined, and logs and procedures were designed. Schmid's project team quickly learned to appreciate additional advantages offered by SAP Ramp-Up. In Schmid's words, "With SAP Ramp-Up, it's quite possible to pass on feedback and ideas for the solution's further development to SAP's development organization."

Upgraded in no time In just four months, Carl Zeiss Optronics was able to complete its upgrade and accurately customize the new release to meet its own specific requirements. Early on in the project, the four-member team called in all of the key users from across the company to help develop, map, and intensively test every required process. Additional implementation security was ensured by SAP GoingLive Check, which the company received as part of the free SAP Ramp-Up service package for mySAP ERP. This service analyzed core business processes, safeguarded the company's successful go-live with the right performance parameters, and ensured stable technical operation. The internal effort required for the upgrade amounted to approximately 225 workdays.

In addition to the team's high level of SAP competency, intensive collaboration with the developers at SAP also led to the project's rapid success. The SAP Ramp-Up coach assigned to the project ensured that communication between the two camps was simple and problem-free. The coach served as SAP Consulting's main contact person and provided Carl Zeiss Optronics with onsite support; among other things, he ensured that urgent questions and customer messages always reached the right contact people at SAP. "Our SAP Ramp-Up coach played a crucial part in the smooth cooperation between the internal and external parties involved in the project. Because of this, we were able to shorten the duration of the project from five to four months—that's 20 percent," says Schmid. The costs of the project were also 10 percent lower than planned.

During the upgrade, a special header tag identified problem notifications received by Carl Zeiss Optronics as messages pertaining to Ramp-Up customers. Consequently, SAP ensured preferred support and accelerated processing times throughout the project. Direct exchanges with the Ramp-Up coach facilitated and complemented a mutual knowledge transfer while simultaneously supporting rapid problem resolution. This benefited both the IT team at Carl Zeiss Optronics and SAP. Overall, a mere 19 notifications were submitted and subsequently handled with an average processing time of one and a half days.

Fast response to problem notifications

"In the course of the upgrade, we were able to replace around 50 percent of all of our previous release's individual modifications with the standard functions offered by mySAP ERP 2004. To us, this clearly indicates that SAP is getting better at thinking along the lines of other companies' needs and mapping the requirements of industrial processes in its solutions," says Schmid. At the same time, the project team also implemented a new workflow for logistics invoice verification to comply with its parent company's specifications. Previously based on financial accounts, invoice verification is now handled in an object-oriented manner using materials management documents that record the actual receipt of goods.

Carl Zeiss Optronics' new mySAP ERP solution has received consistently positive evaluations from its 220 users and 17 key users. They quickly adapted to the modified appearance of the new SAP GUI 6.40. "All of the standard reports meet with a high level of acceptance," says Schmid, who is also pleased with the system's performance: "The system is stable and performs very well." Daily evaluations of the logs kept by SAP EarlyWatch Alert confirm this assertion. This fully automated diagnosis service monitors the most important administrative areas of the SAP landscape run by Carl Zeiss Optronics and provides current data on the system's performance and stability.

High level of buy-in, stable performance

In the current fiscal year, Schmid's team is mostly concentrating on taking full advantage of SAP NetWeaver BI's potential. Carl Zeiss Optronics wants to eliminate its use of complex, error-prone Microsoft Excel reports: "Our next goal is to map all of our key company figures in SAP NetWeaver BI to provide our decision-makers and employees with a

Developing synergies

comprehensive and user-friendly reporting system," says Schmid. The planning and simulation functions included in mySAP ERP are also a focus of the company's considerations for the future. Schmid sees crucial potential and synergies for more optimized company planning and management in the interaction of these features and SAP NetWeaver BI: "As part of our strategy, we're first amassing the internal expertise we need to gradually approach our goals in the medium term. In the process, we'll be glad to have the support of SAP Ramp-Up to rely on whenever necessary."

6.2.3 China Telecom Corporation, China

At a glance

Industry	▶ Telecommunications
Key Challenges	▶ Build a state-of-the-art IT landscape to support business transformation ▶ Comply with international reporting rules ▶ Integrate all major business functions and achive real-time management
Solutions and Services	▶ mySAP ERP, SAP NetWeaver (SAP Business Intelligence and SAP Enterprise Portal)
Implementation Partner	▶ Bearing Point
Implementation Highlights	▶ Implemented at three sites with 1,000 users in seven months ▶ Will grow to 30,000 users in 20-plus offices over two years ▶ Built a new IT infrastructure from HP ensuring uninterrupted operation
Key Benefits	▶ Scalability and flexibility of mySAP ERP and the underlying HP infrastructure allowed an initial focus on essential business needs, enabling fast implementation while maintaining full adaptability ▶ Comprehensive business insight and analysis, supporting faster decision-making and tighter operational control ▶ Faster information flow, enhanced internal collaboration, and increased employee productivity
Hardware	▶ Multiple HP 9000 servers: HP server rp5470, HP server rp8400 ▶ HP Storage Area Network (SAN) on HP StorageWorks XP128 Disk Array
Operating System	▶ HP-UX with an Oracle Database

China Telecom Corporation, the world's largest fixed-line operator, has a vision: to turn the company into a world-class telecom powerhouse within five years. To turn that vision into reality, China Telecom teamed up with SAP and HP to build a state-of-the-art IT landscape. The company took a huge leap forward to gain business insight, achieve organizational efficiency, and increase productivity.

China Telecom was formed as part of the reorganization of the former China Telecommunications Corporation, a state-owned enterprise. Today, China Telecom has over 350,000 employees across China; operates domestic and international fixed-line networks; provides fixed-line voice, data, and information services; and is engaged in international telecom accounts settlement.

Turning a challenge into an opportunity

Despite the worldwide slowdown in the telecom industry, China Telecom has maintained sustained growth over the last two years, with 17.6 billion USD in sales and an 8% increase in 2003. In 2002, China Telecom successfully launched its IPO at the New York Stock Exchange to become the third Chinese telecom company listed on an overseas stock market.

China Telecom has undertaken challenging reforms to transform itself from a traditional state enterprise into a customer-focused, profit-driven modern enterprise. This process has posed an enormous challenge to IT within the company. And as a publicly traded company, China Telecom must comply with international reporting rules.

Looking at these challenges as an opportunity, China Telecom decided to build a new IT platform, based on best practices, with cutting-edge technology.

China Telecom set an ultimate goal for this initiative: The new environment needed to help the company increase organizational efficiency, achieve transparency and real-time management, tighten internal control, and enhance collaboration between departments. The software had to integrate within and beyond its functions and meet the industry-specific business requirements of a telecom operator.

Strategic tie with SAP and HP

After careful evaluation of several global ERP vendors, the company chose mySAP ERP as the backbone system. "We chose SAP because of its broader range of functionalities and integration capabilities. It is best equipped to deliver solutions for a large enterprise and provides much-needed industry expertise for a telecom business," says Shiping Liang, director of the application division at China Telecom.

mySAP ERP supports several core business processes, including finance, controlling, human capital management, procurement, and engineering project management. To build an enterprise-class data integration platform, China Telecom also chose to leverage the SAP Business Intelligence (SAP BI) and SAP Enterprise Portal (SAP EP) components of SAP NetWeaver.

To ensure maximum ROI, China Telecom required an infrastructure platform with exceptional reliability, performance, availability, and scalability to power mySAP ERP. Equally important, it needed a flexible solution to allow IT to keep pace with changes while offering a low total cost of ownership. The vendor had to be able to assemble a broad range of products and services to cover all of China Telecom's requirements—from PCs to powerful servers, from network storage to customer support.

In intense competition among global IT vendors, HP stood out as the best choice for the IT infrastructure. "HP outperformed other alternatives in terms of price-performance ratio. It is a scalable, flexible, and adaptive solution that fully meets our technical requirements in supporting SAP now and for the future, while still offering a competitive total cost of ownership," says Liang.

The company selected HP's HP 9000 server family to support the mission-critical SAP applications. For the network storage infrastructure, China Telecom chose HP Storage Works XP128 Disk Array, a state-of-the-art storage solution that delivers outstanding scalability, availability, reliability, and the highest performance in its class.

With mySAP ERP and its new HP infrastructure, China Telecom is equipped with one common solution that provides the flexibility to respond to changing and growing business needs. This flexible and adaptive platform plays a critical role in enabling the enterprise to achieve maximum business agility and further enhance its competitiveness.

The big move China Telecom will roll out the complete SAP solution over two years at 20-plus subsidiaries. Eventually, the system will have 30,000 users across China. The project is the first large-scale SAP deployment in the telecom industry in China, according to Chris Zhao, senior account manager at SAP China.

The countrywide kickoff of the SAP project started in parallel in the Beijing, Guangzhou, and Shanghai offices. The solution successfully went live seven months later in all three locations with a total of 1,000 users. The SAP landscape has been designed to cater to the business needs of each office. At its Beijing headquarters, China Telecom implemented the human capital management functions of mySAP ERP and SAP BI to support centralized human resources management and to provide consolidated information to group management. The Guangzhou and Shanghai subsidiaries, which generate most of the company's business, use the financials, operations, human capital management, and analytics capabilities of mySAP ERP, plus SAP EP and SAP BI.

For maximum computing power and uptime, the application landscape was designed in separate systems supporting mySAP ERP, SAP BI, and SAP EP individually. Each system is composed of a development system, a test system, and a productive system. All have been equipped with HP rp5470 servers for the test and development systems and with HP rp8400 servers for the productive system. All servers are linked into a new storage area network under HP Storage Works Disk Array XP128 and are supported by a Veritas backup system. The landscape is identical in all three locations, and the company will use this configuration in future implementations.

The implementation is considered a huge success at China Telecom. According to Liang, strong and consistent support from top management, excellent project planning, and teamwork contributed to the success. China Telecom also took advantage of the scalability and flexibility of mySAP ERP and the underlying HP infrastructure so it could make tough decisions and focus on essential business needs while maintaining full adaptability to grow the installation and respond to changing requirements. According to Liang, this was critical to managing the implementation and achieving faster ROI.

China Telecom has three building blocks for its corporate information strategy: the Management Supporting System (MSS) to support back-office activities, the Business Supporting System (BSS) to manage customer relationships, and the Operational Supporting System (OSS) to take care of its supply chain. The first phase of the SAP implementation focused on enhancing MSS to optimize internal processes. With the introduction of mySAP ERP, SAP BI, and SAP EP—all complemented by office software—China Telecom's MSS became a powerful platform, delivering a wealth of benefits.

mySAP ERP building momentum

The major advantage for China Telecom is the visibility of information available due to seamless data integration between different functions and data sources, allowing for comprehensive business analysis. Under the new environment in which SAP BI is an integral part of mySAP ERP, the accounting, procurement, and engineering management functions, which used to be isolated, are now fully integrated. This integration accelerates the flow of information and encourages active internal collaboration. "We have more information and a much quicker exchange of information, and that is the decisive advantage for us," says Liang.

In addition, the data integration between the accounting and human capital management functions allows for easy analysis of personnel costs and performance-based payment plans, which used to be an extremely time-consuming process.

Another noteworthy advantage is the ease and speed with which information can be accessed. SAP EP unified data and applications with a central, secure, and role-based access to all mySAP ERP systems. Users have personalized access from a Web browser, and single sign-on (SSO) has resulted in significant timesavings and productivity gains because users have to log on only once.

"mySAP ERP provides us with a single, consolidated, and timely view of our business. This is a major breakthrough for us. With SAP, we can make faster decisions and get a stronger grip on management control," says Liang.

The success of the MSS implementation has built momentum to extend the use of SAP within China Telecom. For a complete view of all operations, as well as internal and external processes, the company plans to extend the use of SAP BI to the BSS and the OSS functions.

HP secures mission-critical applications

At China Telecom, handling large volumes of data between SAP BI and mySAP ERP posed a challenging test for the speed and processing capabilities of the server platform. Making critical data available 24/7 put unprecedented demands on the network storage and backup solutions. "High availability, scalability, and high performance are key features integral to running our SAP applications," says Liang.

HP 9000 servers are built around super fast PA-RISC processors and supported by the powerful 64-bit HP-UX 11i operating system, so they can handle demanding workloads. With HP rp8400s and rp5470s, China Telecom had the speed and computing power it required to generate fast, timely, and accurate reports and analyses.

"The computing performance of HP 9000 UNIX servers meets with our satisfaction and approval entirely. The system is also impressively stable; we didn't receive any complaints in that respect," says Liang. "And on top of that, we benefit a lot from HP's first-class customer support." In addition to an excellent price-performance ratio, the new infrastructure platform gives China Telecom the flexibility and scalability it needs to dynamically respond to future changes in business requirements, as well as the expected growth in system demands.

As planned, China Telecom will continue the rollout of mySAP ERP into its other locations in China. Concurrently, the company will make enhancements and introduce additional developments to further maximize the benefits. **Looking to the future**

The ultimate goal is to integrate the company's MSS, BSS, and OSS on a single platform so the company can see a complete view of all of its processes with customers, partners, and employees. China Telecom has achieved an important first step toward that goal by linking MSS with the billing system in the BSS using SAP BI. The next challenge is to apply SAP BI to integrate disparate data from heterogeneous sources in BSS and OSS, which have legacy systems and third-party applications in place. "With the SAP and HP technology on our side, we will make it," says Liang.

When the project is complete, China Telecom will have a management cockpit with key performance indicators (KPIs) across all internal and external processes, further improving its business efficiency and competitiveness.

6.2.4 Freescale Semiconductor, USA

Managing real estate for the world's newest semiconductor giant

At a glance

Industry	▶ High-Tech
Key Challenges	▶ Replace legacy real estate management system used by Freescale's former parent company, Motorola Inc.
	▶ Manage global real estate portfolio more effectively
	▶ Reduce costs
Project Objectives	▶ Introduce new real estate management capabilities without disrupting existing processes
	▶ Complete implementation before final independence from Motorola

Solutions and Services	▶ SAP Real Estate Management, an application found in the mySAP ERP solution
	▶ SAP Education for training
Why SAP Solution	▶ Consistency and ease of integration with SAP solutions already in place
	▶ History of success with SAP solutions and SAP Consulting
	▶ Minimal cost impact since company already owned software
	▶ Support for a phased implementation
Implementation Highlights	▶ Customized implementation process for organizational specifics
	▶ Met aggressive schedule with small implementation team
Key Benefits	▶ Implemented single solution for managing all real estate holdings globally
	▶ Achieved automatic tracking and flagging of critical real estate-related dates
	▶ Gained protection against accidental deletion of key information
	▶ Automated data cleansing, data archiving, and contract lookup
	▶ Attained cost information visibility at the individual site level
	▶ Improved productivity
	▶ Positioned to automate financial transactions and reporting via integration with other SAP solutions
	▶ Completed implementation prior to final independence from Motorola
Implementation Partner	▶ SAP Consulting
Existing Environment	▶ Homegrown real estate management database supplemented by spreadsheets and paper documents
	▶ Accounts payable and general ledger capabilities of mySAP ERP and the SAP Business Intelligence component
Database	▶ IBM DB2
Hardware	▶ IBM servers
Operating System	▶ IBM AIX

The birth of Freescale Semiconductor came about as a result of a decision by Motorola to end its engagement in semiconductor manufacturing operations. Freescale was formed in April 2004, became a publicly traded company in July 2004, and finalized its independence from Motorola in December 2004. The new company instantly became one of the world's semiconductor giants, with over 200 sites spanning the globe. Managing these real estate holdings is a massive undertaking. In the past, Motorola performed this management using only a homegrown database augmented by a collection of spreadsheets. In July 2004, management of the publicly traded company commenced a project to replace this legacy system with a powerful new real estate management capability. The project had to be completed prior to the company's final independence from Motorola, which presented the team with a very aggressive six-month implementation schedule.

"As an SAP shop for so many of our business needs, we had no doubt that SAP Real Estate Management was right for us," says Glynis Himes, real estate IT project lead for Freescale. "It fit our roadmap and it integrates easily with our other SAP solutions. Since we already owned the software as part of our mySAP ERP solution, the cost impact was small. Another advantage was that it lent itself to a phased implementation, allowing us to enter production with the essential master data on our timeline and integrate with other solutions later on."

Solution fits the roadmap, implements on time

It was just as clear that SAP Consulting was the right implementation partner for Freescale. "We'd had excellent experience using their services in the past," Himes explains, "and they know SAP Real Estate Management far better than other service providers we use." SAP Consulting dedicated a small but talented team to the implementation. Since Freescale could not afford disruption to its business processes at such a critical time, the team customized the implementation to introduce the solution's functionality to fit within these processes. In November, right on time and well ahead of the deadline, SAP Consulting completed the implementation. Himes then attended a training course on the SAP Real Estate Management application conducted by SAP Education. "SAP Consulting went the extra mile for us to make sure they completed the implementation on time. They did an excellent job, and so did SAP Education. The course packed a lot of information into a short period, minimizing my time consumption while conveying everything I needed to know."

Combines global view and individual site specifics

With SAP Real Estate Management, Freescale's eight property managers have a global view of all the company's facilities, including 79 leased sites, 20 owned sites, and approximately 142 contracts, of which three are leased out. Not only can they track the property specifics, but also the personnel in these locations. All financial information is available—including rents, service fees, and maintenance costs. In the future, this data can be easily rolled up to project overall real estate expenses and revenues.

With the previous system, revenues and costs were grouped at too high a level to permit decisions about specific properties to be made effectively. SAP Real Estate Management, however, provides visibility of budgeting information at the individual site level. This is important because Freescale, as a new company, seizes every opportunity to save costs. Critical date tracking is another valuable feature that SAP Real Estate Management introduced. In the past, Freescale's property managers often had too little warning about key events to make informed decisions. Now they are automatically reminded well in advance of a lease expiration, for example, and provided with enough time to properly research and consider cost-effective alternatives to extending the lease.

Automating manual business processes

SAP Real Estate Management has improved and automated several business processes that used to be conducted manually. For example:

▶ Data for unused properties is automatically cleansed from the system

▶ Data archiving is performed automatically, permitting recovery in the case of inadvertent deletion

▶ Contracts that used to exist only on paper can now be looked up electronically

Freescale's next step is to integrate SAP Real Estate Management with the mySAP ERP solutions—already in place for financials—and with the SAP Business Intelligence component for generating reports that include real estate information. The link to the existing accounts payable and general ledger solutions will further automate manual processes, thereby eliminating the duplicate entry of data for making rental and service contract payments. In the long term, Freescale plans to implement the accounts receivable capabilities of mySAP ERP and integrate them with SAP Real Estate Management as well. This will automate the invoicing process for leased-out properties.

Managing change, saving costs in the long term

"We are making many facility changes during our first year as an independent company and SAP Real Estate Management is helping enormously in managing and controlling the change process," says Himes. "After the changes diminish, our focus will shift toward savings costs and SAP Real Estate Management will be our key tool for identifying areas where we're spending too much on facilities."

"We're very pleased with SAP Real Estate Management," concludes Himes. "It has already improved our productivity, and as we get to know it better, we're continually finding new ways to save time. SAP Real Estate Management is a powerful, flexible solution that has helped us to improve our business processes while achieving a global view of our real estate holdings."

6.2.5 Petroquímica Triunfo, Brazil

SAP solutions help a company organize information and give it strategic value

At a glance

Industry	▶ Chemicals
Key Challenges	▶ Optimize costs
	▶ Establish IT as part of the business
Project Objectives	▶ Integrate departments
	▶ Unify information
	▶ Increase operational control
	▶ Achieve organizational efficiency
	▶ Guide strategic planning
Solutions and Services	▶ mySAP ERP solution
	▶ SAP NetWeaver, including the SAP Business Intelligence and SAP Portal components
	▶ SAP Strategic Enterprise Management (SAP SEM) application
	▶ SAP SEM business planning and simulation functionality
	▶ SAP SEM balanced scorecard functionality
	▶ SAP Management Cockpit application
Why SAP Solution	▶ Complete range of management solutions for all company levels
	▶ Capacity for growth and investment in research
Implementation Highlights	▶ Smooth installations and upgrades, with company able to handle the final migration in-house
	▶ Transformation of data input operatives into information analysts
Key Benefits	▶ Transparency and reliability of data
	▶ Operational, tactical, and strategic alignment
	▶ Simulation and forecast capacity

Implementation Partner	▶ MultiVision
	▶ SoftTek
Existing Environment	▶ Legacy Systems
Hardware	▶ HP and Intel
Operating System	▶ Microsoft Windows Server 2003
Database	▶ Microsoft SQL Server 2003

From a fragmented IT structure to an integrated solution, for Brazilian petrochemical firm Petroquímica Triunfo, the adoption of SAP solutions constituted a milestone that marked its ability to control and generate information more reliably and efficiently. Furthermore, data input operators were transformed into authentic business analysts.

It all started in 1998 when the producer of chemicals for the plastics manufacturing industry decided to scan the market for a solution that could integrate its internal processes. The catalyst for this search for an integration solution was dealing with the millennium bug, but Gil Carvalho de Freitas, IT manager at Triunfo, was already considering replacing the decentralized in-house tools with a solid system that could serve the entire company's needs.

SAP solutions justify investment The choice came down to SAP. According to Freitas, "One of the points that caught our attention at the time we were making the decision was that the investment by SAP in research and development was equivalent to the annual revenue of the second-place company."

Triunfo implemented SAP R/3 software and worked on fine-tuning its business management software until the arrival of the SAP NetWeaver platform, which was adopted in November 2005. The initial version of the software was implemented with the support of an SAP partner, MultiVision, and then updated in 2003 with the support of SoftTek. In March 2005, the transition to the mySAP ERP solution did not require external support.

After adopting SAP NetWeaver, the other solutions were gradually implemented, such as the SAP Business Intelligence (SAP BI) component and the SAP Strategic Enterprise Management (SAP SEM) application balanced scorecard functionality, both of which have been integrated into the new platform. The plan is to update all the SAP solutions rapidly so that the migration to SAP NetWeaver can be finished in eight months.

Petroquímica Triunfo's investment in SAP exceeds 1 million BRL (0.4 million Euro, 0.5 million USD) per year. In the next three years, he expects to invest a total of 3.5 million BRL (1.4 million Euro, 1.7 million USD). Freitas' justification for the increase is simple: "It would be difficult to find another solution on the market that serves all the corporate management levels." The investment has proven to be money well spent. "Today our IT costs are the same as before we adopted SAP, however, we have gained many more valuable benefits," says Freitas.

The evolution of Petroquímica Triunfo's IT management involved three phases, which addressed operational, tactical, and strategic concerns.

Addressing operations, tactics, and strategy

The first phase, the implementation of mySAP ERP, defined the best business practices and rules to improve operations. "Previously, each data-entry operator input data into Excel spreadsheets in his or her own way, leading to variations in data pertaining to the same information. This, in turn, led to many errors, and the information was unreliable," points out Freitas. Today it is possible to ascertain precisely when data was produced, in what quantity, and for which client.

Another example of significant improvement can be seen in the monthly balance sheet; previously, this required as many as 15 days to be completed. Now the balance sheet only need be consulted on the second working day of each month. "The rules are essential to control the data. For us, this proved to be a huge benefit in methodology, given that people dealing with transactions have to produce consistent, reliable, and transparent work, complying with the business rules of the company," adds Freitas.

With operations addressed, Triunfo embarked on the second stage for IT management: the quest for organizational efficiency. A tactical component was necessary, and for this Triunfo chose SAP BI and SAP SEM business planning and simulation (BPS) and balanced scorecard functionality. Now company managers, coordinators, and business analysts can analyze information collected in all areas, from the factory floor to the financial department, both inside and outside the company, via remote access. This represents a tremendous leap ahead in Triunfo's business management capabilities.

Petroquímica Triunfo began to use SAP BI in 2002, and it was fully up and running in 2003. In 2005, the entire integrated IT management project based on SAP was fine-tuned across all levels of the company.

Strategic planning enabled across the company

With SAP SEM balanced scorecard functionality supporting strategic planning, the executives and directors can use the range of information generated in the operational and tactical phases to draw precise growth targets for the company, controlling the pace, and thereby fulfilling the third, strategic stage of the Triunfo plan. "One of the strong points of BPS is that it makes simulations possible. At any time, it is possible to know exactly what impact an increase in a given production line will have on the company margins, for example," says Freitas.

Accessible infor-
mation for opera-
tional efficiency
With the SAP system, the business vision has become clear for managers, who are now able to access any data from the production and sales cycle quickly, with a time lag of only four hours. The next step is to achieve real-time data, which will be possible with new analytics functionality, implemented in October 2005.

"There is a lot of talk about operational efficiency to obtain a leading edge; for us this is evident," says Cezar Augusto Mansoldo, managing director of Petroquímica Triunfo.

"Organizational efficiency will give us a competitive advantage. To achieve it, one requires a management model, qualified staff, and necessarily a business intelligence structure, like SAP BI, which enables top management to manage the performance of the organization."

SAP NetWeaver has proven its worth to Triunfo over the last two years. At the current strategic stage of the project, the company is making IT a business driver—"IT embedded in business," as SAP puts it. "When the users have access to timely, reliable information, the login becomes an act one does not just to 'find out' but rather to 'carry out,'" concludes Freitas.

6.2.6 University of Westminster, Great Britain

Supporting innovation with the power of automated human capital management and payroll solutions from SAP

At a glance

Industry	▶ Public Sector—Higher Education
Key Challenges	▶ Improve efficiency of payroll and HR operations
	▶ Reduce the cost of HR and payroll activities
	▶ Improve management control and reporting capabilities

Key Challenges (cont.)	▶ Enhance visibility and decision making
	▶ Eliminate duplicate data entry and improve data accuracy
Project Objectives	▶ Automate manual HR and payroll operations and provide employee and manager self-service functionality
	▶ Implement an integrated and scalable solution to consolidate data entry and enhance reporting
Solutions and Services	▶ mySAP ERP Human Capital Management (HCM) including the SAP Employee Self Service (ESS) application
Why SAP Solution	▶ Powerful HCM, payroll, and ESS functionality
	▶ Strong track record at numerous universities
	▶ Support for future expansion, thanks to software's scalable, flexible architecture
Implementation Highlights	▶ Implemented solution in nine months
	▶ Involved 450 users, with more to come
	▶ Eliminated multiple legacy systems
	▶ Deployed a variety of customer interfaces for other applications, including a homegrown online recruitment tool
	▶ Created numerous customized reports
Key Benefits	▶ Enhanced speed and accuracy of payroll processing and increased flexibility
	▶ Reduced HR and payroll costs
	▶ Provided online access to HR data through SAP ESS
	▶ Improved management reporting and access to information
	▶ Reduced data entry and data errors
Implementation Partner	▶ Pecaso
Existing Environment	▶ Discrete, nonintegrated legacy systems
Database	▶ Microsoft SQL Server Enterprise 2000
Hardware	▶ Dell Power Edge 2650
Operating System	▶ Microsoft Windows

A widely respected educational institution, the University of Westminster was formerly Britain's oldest polytechnic institute and is now a leading university. With a history of developing new technologies, the university is closely aligned with the business, professional, and academic life of

London. This vibrant institution is also dedicated to recognizing the needs of its diverse population of over 23,000 students, as well as creating imaginative educational offerings to serve its target markets.

Yet when it came to processing payroll and managing human capital, the University of Westminster struggled to introduce innovative business approaches. Using its legacy business systems, the university was unable to automate routine processes or to get the information it needed in reports. "We had an integrated HR and payroll system, but it was limited in its capabilities and completely static," says Fiona Sinclair, project manager at the University of Westminster. "We could not get any management information from it, and it could not support our employee self-service plans. We had to run recruitment separately and administer training manually." Seeking a powerful business system that could support its payroll and HR operations, as well as innovative plans for Employee Self Service (ESS) applications, the university selected software from the SAP for Higher Education & Research solution portfolio.

New business requirements   The university's labor-intensive COBOL-based business systems, in service for several years, could no longer meet the requirements of an innovative institution of higher learning. "Many calculations needed for payroll, for example, had to be done manually," says Sinclair. "The systems we were using simply could not handle them." This added significantly to the cost and time required to process payroll and to perform other HR activities.

At the same time, the university faced a rapidly expanding list of reporting requirements. Statutory reporting to meet governmental mandates was growing annually, and funding regulations also demanded additional data and reports that the old HR and payroll systems could not generate.

It was also becoming increasingly difficult to locate IT professionals who were willing or able to work with the outmoded technology of the university's systems. "Finding staff with the necessary skills like COBOL or people willing to work with something so old was a challenge," says Sinclair. "SAP expertise is easy to find, whether we're looking for an employee or a consultant."

Finding the right technology fit   The university then formed a small team to investigate IT solutions. The team asked vendors with appropriate solutions to send information packages, and then selected 10 vendors from those that responded to submit formal proposals. "We evaluated the proposals against the criteria that we had established—cost, functionality, and so on," says Sinclair. "We also wanted a vendor who had experience working with universities, because we know our requirements are very different from those of organizations in the private sector."

After reviewing the proposals, the university's team invited four vendors to deliver full presentations. Following an intensive period of vendor demos and site visits, the university chose the SAP human resources solution, which is now available as the mySAP ERP Human Capital Management (mySAP ERP HCM) solution. "SAP software best met our functionality requirements by a long shot," says Sinclair. "SAP's people had the most professional presentations, their demonstrations always worked, they were there on time, and they answered all of our questions better than any other vendor."

Other critical factors: the SAP solution could run with the university's existing Microsoft SQL Server database, and it could produce the customized reports that the university required to meet mandates from both the government and funding sources. The SAP solution was also capable of handling UK public-sector-specific payroll requirements. The ready availability of SAP knowledge and SAP-experienced IT professionals and consultants also contributed to the decision.

The university considered SAP's reputation for innovation as well. "We implemented SAP software because we thought it would be future proof, and because we thought that SAP would always be developing ahead of our requirements," says Sinclair. "We did not want to be saddled with yet another legacy system in five years, which would force us to go through this whole process again. We felt that SAP would protect us from that."

Having selected SAP software, the university assembled a small internal implementation team. Lacking SAP implementation experience, the team elected to bring in a consulting partner to streamline the installation and go-live processes. "Prior to this project, the team had limited implementation experience so we knew we'd need a lot of help," says Sinclair. "We picked Pecaso, because it was SAP's preferred implementation partner for HR and payroll in the United Kingdom, and because it had previous experience in the higher education sector."

Rapid implementation, comprehensive training

In addition to assisting with the implementation, Pecaso spent a great deal of time transferring the necessary knowledge to the university's team and training them to train university personnel on how to effectively operate the HCM software. "We wanted to learn as much as possible so that we did not have to call in a consultant every time we wanted to do something simple," says Sinclair. "Instead of doing everything for us, Pecaso showed us how to do it. This made implementation easier, because we were not waiting for consultants to do everything. And when the implementation was complete, we were better prepared to operate the system." With Pecaso's assistance, the university was able to implement the HCM software, including payroll, recruitment, and training and events, in about nine months.

Enhanced productivity and reporting accuracy The payroll-related calculations that were performed manually under the legacy system are now handled automatically by the SAP software for human capital management. This improvement has reduced the amount of time and effort that the university spends preparing payroll and has increased accuracy.

Using the SAP Employee Self Service application, university employees can now update much of their own personnel information. Once all employees are using the self-service software, HR staff will be able to concentrate on activities that offer more value to the university, such as recruitment and employee relations.

With more flexible and HR-specific reporting capabilities, the university has experienced a dramatic improvement in the quality and accuracy of its reporting. Administrators can now generate timely, accurate, and more detailed reports, resulting in improved planning, budgeting, and decision-making. "The SAP software gives us greater reporting potential and better access to management information," says Sinclair.

Because the SAP software implementation consolidated multiple discrete applications, the university now enters data only once; this change has reduced data-entry errors. A simpler, uniform interface has made the system easier to use and has reduced user error rates further. Data cross-checking capabilities and audit reports help users quickly identify any inaccurate information so that it can be corrected before being disseminated.

A centralized system resource Taking advantage of the role-based security capabilities of the SAP solution, the university has granted wider access to the system while establishing more clearly defined responsibilities among the HR and payroll staffs. The university has also created interfaces between the SAP solution and a number of its non-SAP applications. "Our online recruitment website and our financial system are two examples," says Sinclair. "The interface to the recruitment site allows us to create vacancy descriptions using the HCM software. Then, we can export them onto the website and import information that applicants submit back into the SAP solution."

The university also built interfaces for its card access system for staff, an online staff directory, and email and user account creation programs. This allows the university to integrate data from a wide variety of applications into the SAP solution. "The SAP system has basically become a central source for providing information to other systems," says Sinclair. "We even have an interface between our library systems and the SAP system."

As a result of its success with the employee self-service functionality— including the positive employee response and the timesavings in the HR department—the university is thinking about expanding its use of SAP technology. For example, it is considering using the SAP NetWeaver Portal component with the SAP NetWeaver Application Server component to support its ESS initiatives and to deliver further value to its employees. "Our initial ESS implementation was limited," says Sinclair. "Although people can view pay slips, update their personal data, and book training, for example, where we think we'll get our real benefit from the HCM software is with online submission of timesheets, sick days, annual leave, and expenses. And we really want to push out more on the training and development side, offering capabilities such as online employee appraisal and personnel development plans. We see a lot of opportunities to use SAP software to make life easier for both our employees and our HR staff."

Building on immediate success

Having deployed the manager's desktop capabilities, the university plans to eventually upgrade to the SAP Manager Self Service (MSS) application. "The response to the manager's desktop has been positive, but we are not doing anything sophisticated with it right now," says Sinclair. "We fully expect to introduce workflows, so that the managers can use automated processes to do approvals and reporting. We see a real benefit there."

After only a few months of using the new solution, the University of Westminster considered the implementation a success. "Our experience with SAP and its implementation partner Pecaso has been positive," says Sinclair. "We have some tight budget constraints, but we expect to continue to expand our SAP implementation and add more functionality in the near future."

7 Outlook

This final chapter describes SAP's vision, strategy, develop-
ment, and commitment for mySAP ERP and its future role
and position within SAP's overall solution portfolio. The vision
and roadmap described are those that SAP currently plans to
realize within the next three years.[1] The most important inno-
vations will occur for Enterprise Services Architecture and the
Business Process Platform, which have both been introduced
in this book. In this chapter, you'll learn about the future
developments that you can expect.

7.1 Enterprise Services Architecture Adopted within mySAP ERP

The Enterprise Services Architecture (ESA) will gain even more importance in the future. Until 2007, all SAP solutions will conform to ESA. This
section deals with the changes that you can expect with regard to ESA.

7.1.1 Introduction of Services

mySAP ERP is one of the major contributors to fulfill on the promise of
the Enterprise Services Architecture (ESA) blueprint. Recently published
by SAP, this roadmap will enable organizations to benefit from a service-
oriented architecture, one that allows for high flexibility while ensuring
that related costs of change could be contained.

ESA roadmap

In brief, Enterprise Services Architecture is SAP's open architecture for
adaptive business solutions. The fundamental premise of ESA is the
abstraction of business activities or events, modeled as *Enterprise Ser-*
vices, from the actual functionality of enterprise applications. Aggregating
Web services into business-level enterprise services provides more meaningful building blocks for the task of automating enterprise-scale business
scenarios (see Figure 7.1).

Building blocks for business processes

---

1 This implies the possibility that, due to any number of reasons, SAP may have to
   postpone or cancel some of the planned capabilities.

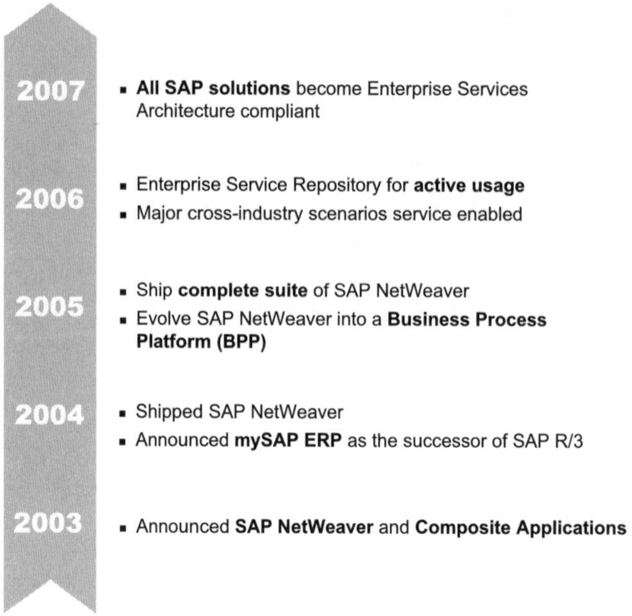

2007
All SAP solutions become Enterprise Services Architecture compliant
2006
Enterprise Service Repository for active usage
Major cross-industry scenarios service enabled
2005
Ship complete suite of SAP NetWeaver
Evolve SAP NetWeaver into a Business Process Platform (BPP)
2004
Shipped SAP NetWeaver
Announced mySAP ERP as the successor of SAP R/3
2003
Announced SAP NetWeaver and Composite Applications

Figure 7.1 Enterprise Services Architecture Roadmap

Leverage, extend, and innovate

Business applications that are based on ESA principles can reduce costs by lowering total cost of ownership (TCO) for the operation of existing IT solutions and freeing up capacity to invest in new solutions to stay ahead of the competition. This is achieved through a major shift in development, deployment, and maintenance paradigms across the overall IT landscape, enabling innovative customers to move from a traditional "Rip & Replace" to a "Leverage, Extend, & Innovate" methodology (see Figure 7.2, Figure 7.3, and Figure 7.4). This is achieved through a common set of standards, which allows integrating other open standards or platforms.

Composites
Enterprise Services
Platform

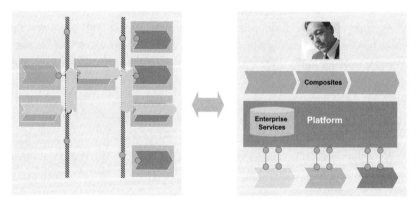

Figure 7.2 Enterprise Services Architecture

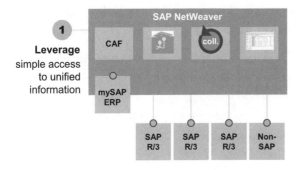

Figure 7.3 Leveraging Enterprise Data via Enterprise Services Architecture

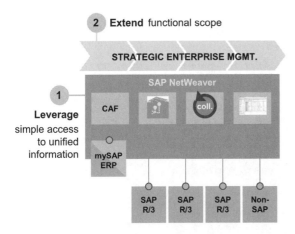

Figure 7.4 Scope Extension via Enterprise Services Architecture

In mySAP ERP 2005, SAP invested heavily into the seamless integration of various SAP NetWeaver components with SAP business solutions within the mySAP Business Suite family of business solutions. The SAP NetWeaver components and capabilities that are fundamental to support our service-oriented approach include:

▶ Transparent service definition through the *SAP NetWeaver Exchange Infrastructure* component

▶ Flexible process definition through *guided procedures* and integrated Adobe forms

▶ Fast and user-friendly master data search with SAP's *search engine*

▶ Enhanced flexibility through *Web Dynpro*-based user interfaces

▶ Increased efficiency by leveraging the *SAP NetWeaver Portal* features

▶ Better insight with embedded *analytics* and integrated analytical applications

NetWeaver components

From a business point of view following the ESA roadmap, mySAP ERP 2005 enables:

▶ Improved efficiency, greater automation, increased productivity, and better IT asset utilization that can save time and money while reducing the number of process steps

▶ Greater flexibility with better optimization and easier integration that enables growth of end-to-end business processes and reuse of existing assets

▶ Faster innovation with new processes that benefit from collaboration inside and outside the organization

The first package of services for mySAP ERP will be made available at the beginning of 2006, when several hundred services will be published. These services will be available for mySAP ERP 2004 and, shortly thereafter, for mySAP ERP 2005.

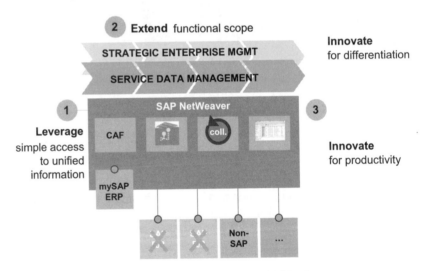

Figure 7.5 Enabling Innovation via Enterprise Services Architecture

7.1.2 Composite Applications

Quick modifications Future development of mySAP ERP will emphasize the creation and use of *composite applications*. Composite applications use the functional application building blocks made available through Enterprise Services Architecture to create more flexible business processes and task-oriented applications that can be created and modified faster. These enhanced capabilities—through the exploitation of composite applications—will not only improve collaboration within enterprises and organizations' ecosystems, but will also offer new opportunities for higher efficiency. This higher efficiency can be achieved via new capabilities in the composite applications that SAP will deliver to enhance future mySAP ERP versions. Organizations can more easily adapt the supplied business and workflow processes, and optimize the supplied user interface to the applications with the SAP process modeling capabilities and the visual toolset that is part of the SAP Composite Application Framework (CAF) tool. For streamlined processes, SAP will offer the concept of guided procedures, which is especially helpful for uncomplicated processes.

SAP is already working on a variety of composite applications that will be showcased at the beginning of 2006, when the first batch of enterprise services are made available for mySAP ERP 2004, and later on for mySAP ERP 2005.

7.1.3 Analytical Applications

For organizations that require even more flexibility, SAP will provide new analytical functionality, as well as visual tools that enable authorized individuals within organizations to produce new analytical applications, such as dashboards, or enhance and adapt existing applications by integrating additional information via these new services. These dynamic analytical processes, with the typical pattern of "event–analysis–resolution," require more flexibility and fast project delivery by an IT organization. Ideally, power users will be able to adjust this new type of application to their team needs, which is possible only with an increasing number of enterprise services that will be delivered with the next mySAP ERP versions. **Visual tools**

Integration of analytical information will be much more flexible with the service-oriented approach. Today, integrating interactive reports into user roles already delivers the necessary information in one view. SAP will deliver more services that push important events to users, regardless of the form used or the context of the user environment. New dashboards will not only provide the relevant information at a glance, but will also enable users to react to these events immediately. Integrating office documents and other unstructured data, as well as being able to search and retrieve relevant information across object and media boundaries, will allow for a new level of quality in decision-making processes. This added value, along with faster reaction capabilities and the opportunity to be more proactive in areas such as planning and forecasting, will be key benefits for SAP customers. **Interactive reports**

7.1.4   Common Repository for More Flexibility

Firsthand information A common repository offers many benefits. A common shared enterprise services repository can integrate mySAP ERP enterprise services with other services in an enterprise's individual landscape. This is where business knowledge on processes and enterprise services resides, which offers clear advantages. The tools provided in SAP NetWeaver and tighter tool integration in the near future provide flexibility for both IT and power users.

mySAP ERP will also offer services and tools that enable enterprises to define and build individual processes using a model-driven approach, with their own in-house staff or with the help of specialized partners. The key is that SAP provides interoperability because our customers typically run a mix of SAP and non-SAP software.

Flexibility for processes is not enough. Enterprises need the ability to consolidate and scale where appropriate. With well-defined deployment units, SAP enables enterprises to be more effective in areas where shared-service centers and business process outsourcing are common. With the flexibility of a service-oriented architecture, it is much easier to change models and integrate additional tasks while maintaining control. You should expect additional services to be provided in subsequent mySAP ERP releases, for example, in the areas of payroll, financial processes, manufacturing, and warehousing.

7.1.5   Supporting Open Standards

Open standards across boundaries Building on the open architecture of SAP NetWeaver, mySAP ERP automatically benefits from the improvements of open standards for business applications. SAP actively participates in the definition of international standards, including Business Process Management Initiative (BPMI); Organization for the Advancement of Structured Information Standards (OASIS); Universal Description, Discovery, and Integration (UDDI); World Wide Web Consortium (W3C); and United Nations Centre for Trade Facilitation and Electronic Business (UN/CEFACT). This ensures the interoperability and reach of ERP solutions beyond the boundaries of enterprises in a cost-effective way. SAP invests in the most important industry standards, which means our customers can expect additional out-of-the-box integration in that area.

Open standards allow our partners to smoothly transfer their existing solutions or build new ones based on these standards. Decoupling of previously integrated monolithic or individual approaches through common Web service–based standards enables the flexible upgrade of components in IT landscapes. As the typical backbone of such a landscape, mySAP ERP will contribute to and benefit from this new service orientation. The service paradigm not only helps customers to become more flexible, but also enables them to grow their processes as needed.

Within the 2005–2007 timeframe, mySAP ERP will see more integration scenarios and composite applications. Enhancing processes and increasing flexibility in a step-by-step approach will lead to faster innovation while keeping projects under control and achieving a faster return on investment (ROI) for SAP customers.

7.1.6 People Productivity: Continued Focus on Users

The future direction of people productivity within mySAP ERP will be to continue support for bottom-line improvements by increasing user efficiency and effectiveness, as well as to increase support for top-line growth by providing adaptable composite applications. As with mySAP ERP 2005, future versions will provide easy-to-use and intuitive access for all authorized employees to all information, applications, and services they need for their work. Intuitive interfaces and online access to broader, more accurate information support employees—even occasional users—to make decisions more quickly and complete their jobs more effectively than before.

Intuitive access

SAP will continue its user-centric engineering approach when developing future versions of the mySAP ERP solution, focusing on productivity of people. Improved productivity means greater efficiency and quicker responsiveness. Extending the reach of real-time business processes lets enterprises engage and connect with more users both within and beyond the enterprise, including customers, suppliers, and partners. The solution's easy-to-use and intuitive role-based portal environment ensures easier system wide access to a consolidated and consistent process view that increases user adoption and collaboration.

With improved efficiency, enterprises can empower everyone in the organization with the information they need to react and respond proactively to market changes more rapidly than their competitors. In previous versions of SAP software, the focus was on data and process consistency. This is still true in mySAP ERP. But to proven track records in functionality, performance, and reliability, SAP adds convenience for the user, flexibility, and speed. While the solution still supports users in "doing things right" through work centers, SAP supports them even more in "doing the right things."

7.1.7 Industry Availability with mySAP ERP 2005

Because of the different delivery streams listed in Section 4.2, there are now many components and release schedules unique to each industry, which makes it a time-consuming and costly exercise for customers to deploy a solution for an industry. In general, it is not possible to deploy multiple industry-specific components as Add-ons to the same core release, so customers who don't fit into one industry category are limited in the value they can extract from SAP's industry portfolios.

Retrofit of industry solutions
With the ERP market maturing and focusing on total cost of ownership (TCO), there is pressure to streamline the delivery of industry solutions. Furthermore, there are a number of generic functions in industry solutions, which are valuable for customers using only mySAP ERP. In addition, there is a strong demand for deep industry-specific offerings in the ERP market.

This is why SAP has decided to deliver several industry-specific functions as part of mySAP ERP in the future.

The prerequisite for retrofitting industry-specific Add-ons into mySAP ERP is a technical layer known as the SAP Switch Framework (see Figure 7.6). Current restrictions still apply. The goal is to retrofit all industry-specific Add-ons into mySAP ERP for the 2005 release. Each industry-specific Add-on follows a specific migration path to reach this goal, depending on its current delivery stream.

Switch Framework and Business Function Sets

Switch Framework
The Switch Framework is a versatile tool, which offers great benefits; especially since industry solutions become available at the same time that core functionality is delivered. The switch setting is activated at the beginning of the implementation phase for a specific industry solution. Functions can be shared between different industry solutions.

Business Function Sets
With mySAP ERP 2005, and therefore SAP ECC 6.0, industry extensions are represented in Business Function Sets. Depending on the industry, the specific functionality is delivered as an industry extension, technically represented in the so-called Industry Business Function Sets, or as an enterprise extension, technically represented in the so-called Generic

Business Functions. The main difference between these two sets is the possibility to activate the industry-specific functionality via the Switch Framework. While only one Industry Business Function Set can be activated out of all the industry extensions, several Generic Business Functions can be activated in parallel via the Switch Framework. One of the benefits of this tool is an as-needed solution enrichment. Industry solutions can now be enriched by generic functions from other industries. When the activation of a Business Function Set is generating data, there is no way to deactivate a Business Function Set, as this would cause data inconsistencies.

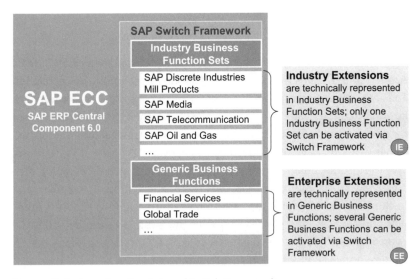

Figure 7.6 Business Function Sets and Switch Framework

With mySAP ERP 2005, industry solutions will be delivered within the standard release cycle and can be activated on an as-needed basis. Through a consolidation of the system landscape (hardware, interfaces, and maintenance), the total cost of ownership can be reduced. In addition, future upgrade costs will be reduced, because there will be no more separate handling for Add-ons.[2] The immediate availability of industry solutions via the standard release implicates no more delays of support packages and legal changes of industry Add-ons. New industry functionality will only be developed on SAP ECC (see Figure 7.7).

Activation on an as-needed basis

---

2 Technical and license restrictions may apply.

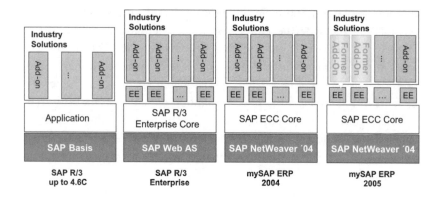

Figure 7.7 Evolution of Industry Solutions in mySAP ERP 2005

Figure 7.8 shows the synergies of industry solutions in mySAP ERP 2005. As mentioned, there will be a difference between an exclusive activation and a multiple usage of industry-specific functionality. For example, a customer can activate SAP for Insurance and concurrently activate SAP for Banking and SAP for Financial Service Providers, whereas another customer wouldn't have the opportunity to activate SAP for Automotive and SAP for Insurance concurrently. These considerations are becoming progressively more important, because increasingly more companies and institutions are expanding their portfolio with non-industry specific products and services, and even strategically investing in other industries. Of course, SAP will further leverage the retrofit of industry-specific functionalities in mySAP ERP for future releases.

Exclusiv Activation		Multiple Usage	
A	SAP for Aerospace and Defense	C	SAP for Chemicals
A	SAP for Automotive	C	SAP for Consumer Products
A	SAP for Engineering, Construction & Operations	C	SAP for Financial Service Providers
A	SAP for High Tech	C	SAP for Global Trade Management
A	SAP for Mill Products	C	SAP for Industrial Machinery & Components
A	SAP for Public Sector	C	SAP for Pharmaceuticals
A	SAP for Utilities	C	SAP for Professional Services
A	SAP for Healthcare	C	SAP for Retail
A	SAP for Higher Education & Research	C	SAP for Service Providers
A	SAP for Insurance	C	SAP for Life Sciences
A	SAP for Media	C	SAP for Logistics Service Providers
A	SAP for Mining	C	SAP for Postal Services
A	SAP for Oil & Gas	C	SAP for Railway Services
A	SAP for Telecommunications	E	SAP for Banking
		E	SAP for Beverages
		E	SAP for Defense and Security
		E	SAP for Public Sector - Management
		E	SAP for Utilities - FERC 2.0
		E	SAP for Oil & Gas - JVA

Figure 7.8 Synergies of Industry Solutions in mySAP ERP 2005;
A = Add-on, E = Extension, C = Core

7.2 mySAP ERP—Embracing the Business Process Platform

Over the next few years, mySAP ERP will continue to build on SAP NetWeaver and embrace the Business Process Platform. Let's quickly sum up the main evolutionary steps, as already outlined in more detail in Chapter 4, focusing now on what will happen with mySAP ERP 2005 and beyond.

Development towards Business Process Platform

SAP R/3 (up to version SAP R/3 4.6C) was a standalone system in which people, rather than technology, acted as integrators in business processes. SAP R/3 was a clearly defined application, with strong ties to other SAP applications. With the introduction of SAP R/3 Enterprise, the technology layer of SAP R/3 used SAP Web Application Server (SAP Web AS) for the first time. SAP Web AS, now called SAP NetWeaver Application Server (SAP NetWeaver AS), formed the new technology basis for all SAP applications, and future versions of SAP applications didn't just use SAP Web AS, but were actually built on it. This is true for mySAP ERP 2004, which also uses other SAP NetWeaver components extensively, such as SAP Enterprise Portal,[3] or SAP Business Intelligence,[4] to offer role-based access and integrated analytics.

In future versions of mySAP ERP, additional integration of SAP NetWeaver is a given. Analytics will play an increased role to ensure all information on an organizational, individual, and process level is available to those who need it. Information from multiple distributed systems can be consolidated more easily within SAP NetWeaver. Tighter integration with the portal will offer a much improved user experience with role-based information actively pushed to users.

SAP NetWeaver integration

mySAP ERP 2004 was one of the first SAP solutions to utilize composite applications. The idea is that flexible applications can be built quickly and maintained easily on top of the existing infrastructure. Composite applications will be a major focus of development in future mySAP ERP releases. Processes already in mySAP ERP, such as creating or changing a product and hiring new employees, act as composite applications. In mySAP ERP 2005, more composites will be introduced, such as guided procedures in self-service applications. All composites use SAP NetWeaver as the underlying technology.

Composite applications

---

3 From mySAP ERP 2005 on, SAP Enterprise Portal will be known as SAP NetWeaver Portal.
4 From mySAP ERP 2005 on, SAP Business Intelligence will be known as SAP NetWeaver Business Intelligence.

Additionally, partners can use the infrastructure to create and develop their own composite applications, and organizations can leverage both SAP and partner composites to create their own applications.

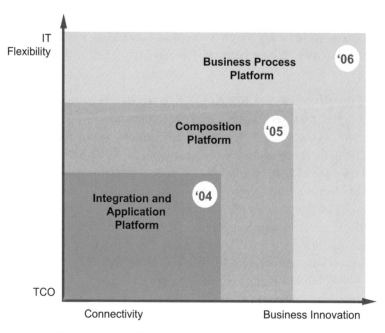

Figure 7.9 Business Process Platform

SAP Developer Network Future development of mySAP ERP will start to embrace Web services as a foundation of Enterprise Services Architecture (ESA). By leveraging the 2005 enterprise services inventory, and directing customer and partner feedback via the SAP Developer Network ESA preview system, increasingly more Web services will be developed. In 2005, plans were announced to introduce a first package of several hundred services. Services will include basic functionality, such as currency conversion; user-interface services, such as sales order status; and complex services, such as purchase order creation or listing absent employees.

Orchestration of business processes   Finally, with the repository complete, SAP NetWeaver will become a platform for orchestrating business processes (see Figure 7.9). Functionality will be moved from some applications and centralized within the platform, making it available for use by a variety of different applications. For example, when functionality for a call center is moved to the platform, it can be used by ERP applications for an employee call center and by a Customer Relationship Management (CRM) application for a customer interaction center. Along with the completion of the ESA Roadmap in 2007, the complete suite and all industry solutions will be based on the Business Process Platform (see Figure 7.10).

- **Complete Suite** and all Industry Solutions on **Business Process Platform**
- Enterprise Services Architecture roadmap completed

- **Business Process Platform** available for ISVs
- **All-In-One** available on Business Process Platform

- **mySAP ERP** general availability
- **Complete Suite** and all Industry Solutions on **SAP NetWeaver**

Figure 7.10 Business Process Platform Roadmap

With this approach, mySAP ERP, as well as other applications, will use common elements within the platform. This means reduced landscape complexity and increased system flexibility, as new composite applications can be built around the services offered by the platform, either from SAP or from partners.

In the long term, this means greater flexibility for organizations and the ability to react quickly to the demands of the market and customer needs while maintaining costs.

A   Websites and Resources

For additional information and insight on specific topics, we recommend exploring the following resources.

▶ SAP website: *www.sap.com*

▶ mySAP ERP site: *www.sap.com/erp*

▶ SAP Community: *www.sap.com/community*

▶ SAP Events: *www.sap.com/events*

▶ SAP Partners: *www.sap.com/partners*

▶ Meet SAP Customers: *www.sap.com/community/pub/success* (registration necessary)

▶ SAP Service Marketplace: *http://service.sap.com* (registration necessary)

▶ America's SAP Users' Group (ASUG): *www.asug.com*

▶ German-Speaking SAP User Group (DSAG): *www.dsag.de*

B Acknowledgements

Without the help and support of several colleagues, writing this book on mySAP ERP would have been an even bigger endeavor for us.

Special acknowledgements go to the mySAP ERP customers referenced in the customer reports, as well as to the following individuals for their contribution: Thomas Baur, Andreas Brandt, Juergen Helmle, Oliver Hid Arida, Daniela Menger, Nis Boy Naeve, Juergen Roehricht, Juliana Vargas, and Frederike Zeier.

We appreciate the efforts and support of our publisher Galileo Press, especially our editor Nancy Etscovitz for her continued dedication.

Last but not least, a special mention to our families for supporting this project.

Frank Forndron, Thilo Liebermann,
Marcus Thurner, and Peter Widmayer
Walldorf, February 2006

C   The Authors

Frank Forndron is the Program Director and Head of Program Management for the Global ERP Initiative at SAP AG, a dedicated team responsible for the overall strategy, global sales programs, and global field rollout of the mySAP ERP solution. Prior to this position, he gained in-depth product knowledge of mySAP ERP as Program Manager in the User Productivity group. From 1999 to 2003, he held several project management positions at global SAP implementations. In 1997, after having received a diploma in economics, he embarked on his career at a SAP consulting partner focusing on mid-market accounts before joining SAP in 1999.

Thilo Liebermann is a Business Solution Architect within the EMEA Field Services Team of the IBU Banking at SAP AG, where he is in charge of Enterprise Management (ERP) for Financial Services institutions. He is also involved in the positioning of Supplier Relationship Management for Banking. Prior to his current position, he worked within product and program management for the Global ERP Initiative for three years. His knowledge of mySAP ERP is also based on his former involvement in several SAP R/3 Enterprise projects, where he supported various cross-regional field enablement processes. Thilo holds a diploma in geography, economics, and sociology from the University of Heidelberg.

Marcus Thurner works as Program Manager within the COO Management Office at SAP Field Services since September 2005. Prior to this position, he was responsible for the proactive reference generation and the operational management in the Global ERP Initiative at SAP AG. Before that, he worked six years as project manager and HCM application consultant, of which he spent three years at SAP Deutschland AG & Co. KG. During this time, he was also the SAP consultant responsible for SAP Travel Management. In addition to completing his degree in mechanical engineering at the University of

Kassel, he spent two years working as an independent consultant for an automotive supplier.

Dr. Peter Widmayer works as ERP Program Manager who is leading the SAP Small and Medium Business Initiative from an ERP solution perspective. In addition, he oversees ERP development during the Ramp-Up of mySAP ERP 2005. Earlier, as part of the Global ERP Initiative at SAP, he was responsible for the global field rollout of the mySAP ERP solution, where he led the Ramp-Up of mySAP ERP 2004 to a global success. He gained his in-depth SAP experience while in charge of the SAP Product Standard Globalization, as well as during the successful market rollout of Unicode technology. He joined SAP in 1999 as application and technology consultant at global implementation projects. Peter holds a PhD in experimental physics.

Index

The official guidebook to SAP CRM 4.0

462 pp., 2004, 59,95 Euro
ISBN 1-59229-029-9

mySAP CRM

www.sap-press.com

R. Buck-Emden, P. Zencke

mySAP CRM

The Official Guidebook to SAP CRM 4.0

Discover all of the most critical functionality, new enhancements, and best practices to maximize the potential of mySAP CRM.
Learn the essential principles of mySAP CRM as well as detailed techniques for employing this powerful SAP solution. Practical examples highlight important functional aspects and guide you through the complete Customer Interaction Cycle. Plus, you'll also discover the ins and outs of key functional areas and benefit from expert advice illustrated throughout with mySAP CRM business scenarios. A fully updated presentation of the implementation methodology, as well as the technical fundamentals of SAP CRM 4.0, on the basis of SAP NetWeaver, serve to round out this formidable resource.

Collaborative Processes, Interfaces, Messages, Proxies, and Mappings

Runtime, configuration, cross-component processes, and Business Process Management

Incl. technical case scenarios on cross-component BPM and B2B- Communication

270 pp., 2005, US$
ISBN 1-59229-037-X

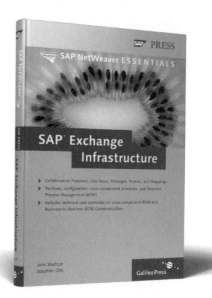

SAP Exchange Infrastructure

www.sap-press.com

J. Stumpe, J. Orb

SAP Exchange Infrastructure

If you know what SAP Exchange Infrastructure (SAP XI) is, and you have seen the latest documentation, then now you will want to read this book. Exclusive insights help you go beyond the basics, and provide you with in-depth information on the SAP XI architecture, which in turn helps you quickly understand the finer points of mappings, proxies, and interfaces. You'll also benefit from practical guidance on the design and configuration of business processes. Additionally, in a significant section devoted to step-by-step examples, you'll discover the nuances of various application scenarios and how to tackle their specific configurations.

>> www.sap-press.de/934

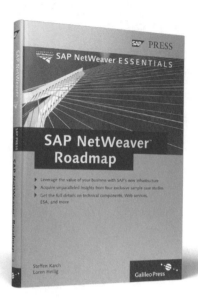

**How to succeed with
InfoObjects, InfoProviders,
and SAP Business Content**

**Step-by-step instruction to
optimize your daily work**

**All new and up-to-date
for SAP BW 3.5**

437 pp., 2005, 69,95 Euro
ISBN 1-59229-043-4

SAP BW Data Modeling

www.sap-press.com

N. Egger, J.-M. Fiechter, J. Rohlf

SAP BW Data Modeling

This book delivers all the essential information
needed for successful data modeling using SAP BW.
In a practice-oriented approach, you'll learn how to
prepare, store, and manage your data efficiently.
Essential topics such as data warehousing concepts
and the architecture of SAP BW are examined in
detail. You'll learn, step-by-step, all there is to know
about InfoObjects, InfoProviders, and SAP Business
Content, all based on the newly released SAP BW
3.5.

Expert advice to implement key ETL processes

Complete coverage of master data, transaction data and SAP Business Content

Step-by-step instruction and field tested solutions

552 pp., 2006, 69,95 Euro
ISBN 1-59229-044-2

SAP BW
Data Retrieval

www.sap-press.com

N. Egger, J.-M. Fiechter, R. Salzmann, R.P. Sawicki, T. Thielen

SAP BW Data Retrieval

Mastering the ETL process

This much anticipated reference makes an excellent addition to your SAP BW Library. Read this book and you'll discover a comprehensive guide to configuring, executing, and optimizing data retrieval in SAP BW.

The authors take you, step-by-step, through all of the essential data collection activities and help you hit the ground running with master data, transaction data, and SAP Business Content. Expert insights and practical guidance help you to optimize these three factors and build a successful, efficient ETL (extraction, transformation, loading) process. This all-new edition is based on the current SAP BW Release 3.5, but remains a highly valuable resource for those still using previous versions.

Make the most of BEx Query Designer, BEx Web and SAP BW Information Broadcasting

550 pp., approx. US$
ISBN 1-59229-045-0, nov 2005

SAP BW
Reporting and Analysis

www.sap-press.com

N. Egger, J. Rohlf, J. Rose, O. Schrüffer, J.-M. Fiechter

SAP BW – Reporting and Analysis

In this book you'll find everything you need to configure and execute Web reporting and Web applications, as well as detailed instruction to take advantage of the resulting possibilities for analysis and reporting in SAP BW.
First, you'll be introduced to the basic topics of BEx Query Designer, BEx Web Application Designer, BEx Web Applications, BEx Analyzer, and SAP Business Content. Then, expert guidance shows you, step by step, how to master the process of creating custom reports and analysis. That's just for starters. You'll also learn best practices for creating your own SAP BW Web Cockpit and much more.

>> www.sap-press.de/982

Best Practices for Payroll, Time Management, Personnel Administration, and much more

Expert advice for integrating Personnel Planning and SAP Enterprise Portal

Based on R/3 Enterprise and mySAP ERP HCM 2004

629 pp., 2006, 69,95 Euro
ISBN 1-59229-050-7

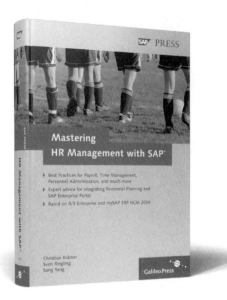

Mastering
HR Management with SAP

www.sap-press.com

C. Krämer, S. Ringling, Song Yang

Mastering HR Management with SAP

Get a step-by-step guide to the entire personnel management process, from recruiting, to personnel controlling, and beyond. This book comes complete with practical examples regarding user roles, and covers all of the new enhancements, improved features and tools that have been introduced with R/3 Enterprise. Uncover the ins and outs of e-recruiting, organizational management, personnel administration, payroll, benefits, quality assurance, rolebased portals, and many others too numerous to list. The book, based on Release 4.7 (R/3 Enterprise), also contains information on mySAP ERP (HCM).

Gain a deep understanding of SAP MM functionality and configuration

Learn from the experience of experts via case studies and practical examples

500 pp., approx. 69,95 Euro
ISBN 1-59229-072-8, April 2006

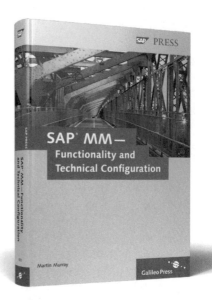

SAP MM—Functionality and Technical Configuration

www.sap-press.com

Martin Murray

SAP MM—Functionality and Technical Configuration

This book will include all aspects of SAP Material Management, including MM Master Data, Purchasing, Inventory Management, Financial Integration and topics that are cross application, but relevant to MM, such as Document Management, Batch Management and Classification. Using practical examples and case studies it will give readers a holistic understanding of SAP MM, how it works and relates with the other SAP modules.

Interested in reading more?

Please visit our Web site for all
new book releases from SAP PRESS.

www.sap-press.com